# Rock Bottom

# Rock Bottom

## A Music Writer's Journey into Madness

Michael Odell

ICON

Published in the UK in 2017
by Icon Books Ltd, Omnibus Business Centre,
39–41 North Road, London N7 9DP
email: info@iconbooks.com
www.iconbooks.com

Sold in the UK, Europe and Asia
by Faber & Faber Ltd, Bloomsbury House,
74–77 Great Russell Street,
London WC1B 3DA or their agents

Distributed in the UK, Europe and Asia
by Grantham Book Services,
Trent Road, Grantham NG31 7XQ

Distributed in Australia and New Zealand
by Allen & Unwin Pty Ltd,
PO Box 8500, 83 Alexander Street,
Crows Nest, NSW 2065

Distributed in South Africa
by Jonathan Ball, Office B4, The District,
41 Sir Lowry Road, Woodstock 7925

Distributed in India by Penguin Books India,
7th Floor, Infinity Tower – C, DLF Cyber City,
Gurgaon 122002, Haryana

ISBN: 978-178578-222-0

Typeset in Scala Serif by Marie Doherty

Printed and bound in the UK
by Clays Ltd, St Ives plc

# Contents

*Author's Note*                                             ix

**1**   I Had Too Much to Think Last Night                   1

**2**   Morris Dancer                                        9

**3**   Panic!                                              40

**4**   Sister of Mercy                                     53

**5**   Mental Health's Backstage Area                      65

**6**   Mrs Henckel                                         70

**7**   Serving the True Believers                          81

**8**   Nicely Does It                                      97

**9**   Hell vs Heaven (Slipknot vs U2)                    105

**10**  In the Event of an Emergency                       129

**11**  Me and Julio                                       146

**12**  Goodbye to Pain                                    164

**13**  Mental Elf                                         174

**14**  American Nihilist                                  191

**15**  To Live and Die in Croydon                         209

**16**  Dark Side of the Loon                              219

**17**  The Teachings of Bowie                             230

**18**  You're Fired!                                      253

| 19 | Magnolia Psyche | 272 |
| 20 | Teacher's Lips | 275 |
| 21 | Man and Van | 282 |
| 22 | Van The Man | 287 |
| 23 | Slash | 290 |
| 24 | What's the Story? | 297 |
| 25 | An Enemy of Rock 'n' Roll | 305 |
| 26 | O, Daddy of Rock! | 308 |
| 27 | Low | 315 |
| 28 | Reasons to Be Fearful | 319 |
| 29 | Foetus on My Breath | 328 |
| 30 | Paul McCartney | 337 |
| 31 | The A-Rockalypse | 346 |
| 32 | Pete, Come Back! | 353 |
|  | *Postscript* | 370 |
|  | *Acknowledgements* | 374 |

"What's up with you, you c***?"
LIAM GALLAGHER

"How dare you!"
DAVID BOWIE

"Get out of my house!"
PETE DOHERTY

"Hey, those are my trousers!"
THE STROKES

"Very good, very good."
NELSON MANDELA

"I'm glad no one checked my mental health when I was starting out – they wouldna f***** found any. Like your pal, rock 'n' roll for me was do or die. My old man said if I didn't make it, I'd end up in jail or dead. Of course we always hear about the winners. But in this game, when you lose, you lose big."

OZZY OSBOURNE, 2017

## AUTHOR'S NOTE

During a period that began in the summer of 2005, I was trying to solve some deep-seated personal issues related to an over-dependence on rock music, while maintaining a magazine job interviewing the world's biggest rock stars. I have tried to tell the personal side of the story accurately and without upsetting too many people. This has meant telescoping some events and changing some names. The interviews with rock stars happened as reported.

# 1
# I Had Too Much to Think Last Night

A bed. South London.

"Stop shouting! Stop shouting, you'll wake Ronnie!"

"What? Wait! Where the hell is the band?"

"The band isn't here. You are home. This is reality."

Reality, I note with a sigh, is not as well-appointed as my dream-life. There is no fancy room service buffet or deluxe hotel chandelier above me but instead a modest Ikea lampshade and a large guitar-shaped damp patch on the ceiling. Before I left on my trip, the patch was about the size of a seven-inch single. Now it has swollen and grown two long tentacles. It's about the size of the preposterous double-necked guitar Jimmy Page used while Led Zeppelin were in their 70s pomp.

The pretty, freckled face of my girlfriend Nicola peers down at me, a scientist examining a specimen. The fringe that makes her look like the dark-haired one from the Human League swishes into her eyes. She flicks it away to improve her view.

"Morning," she says jauntily enough but her eyelids flicker, betraying a reading on the spectrum between curiosity and trepidation.

"Hello, you," I say, blinking myself fully awake. "Sorry, I thought I was ..."

"Michael, you were having a bad dream."

"No, I was asleep," I say.

"But you were shouting, 'Pete! Pete!'"

"Who's Peter?"

"How the hell should *I* know? It was your dream!"

Peter Townshend. Peter Doherty. Peter Hook. These are all Peter rock stars. I know this because I am a rock writer. I have been interviewing rock stars for twenty years. In fact, I have just returned from a testing international assignment. Thrombosed by the contortions of an Economy seat, blunted by in-flight refreshments, I climbed into bed next to Nicola late last night. I slept terribly and woke feeling vexed and haunted. I was dreaming about rock stars. I was on a tour bus with a band. There was music, beer and louche pterodactyl laughter, but the precise details evaporate upon probing. I certainly don't recall any Peters.

"Get up. Have a bath. You'll feel better," Nicola advises.

"Yes, good idea," I say catching the fug of my own long-haul traveller armpit.

Nicola is very good about indulging the peculiarities of my job. You might say it comes naturally to her. She works in mental health, running a South London day centre where she helps a varied clientele adapt to a self-supporting life in the community. It's not so far from living with a rock journalist: if I need rousing or cajoling, she has the skill set to do it.

"So, where did you stay?" she asks, drawing back the curtains.

"The Four Seasons," I say, "Toronto."

"And the weather?"

"Cold as a witch's tit."

"But they were nice?"

"Who?"

"Were the band nice?"

I wince at the question.

"Nice? Why are you asking me if they were *nice*?"

"You went all that way; I'm just asking if they were nice to you."

"Come on," I say, "you don't really want people like that to be *nice*."

Rock stars are combatants in important cultural wars. They are required to be many things but "nice" isn't pre-eminent among them. However, Nicola is less bothered by the complex code of how rock stars should behave than I am. To her mind, they should assume the off-stage persona of cordial and respectful citizenry. Nicola is for common decency. She is for manners.

"What was Mick like?" she asks, with a cautious elevation of one eyebrow.

"A businessman. Emotionally disconnected from his product. Very much focussed on maximising profits," I shrug.

"Oh," she says with distaste.

I have been to Toronto to interview the Rolling Stones. In his dressing room, Sir Mick directed me to a seat ten feet distant from his. Across this chasm of empathy, he offered a wily, craggy defence of the Stones' legacy. He's been their frontman for over 40 years now. No wonder he feels more like a brand ambassador discussing augmentations to the product line than a rock star.

I went for broke. I lobbed in my hand grenade question: "Is it possible, as Keith and I discussed earlier, that the Stones' sexual threat and perhaps even the entire permissive 60s may have originated with your cock?"

"Great quote. No comment."

In most interviews the "grenade question", something incendiary dropped onto the floor and left to roll around with the pin out, opens things up. But not this time. He was too good. Nevertheless, eyeballing the walnut-faced Jagger up close was a solemn and special occasion for me. Jagger and Keith Richards are members of the Big Six, the giants, the founders even, of modern rock whom every rock writer would like to interview. The others are Bowie, Townshend, Page and McCartney. They are getting old now and soon they will all be dead. It is my sworn aim to find the big beasts before they go extinct. And before I do too. In six months I will be 42.

"After the Stones, I expect you're feeling tomorrow will be a bit of a come-down," Nicola says.

"Tomorrow. What's tomorrow?"

"The Q Awards."

Oh yes, I remember now. Tomorrow Q magazine is holding its annual awards bash. Each journalist must chaperone one of the star guests up the red carpet, through a global media maelstrom and into a hotel ballroom where gongs will be handed out. I have been allotted Britpop titans Oasis. Oasis are not in the Big Six, but they are still a major force in rock. Just thinking about chaperoning them makes me feel anxious. I have spent quite a bit of time with the band in the past and, although they are funny and charismatic, they can be wildly unpredictable.

"I think you should get a new suit. And new shoes," Nicola advises, after studying my outfit for the awards.

"Why? Those are fine."

"Come off it," she says. "The shoes are so 1980s, and the suit's ridiculously small."

"I don't care. I am wearing them."

Last year, as I chaperoned the exquisitely tailored Elton John up the red carpet, one of the magazine's top brass hissed at me coldly. "Why aren't you wearing a suit?" she said. "You look like his bloody roadie!"

It pisses me off that this year she has stipulated all writers should attend in formal wear. I will wear the ridiculous suit as a protest. A suit that brazenly refuses to do the conformist work of a suit. I do not believe rock writers should conform. Why should we, mavericks who articulate the voices of the counterculture, ape the dress code of The Man?

"For God's sake, just go and buy one," says Nicola, holding it up with clear distaste. "There's nothing wrong with looking presentable."

I sense we are about to argue, once again, about the place that conformity has in rock 'n' roll culture. But we are interrupted by a noise outside the bedroom door. The tentative *rat-a-tat* of a small human knuckle.

Nicola winks at me as a cue to prepare myself. "Heeeeereee's Ronnie!" she cries, like an MC introducing an act on an old-time TV rock show, and our nine-year-old son Ronnie shoulders through the door. He is wearing his Who pyjama set with a toy plastic guitar slung round his neck. Nicola gently guides his back as he hops onto the bed, as if onto a low stage. Then, with apple-cheeked intensity,

5

ROCK BOTTOM

he begins mimicking the riff to "My Generation". Instead of electricity and amplification, he deploys growls and phlegm for effect. When he gets to the line "Hope I die before I get old", Nicola arches a quizzical eyebrow. When he has finished, he waves to the imaginary crowd, takes off the guitar and assumes his ordinary persona.

"Hello, Daddy. Did you have a fun time in Canada?"

"Yes, I did, thank you."

"Did you meet the real me?"

"Yes, I did."

"Was he nice?"

"Yes," I say.

"Are they paying him more pocket money?"

"Yes. He's getting the same pocket money as everyone else."

Our son is called Tom, but he takes his middle name from the Rolling Stones' Ronnie Wood and likes to use that instead. He is heavily invested in the welfare of his namesake. I have told him that when Wood was drafted into the Stones in 1975, instead of making him a full member of the band, Jagger kept him on a wage for the following nineteen years. Our Ronnie has been indignantly curious about Wood's financial package ever since.

"Did you bring me a souvenir?" he asks.

"I did. We'll hang it in the bathroom together later, shall we?"

Whenever I return from an assignment, Ronnie and I enjoy curating any new rock memorabilia I have acquired. Our bathroom is a rock 'n' roll shrine, and the placing of new artefacts is a tradition, a harmless bit of father–son bonding. At least I think it is.

"What did you bring him this time?" Nicola whispers to me. "Please, God, I hope it's appropriate."

I can understand Nicola's concern. On a recent trip, I made a mistake. I was on tour with New Order on the west coast of America, and on the final night in California there were a few drinks. Late in the evening, I lurched about the dressing room looking for a souvenir and slipped what I thought was the duster used for wiping down Peter Hook's bass strings into my bag. Peter Hook's bass playing, especially on Joy Division records, is some of the most legendary in rock. I wanted a connection with it, even if it was just a rag. But when I got home and unpacked my trophy, I discovered it was a pair of underpants.

Owning a pair of Peter Hook's underpants would still give me a solid connection with legendary New Order and Joy Division bass lines. But Ronnie didn't agree. "Why have you brought home someone else's pants?" he asked me. We didn't hang them up in the bathroom. I threw them away.

Ronnie is growing up fast. He is taking rock 'n' roll increasingly seriously, so we have to monitor his exposure to it carefully. Rock is not like other art forms, like, say, pottery or theatre or ballet. Its core values – seditious hedonism, emotional extremity and nihilistic torpor – need to be managed carefully in the domestic sphere.

And so, I am not sure about my Ronnie Wood souvenir. I know this new artefact is a borderline case.

"A cigarette butt," I say finally.

"Jesus, Michael," Nicola says under her breath, "why on earth have you brought your son a cigarette butt?"

"It's Ron Wood's. That means it's been held in the very same fingers that played guitar on the Stones' 'Miss You' and 'Start Me Up', not to mention Rod Stewart's 'Maggie May'," I explain.

Nicola's shoulders drop as though she has been the recipient of bad news. "You are insane," she says quietly to herself.

I do not agree. For me, a fag butt with a direct physical connection to such music puts the owner in touch with immortality.

"Daddy, why were you shouting in your sleep?" Ronnie asks suddenly.

I look at Nicola. She shrugs. "It was quite loud," she confides to me gently.

"Daddy's not shouting now. He wants to get up," I say.

"Pete! Pete!" my little boy shrieks, giggling. Then draping himself around me he adds: "Come back!"

"Come back?" I ask. "Did I actually say 'Come back'?"

Nicola nods. "'Fraid so, you weirdo."

"Yes, you sounded scared, Daddy!" says Ronnie.

"Alright, alright," I say, unpicking his sausage fingers from around my neck. "Daddy was just having a bad dream."

# 2
# Morris Dancer

It is the morning of the awards and I am in the bath. As a roving rock writer, I have amassed quite a range of high-end bathroom unguents from quality hotels around the world. I wallow in an astonishing afro of suds.

I look around the bathroom walls for a space where Ron Wood's fag butt might go. There is not much space left. The walls are already well-upholstered with rock ephemera. In pride of place are my Big Six trophies: a health-promoting tea tree stick from David Bowie, a napkin with which Pete Townshend once dabbed his mouth, and a jar of peanuts from Jimmy Page (he offered me one, I said thanks and then, as he continued talking, slipped it into my bag). Then the lesser artefacts: two French fries I stole from Sting, a salt cellar Joe Strummer from The Clash threw across a café in a rage (additionally I have the spoon with which he stirred his tea), and a doodle on a pad by Jack White from The White Stripes.

Then there's the slightly weirder stalky stuff: one of Mariah Carey's hotel slippers, a fag packet of Paul Weller's, a clump of hair belonging to one member of Duran Duran, a sock from Roger Daltrey and a heavily chewed cigar stump from Jay Z. I also have a pair of trousers that once belonged to Nick Valensi of The Strokes and a mini sausage roll I stole from Nelson Mandela. Mandela is not a rock star in the traditional sense but, with his fist-pumping cries of "Amandla!", very much an embodiment of its spirit.

I think about the journey in rock that has brought me such riches. I have walked into hundreds of hotels, usually at the tail end of an entourage, trying to appear as though I am "with the band". But then, more often than not, a flint-hearted manager will stand on tip toes overlooking the melee in the lobby and point me out to reception staff with a clear slicing motion of the hand.

"This guy pays for his own drinks," he will say. "He's not with us."

Reception staff henceforth fix me with the sceptical, pitying air reserved for the fan, the hanger-on. This is always the moment when I remember I am not a rock star. And so, I need memorabilia to prove I was there. I need somehow to establish that I am on the *inside* and not the type of bottom-feeder who asks for autographs. *God damn it, I bear witness! I shape the narrative!*

Some of my stuff, I must admit, is starting to look a bit dodgy. A hand towel on which a sweat-drenched Ozzy Osbourne once wiped his face hangs in front of me. It stinks. Once, when Ronnie had his friend Jack to stay for a sleepover, he pulled it down and gave himself a once over with it after a shower.

"Holy shit, Michael, Jack's dried himself with Ozzy Osbourne's towel!" Nicola reported with horror. We didn't tell his parents, just waited in terror for news that Jack was off school with rabies.

My most astonishing piece of rock memorabilia is the half-eaten sandwich I stole from the plate of James Brown, the Godfather of Soul. Sprayed with art fixative and mounted on a wooden plaque, it is a deathless memento of a soul legend's snack habits. Sometimes I reflect that I am the only rock writer I know with a James Brown sandwich remnant, and it gives me a thrill.

But not today. I am soaking in the bath and wondering if Ron Wood's fag butt might go next to it when I detect a slump in mood. I do not derive the usual pleasures from my memorabilia collection. I stare at the James Brown sandwich. I see the Godfather of Soul's uneven teeth marks on the bread crust. It emits no wattage of legendariness. It's just a sandwich.

Something is not right. I'd like to think it's jet lag but it's not. I feel spooked, edgy and low. I drank too much on the plane. I suffered a fitful, nightmarish sleep. Also, I was not very pleased with how the Rolling Stones interviews went. Talking to Jagger was like addressing an AI robot, albeit one installed with state-of-the-art cockney-talk software and a weathered-look latex face. Every question drew a perfectly polite, automated response. Ron Wood was okay, cackling poolside at his rented Toronto mansion. Charlie Watts was a bit grumpy – but, then again, he had just survived a car crash and cancer.

No, it was Keith. Keith Richards, the Rolling Stone who perhaps more than any living star embodies the spirit of rock 'n' roll, was the problem. He is one of the Big Six. I was more excited to meet Keith than all the others put together. However, a conversation with my sister just before I flew out ruined it for me.

On the morning of my trip, I drove my campervan to short-stay parking at Heathrow airport. My van is an old heap with 260,000 kilometres on the clock, but it has a state-of-the-art stereo. It's a private world where I can rock out. I was early for check-in and so, sitting in the car park, I finalised my Keith interview questions and binge-listened one final time to his immortal riffing. I wanted to share my joy with someone. Nicola is increasingly sceptical of my work as a rock writer, so before leaving the van to enter the terminal, I rang my sister Charlotte in Brighton. She used to be a rocker. She would get it, I reasoned.

"I can't believe I'm actually going to meet Keith," I said to her, "one of the Big Six!"

"Where *are* you?" Charlotte asked. "In a toilet?"

"I'm in the van."

"Jesus, you still have that old heap? And you're calling me to what ... to show off?"

"I'm going to meet Keith," I snapped. "Nicola's not interested. I thought at least *you'd* support me."

"Go on then, you star-fucker," she grumped, "what will you ask him about?"

"I'm going to focus on the dark shit," I said, "attacking Ron Wood with a knife, and the heroin years, for starters."

Charlotte sighed heavily down the phone. "Is that really still your job? Asking rock stars a load of laddish questions?"

"What do you suggest then?" I sulked.

"I dunno. Why don't you ask him about Brian Jones?"

"Oh, great idea," I said with acid sarcasm. "*So, Keith, setting aside the new album and tour, let's talk about your old guitarist's inability to do the breast stroke ...*'"

"Well, he was the talented one, wasn't he? Until he ended up dead ..."

I was no longer excited about meeting Keith Richards. Instead, I could only picture Brian Jones, floating star-shaped in the pool of his Sussex mansion, the tendrils of his water-logged bouffant spreading like weeds across the surface of the water.

"Fuck!" I said rubbing my eyes.

"What's the matter now, you big baby?" asked Charlotte.

"You made me think of Brian Jones! And now I can't get the image of his corpse out of my head!"

"Well, it wasn't so great for him either!" she countered. "It's not always all about *you*, you know."

"Why do you have to piss all over my big moment?!" I raged.

"Why do you have to be such an arrogant prick? Why did you even ring me?"

I shouldn't have rung my sister. She used to be a rocker but then she got all po-faced and serious, dumped all her records, moved to Brighton and started doing lots of therapy and eating mung bean casserole. These days she listens to a lot of whale song. She's over rock.

"Thanks for your downer suggestions," I sneered finally. "Email me at my luxury five-star hotel if you think of anything more upbeat to ask him."

"Enjoy another tough day at the office, celebrating narcissists, freaks and nihilists!" she snapped and hung up.

THE ROLLING STONES were rehearsing for a world tour at Greendale School in Toronto. The kids were on holiday, and the band were making a racket in the hall. I arrived by cab and shouldered through the fan scrum at the gates.

"I'm here to see Keith and the boys," I announced loudly to security, enjoying the waves of fan hate at my back. They looked boggle-eyed with anticipation, clutching their pens and autograph books. I chewed gum wildly and flashed my Access All Areas laminate. *Let me through! Cultural gate-keeper at work!*

I did not think about Brian.

I found Keith, in his backstage nook. He was ensconced in a heavily incensed tent, smoking a fag – every so often leaving it to dangle from his lips as he fiddled with the beads and baubles in his hair, like a human Christmas tree on a tea break, primping its own decorations. We talked amiably enough about the new Stones tour and album. I giggled a little light-headedly when, despite being a multi-millionaire rock star, he discussed the thrill of stealing apples from his neighbour's garden. I cackled a little gauchely when he said that, yes, he had once or twice attacked Ron Wood with a ratchet knife.

"He can be an annoying little cunt, and I have to show him the blade!" he said. There was a lull. I accepted a hand-ful of jelly beans.

But then, out of nowhere, I found myself asking about Brian Jones. "Poor Brian, he was the band's genius," I said. "He thought of the name and created the sound, but he just fell to pieces. Do you ever think about him?"

"Brian? Nah, he was an arsehole," said Keith. Simple as that. History re-written by the winners. I nodded gravely, but I heard Charlotte's voice in my head: *Another tough day in the office, celebrating narcissists, freaks and nihilists!*

I CONSIDER ALL this while scrubbing and soaping in the bath. Then I submerge myself to rinse and, making just-above-the-waterline hippo nostrils, stare at the world through water above me. I panic and lurch upright with a gasp ... *Jesus, is that the last sight Brian Jones saw?!*

Having spooked myself, I exit the bath and towel off in the bedroom. Nicola is already up and dressed. I watch her in the mirror as she brushes at a spot on the bib of her flame-retardant dungarees, head cocked like a wading bird eyeing a fish. She looks good in utilitarian workwear, like a glamorous new member of Slipknot, but she gets through a lot of it because at the day centre there are numerous laundry hazards: thrown food, inappropriately deployed fire extinguishers, floods.

"Somewhere in this city, the Gallagher brothers are putting on smart suits," she says. "Is this really what you are wearing?" She stands by the bed holding my outfit up on a hanger, twirling it slowly in disparagement. I look at the suit and swallow hard. It's a suit made for someone short and stumpy, possibly on a high meatloaf diet. Meatloaf, for example. Nevertheless, it is the suit I have decided to wear to the awards.

"Here is a list of autographs Ronnie has promised his classmates," she says waving a piece of paper. I look at it. The list comprises a new crop of rock lightweights: Keane, Snow Patrol, Coldplay and James Blunt.

I feel a bit sorry for my son. Rock seems to be dying, and these are the bands he and his generation must learn to love. They are not in the Big Six.

"See what you can do," says Nicola. "He's told the whole class his dad knows all the rock stars."

I nod, but I still don't feel right. I do not feel like going to the awards.

"Come down for breakfast, Ronnie has made you a card," Nicola says.

Ronnie is good at art and is always making me cards, no matter how trivial the occasion. Once he made me a Good Luck Meeting Shaun Ryder card. On the front, he drew a stick man lying in a ditch next to a bottle of vodka. His mother told him off.

"We do not make light of people with problems, now do we?" she said. He bowed his head and said sorry.

Downstairs I look at his latest offering. The card says "Good Luck at the Awards". On the front a small stick man carries a tray of drinks to a cluster of larger stick men, all waiting belligerently with hands on their hips. I am annoyed at the inference that this is what I do.

"That's a lovely card. Thank you, Ronnie," I say tightly.

I sigh and take a sip of coffee. I think about eating breakfast, but my suit is so tight it feels like if I put anything in my mouth it will come straight out through my nostrils. Instead, I load a wad of gum, as befits someone in the music industry.

"Don't chew in front of Ron," Nicola hisses. "You know he's been in trouble for that at school."

"But I'm going to a music industry awards. I need to chew gum."

"That's the most ridiculous thing I've ever heard."

SOMETIMES I FEEL Nicola doesn't fully understand the stresses of my work. I am a rock writer. I chew gum to project a more belligerent persona.

At one awards ceremony, I looked after U2. Their security chief manically worked a bolus the size of a golf ball, while inspecting fire exit provision with flint-faced urgency. It was infectious. The more gum he chewed, the more I chewed.

"Give me another piece of that," I said as he questioned the suitability of seating the band next to the Sugababes. Then I marched about looking for snipers.

Today I am looking after Oasis. I will need even more gum. The reason I feel odd about chaperoning Oasis is because, just before the Rolling Stones, I was on tour with the Gallaghers for a cover story. That one was a bit of a weird experience too. "Are you looking for a slap?" was the Liam Gallagher quote that *Q* put on the cover.

I feel queasy just thinking about the circumstances in which he said it. It was our final night in Milan, Italy. I crossed the line. I was unprofessional. I did not maintain control of the interview environment. I know this because I allowed Liam Gallagher to steal my glasses, tie a tea towel round my head and parade me around a five-star hotel bar claiming he had just captured Osama Bin Laden. Afterwards, amid chaotic scenes involving disgruntled hotel guests and staff, I tried to give him and his brother Noel relationship counselling.

"Are you some kind of fucking *Morris dancer*?" Liam Gallagher asked me when I began probing for the emotional core of the brothers' relationship.

"I just want you two to *love* each other," I slurred.

"ARE YOU OKAY?" asks Nicola, straightening my tie. "You look a bit anxious."

"It's only Oasis. No big deal."

But it *is* a big deal. I wince at further memories as Nicola battles with my collar. I haven't fully come to terms with what was going on for me that night in Milan.

Now I come to think of it, the trouble began when I became worried that Oasis were giving up on rock 'n' roll. I had bumped into Liam Gallagher on Milan's Via Tommaso Grossi. He was on his way home from a visit to the local cathedral.

"You've been in a bloody *cathedral*?" I demanded, shriller than I intended.

"Yeah, what's the matter with that, soft lad?"

In 2005 rock is changing. There are a lot of weedy and emotionally literate bands coming through. But Oasis are still angular and spiky and committed, as Noel once put it to me, to "scaring children's parents". I cannot bear to inform *Q*'s readers that their talismanic lead singer has just visited a cathedral.

"I was having a chat with the Big Guy," Liam went on. "You should try it. Sort yourself out."

I'd long thought that Liam Gallagher should calm down a bit. But becoming a Christian was a step too far. I felt weird, as though he had personally let me down.

After that night's show at a venue called Alcatraz, we met in a bar and a chaotic night ensued. No, a *dysfunctional* night ensued. You can over-invest in a band. You can project too much of your own stuff onto them – without doubt, I found the idea of Liam Gallagher accepting a disc of Holy Communion wafer onto his (hopefully forked) tongue, or even just admiring a stained glass window, too much to bear. I was in a bad mood. As alcohol was served and the interview began, we couldn't seem to agree about anything. I was rude and mumbled something inflammatory about how regular church attendance might staunch Oasis's anarchic fire. Then we argued vigorously about the grammar used in the title of their new album, *Don't Believe the Truth*. I said the title didn't make sense.

"What's the matter with you, ya twat? 'Course it does," said Liam.

"What does it mean, then?"

"It means, don't believe the truth the media tells ya."

"If you are implying an ironic mood, then maybe 'the truth' needs to be in inverted commas," I suggested with a wheedling rising tone of drunken haughtiness.

Noel called me a "fucking student". Liam said I must have a "small willy". That's when he pinned me to my chair and dressed me up as Osama Bin Laden. "I've found him!" Liam Gallagher told well-heeled Italians in the bar enjoying late evening intimacy. "I've got Osama, the most evil cunt in the world. Where's my fucking reward?!"

Hotel management moved us into the hotel's lounge. Liam Gallagher was so drunk he began addressing me as "Colin". The interview situation was clearly out of control. I should have gone to bed. But I was drunk, and the journalist's objective rigour fell away. Out of nowhere I soon found myself exploring a completely different agenda.

"Why do you two fight so much?" I asked.

"We like it," said Liam. "Why are you such a fucking hippy?"

"Is Noel the dominant father-figure in the relationship?" I demanded. "Is he the dad you never had?"

"Course he's not my dad," he retorted. "My dad's a bald wanker from Manchester."

"He's from Ireland actually," corrected Noel.

I told the brothers I wanted Oasis to survive, for them to love each other a bit more, but under no circumstances should this mean joining a local church congregation. I told them I knew it was stressful being in a band. I was in one too once, and I clearly remembered the clash of egos, the battles over creative direction.

"When you commit to a band, it should be do or die. Death or glory," I slurred.

"That is so fucking cheesy," Noel said.

"Who talks like that? Only a dick," said Liam, "besides, you can't look like the world's most wanted terrorist *and* be in a band."

Not looking like a rock star has been one of the greatest obstacles to living my life in the way I wanted. I found myself mounting an embittered defence. "It's what's in your heart!" I yelled at them. I crossed the line. I wasn't being a journalist anymore. A member of their entourage escorted me to the lift and shot me skyward to my room.

"It was a bit embarrassing because I compared their experience in Oasis to mine in Mental Elf," I say to Nicola. She is giving me a final pre-awards primp, brushing lint off my shoulder, digging a yellow crystal of sleep from my eye.

As soon as I've said it, I realise I've made a huge mistake. Even though she didn't even know me at the time, Mental Elf is a band name about which Nicola manages to get retrospectively very annoyed.

"I still can't believe you took the piss out of mental health by calling your band Mental Elf," she says.

"It was a play on words," I explain. "It was named after someone short and a bit unpredictable."

Nicola doesn't look convinced. She continues making Ronnie's school lunch, stacking sandwiches with neat symmetry on a chopping board. They look like little Marshall amps being loaded into a truck.

"I'm glad I didn't know you when you were seventeen, and I'm not surprised you didn't make it."

"Give me a break," I say. "Didn't you do anything silly when you were seventeen?"

"Who was the elf?" Ronnie asks.

"A teacher," I say.

"Oh, that's mature, that's sensible," snaps Nicola. "Tell your son how you openly ridiculed a member of staff at school!"

"She didn't know it was about her!"

"Who did she think it was about then?"

"I don't know! An elf probably!"

"But elves don't really exist, do they?" asks Ronnie, perplexed.

"Can we please just stop this conversation?" says Nicola. "It's time for you to get to school." She collects Ronnie's bag, flicks his hair straight, and they head for the door.

"I bet you were a bloody nightmare when you were younger," she says into my scalp, kissing the crown of my head. She is half-smiling. I think that, secretly, Nicola quite likes the idea of me being a bloody nightmare when I was seventeen, but only on the proviso that I am not one anymore.

I hear the front door shut and their happy chatter outside on the path. In the silence of the house I reflect: it's probably a good thing Nicola didn't know me when I was seventeen. I was a half-Bolivian teenager living in the London borough of Croydon. I was clueless and grasping at life. I really did not know what I was doing.

However, I am certainly not glad Mental Elf didn't make it. I would like to have been a rock star. Not necessarily one of the Big Six, just a one-hit wonder. I would like to have attended an awards at least once, even as a rank outsider, and had a journalist serve me a drink. I would like to have ambled up to the stage to applause, collected an award while saying something apposite about world affairs or goading a rival rock band.

But Mental Elf arrived on the scene at a difficult time in rock. Our lead singer Pete Bannerman was an angry punk who brooked no dissent, and our bass player Foetus was his loyal lieutenant. Music was going through one of its periodic shifts in zeitgeist, just as it is now. I urged them to embrace the new mood: the move from guitar to synths signalled by Gary Numan, Depeche Mode, Ultravox and others. Pete said Numan was "the Argos David Bowie". We fell out about it, the band split, and I gave up trying to be a rock star.

In fact, if I wasn't feeling so embarrassed about Milan, I realise I would like to discuss this and much else with Liam and Noel. With Ronnie growing up fast and determined to become a rock star himself, it would be useful if I could make sense of my short career as a teen rocker. My formative teenage years are returning to me; they demand re-evaluation.

But there never seems to be time to look back properly. When you hit 40, life's ratchet only cranks one way. I prepare to leave for the Grosvenor House Hotel strait-jacketed in my bad suit. I do not feel good. I do not feel right. I sense I am going to have a bad time at these awards.

➤

I DRIVE MY campervan to the hotel's entrance. Its ornate columns and cornicing are, I note, a distant architectural nod to licentious Roman feasting. A liveried teenage doorman coughs theatrically in the van's diesel fumes.

"Guest limos only, mate. Sorry," he says and refuses to valet park it for me. As I crunch the gears angrily, a colleague sidles up to him and says: "Who's come in that old heap, then? Supertramp?" They laugh and then slip away behind me to offer deferential white glove treatment to a blacked-out Mercedes.

I am furious. It amazes me that minimum wage drones are happy to sneer at a van with soul and then brazenly fawn over the limo of the oppressor rock pig. They don't get rock 'n' roll. *Bastards!*

Twenty minutes later I have dumped my van in an NCP car park. I am moodily patrolling the red carpet, chewing gum. I am waiting for Oasis.

"There'll be drinks for you in the pub afterwards," says Dave Henderson to the assembled writers, "but for now though you are *hosting*. Please keep an eye on the schedule and your guest."

Dave Henderson is *Q*'s Creative Director of Rock. I've always envied the job title. I've often imagined what it must be like to say "I am the Creative Director of Rock" across the counter at a bank when applying for an ISA, say, or to the police when they have pulled you over on the motorway.

But today I am not imagining being a Creative Director of Rock. I feel edgy and gloomy. I look around for people with more reason to panic than me. Editor Paul Rees is looking over the notes for his speech. I would hate to give a speech to this awards crowd. All year *Q* has taken these rock stars to task, barging in to their concerts, their recording studios and even their homes, to audit their rock 'n' roll credentials. Today they come to us, many bearing grudges, super-charged with free booze. By the time it comes to the Editor's welcome speech, the awards ambience is often that of a public hanging.

I consider telling Rob Fearn, *Q*'s feature editor, that I feel unwell. Rob is possessed of a forensic rock mind, always insatiable for more detail. He has these super-dilated blue eyes that never seem to blink. I sometimes think this is because he fears missing out on some important micro-event in rock. After all, his notes to me are always a variation on the need for more granular specifics.

Once I had gone to interview the Killers in Paris and mentioned that we had eaten a meal of *moules et frites* together. Rob sent me an e mail: "What kind of chips were they? What *cut*?" I remonstrated that I didn't know what kind of chips they were. "But that's the sort of detail that brings us closer," he said. "It's what puts *Q* readers into the *room*."

I decide not to tell Rob because, feeling simultaneously lethargic and wired, I sense he will want to examine a sample of my DNA to find out why.

Instead, I take my place in a wall of gum-chewing *Q* rock writers and wait for the first limos to arrive. There is light banter and winks of encouragement, like troops limbering in a trench, waiting for the signal to go over the top. The gossip is about the new award categories. There is concern that this year we have overdone the superlatives. There's to be a *Q* Inspiration Award, a *Q* Outstanding Contribution Award, a *Q* Icon Award, a *Q* Legend Award, a *Q* Lifetime Achievement Award and a *Q* Special Award.

"The engraver must think we're a right bunch of arse-lickers," opines Ben Mitchell. Phil Sutcliffe, *Q*'s elder statesman, nods in agreement. He speaks in a wise and commanding baritone like the Stranger in *The Big Lebowski*. I admire Phil. He ignores all calls to wear a suit, always turning up in a multi-coloured poncho.

"Michael, you've got glitter on your chest," says Mitchell, analysing the lapel of my suit.

The glitter is from Ronnie's Good Luck card. I had stuffed it into my top pocket as I left the house. I push it down so the craven little stick man serving the bigger stick men can't be seen.

*I feel like a little stick man today, and the big stick men are real!* But I do not say this. I am silent, consumed by further doubts. *Why didn't I take Keith Richards to task in Toronto? And why the fuck did I try to offer Oasis family therapy in Milan?*

This last thing is particularly niggling. I like to think I have been employed by *Q* specifically because I do not act weird around rock stars. I do not try to be their friend, much less offer free psychoanalysis. The magazine has more than 100,000 dedicated readers and it is they whom I serve. I don't know them. I have never met them. And yet, whenever I am on assignment, I feel the presence of the readers, the true believers in rock 'n' roll. When I stride into the rock star mansion, onto the yacht or aboard the private jet, the 100,000 do not want me to gush, smile or flatter, much less sip a cocktail or load up on freebies. They want me to take these motherfuckers to task.

But this service comes at a price. It means making enemies. At last year's ceremony, for instance, Robbie Williams took to the podium and thanked the readers for voting for him. But he made a clear distinction between the readers and the "cocksuckers who write the articles", after an interview I had written. Then, with shambling ironic detachment, Radiohead accepted an award via video-link but also refused to speak to the magazine, again after an interview I had written. Michael Bublé has also refused further contact with the magazine after I reported he had, entirely accidentally, touched one of my testicles during a backstage massage in Manila. He objected to that and other aspects of an interview I had written.

It was also last year that Ben Mitchell, a *Q* writer noted for his brusque interview style, had been personally congratulated from the awards stage by Christina Aguilera after a particularly positive cover story. Finally, he had softened.

"See, Michael, that's what happens when you make friends," editor Paul Rees had whispered to me as the whoops and applause rang out. "Go easy, or we'll have no one left to put in the magazine."

I SHOULD BE clear: I love rock music. I am not fully alive or functioning at my optimum unless I am blasting it through my cranium so loud that I can feel my meninges swell. It's a mood intensifier. It's an accelerant for the fires of the soul and, I find, serves as an adequate replacement for constructing a more normal mental narrative. For example, when Ronnie had mumps and grizzled all night, I didn't actually experience parental angst. I heard the mournful guitar intro to The Police's "Bring on the Night" on a loop in my head instead. And when Nicola won a little bit of compensation at work after a client at the day centre set fire to her hair, I didn't experience joy. I heard the slashing guitar intro to Generation X's "King Rocker". I don't have a normal emotional range per se, I have an internal jukebox.

But that doesn't mean I love all rock stars. To my mind, they are laying claim to a proud cultural legacy. They must be exotic and seditious, pathfinders and prophets who showcase new modes of thinking and living. They must show considerable voodoo prowess before they are admitted to the pantheon of greats! As a rock writer, I serve as a gatekeeper to the pantheon. *Only the most free-thinking nutters shall pass!*

Sometimes, sitting in judgement of rock stars can be painful, and you have to remind yourself why you do the job. In 2003, after I fell out with Radiohead, one of my favourite bands, Lucian, who is an Oxford educated *Q* writer, took me to the pub and explained the rock writer creed carefully.

"So, tell me what happened."

"It all started when Thom Yorke sat down opposite me wearing sunglasses," I began.

"It meant I could only see a reflection of my face."

"And?"

"That annoyed me. I don't want to see my own nervous, twitchy face when I'm doing an interview. I want to see *their* face. Only Stevie Wonder should wear sunglasses in an interview situation."

"Why?"

"Because, unless you're blind, they make you look like an arrogant prick."

"Good. Excellent. Except, Thom Yorke does have a problem with one eye."

"Then he should wear an eye patch. Like Nelson. Or Gabrielle. Dark sunglasses are antagonistic in the interview setting."

"Okay. What else?"

"He said he knew the government were censoring the media because a flan had been thrown at a politician at Aberystwyth University and the incident had not been reported."

"Was he right?"

"No. I checked."

"In that case, I fully support you," said Lucian. "You have fulfilled your part of the bargain."

"Just remind me. What is the bargain again?"

Lucian explained, with donnish articulacy, why it is essential to sit in judgement of rock stars. Rock stars are priest-god figures, modern iterations of Dionysus, the Greek god of wine and excess, who have shaped post-war Western culture. Rock itself was spontaneously willed into existence by a generation needing new lifestyle information, a manifesto to lead them away from their parents, themselves so spiritually impoverished by the fight against the Nazis. As rock writers, we both promulgate and critique the agenda of these priest-gods. We must always hold them to account.

"We must protect the legacy," Lucian told me, with the gravity of an Obi-Wan Kenobi training the next generation to practise the tenets of the faith.

I immediately felt better. What I took from Lucian's input was that, as long as you are in earnest, it's never wrong to give a rock star, even one you admire, a prod with the culture taser.

But that is also why it makes me angry when journalists collude with rock stars. They get friendly and end up writing books about them or giving them cosy album reviews. Once, *Q* sent a journalist to interview Robbie Williams. The pair became friendly and they ended up writing songs together.

"Jesus. Adrian's co-written a track on the new Robbie album. The jammy bastard will never have to work again," someone in the office noted sombrely. I consulted the album's songwriting credits with barely concealed rage. "They jammed together?! What was he *thinking*?!"

But you should never judge a man until you've walked in his shoes. In spring 2003 I too was summoned to Robbie Williams's LA back garden for a *Q* cover story. Williams's personal chef brought high-end Californian eats to our sun-dappled nook. After our interview, I nervously watched Williams produce a guitar, begin strumming and eye me carefully as his pet wolf ambled over and nosed me in the testicles.

"Do you write songs?" Robbie Williams asked.

"No," I said firmly, "I have never written a song in my life, and I never will."

It wasn't even true. When I was in Mental Elf, I wrote a high-octane punk stomper called "I Peaked as a Foetus". But I wasn't going to tell Robbie Williams that. There is a goddamn *code*.

THE FIRST OF the limos arrives. Paul Weller gets out, his eyelids flickering to a supernova of paparazzi bulb flash. Jimmy

Page breezes past, sporting a little silver ponytail that makes him look like a Georgian aristocrat. The crowd at the crash barrier, a writhing millipede, catches him in its mandibles. I see a momentary flash of desperation in his eyes as he fights for space and puts out an imploring hand to security.

*Pete come back!*

I am usually cool and self-possessed around rock titans. But, no two ways about it, my mental health dial just flicked into the red. I am chewing gum, but I cannot locate my rock persona. I feel panic rising.

I decide that perhaps these first arrivals are too legendary. I must ease myself in, first engaging with rock star talent of lesser cultural suction. *Go and make small talk with the drummer from the Kaiser Chiefs! Then, as you feel better, gradually work up to a cocktail with Nick Cave!*

I stand in a little grouping with the Kaiser Chiefs and a fat lawyer. Music industry lawyers disgust me. They split up The Beatles. Also, they are on 20 per cent. They say hi and study my suit. At an awards, there is a steep gradient of tailoring. It descends from the rock stars down through their management, PRs and security, and eventually it reaches the hotel bar staff. At the bottom, there is Phil Sutcliffe in his poncho and below him, me. But this year it is different. Not only am I at the bottom in terms of couture – my suit is trying to kill me. *Why did I wear this fucking suit?*

It's my dad's suit. My dad is dead. Cancer. Or anger, I always thought. A hard life and a lot of repressed rage. Ironically, pop music, letting go a bit, hanging loose, might actually have saved him. But culturally he was too late for that. He spent his teenage years in the wartime Navy and refused to accept that rock 'n' roll was a powerful emblem of the freedom he'd helped secure. He hated pop music with a vengeance. Needless to say, he wasn't a big fan of Mental Elf.

"These rock stars are just drug addicts and hooligans," he'd say, "taking advantage of the freedoms I and others fought for. And you, you are planning to join in with these layabouts?"

I am wearing his suit in a gesture of anti-authoritarian pique but also private sentimentality. I have been dreaming a lot about my dad lately. Sometimes it feels like he is watching me. I thought it would be a way of showing him my world, showing him that the pop music which he thought would destroy my life (or my "prospects" as he insisted on calling them in a jag of neo-Victorian haughtiness) turned out to be not so bad.

*Fuck it, I'll wear the old man's suit. Even if it does mean I have to hold my breath for four hours.*

But now I see Nicola was right. *You are too fat for the suit!* I head for the lavish hotel toilets for an emergency overhaul. I charge to the urinal and gasp as I loosen the waistband.

"Just calm down, you stupid cock!" I say to myself.

"Nervous, my friend?" a voice next to me says.

I look sideways. It's Bee Gee Robin Gibb. I had some beers with him once after an interview. Actually, thinking about it, it was just me that had the beers. After the first, I told him I loved the cat chorus falsettos on "Stayin' Alive". After the third, I told him a French exchange student let me put my hand down her blouse to it when I was fourteen. Then I really hit my stride and told him the Bee Gees were lucky to make the *Saturday Night Fever* soundtrack at all because punk was supposed to sweep them and all the other

31

cheesy disco ponces into the bin. I got a threatening call from his PR. Nevertheless, I am thrilled he remembers me.

"No, I'm not nervous. It's the suit," I say to him, "it's made my knob go a bit numb."

Robin Gibb doesn't respond. My eyes flick sideways. I see that he was addressing Nick Cave drilling the porcelain further along the stall. They zip up and leave together, throwing judgemental looks backward and muttering inaudible legend talk.

I swallow hard. I stare ahead and hose down my own shoes. *For fuck's sake!*

The toilet doors open. Q's deputy editor Gareth Grundy peers in. Gareth exudes a square-jawed can-do pragmatism that makes him perfectly suited to handling difficult personalities. A hundred years ago he might have worked in a circus, taming lions with a whip and chair to gasps from the crowd. Today, as a key awards organiser, he fights off snarling rock star egos with a clipboard and a wraparound face-mic.

"Michael, are you ok?" he asks through the open toilet door. He looks incredibly disappointed to see me spraying my own footwear and then consults his flat-plan.

"I don't want to rush you, but aren't you supposed to be out front looking after Oasis?"

It comes to me in a tomato-faced sprint along a lavish carpet to the hotel's front entrance. It was Pete Bannerman who said a rock band should stay together no matter what. Do or die! Death or glory!

I spot Liam exiting a car outside the hotel's ornate front gates, his 60s feather cut distinct amid the civilian hairstyles. Noel is next to him, gritting his teeth tightly, his large eyebrows undulating in that way that make him look like Parker from *Thunderbirds*. Noel looks at his watch and then up at the throng, like a man waiting for a date. But it's hard to reach him. There's a market day ambience, with journalists and photographers from global media outlets all shouting, "Jimmy, when are Zep reforming?" or "Chris, who are you shagging?" as icons sidle past with their entourages in tow.

"Noel!" I shout, "I'm here!" but he can't hear me.

Fans swarm the crowd safety barriers: middle-aged men, dead eyed professionals touting memorabilia to be signed for sale on eBay; truanting school children who've camped out since daybreak, looking pained and crazed with the effort of worship.

*I am not a fan. I am in the music industry. I need to find my industry composure. I need to reach Oasis!*

I try to barge past Damon Albarn. He has put his rock band Blur on hold to make world music albums in Nigeria and Iran. You can always tell a rock star who has abandoned rock to make world music by their facial expression. Albarn's face says: *Anyone familiar with my new, pan-cultural oeuvre would know that autograph hunting is an inappropriate fan response. However, I can offer you this ironic half-smile.*

Gareth wheels past me, one hand touching the black bud of his wraparound face-mic, the other raised in a five-finger fan. "Five mins to the first award," he says, furiously chewing gum.

*Five minutes to get "industry"!* I flip a desperate thumbs-up back, but in doing so I lose sight of the Gallaghers. *Fuck!*

Moments later, I catch a glimpse of both brothers

lurching forward with cumbersome hip movements, like men in the sea trying to wade ashore against a heavy current. They are being mobbed. Both are negotiating hands, pens and record sleeves held in the multiple tentacles of a large fan-animal trying to grab and absorb them.

I clock Gareth staring me out. *Three minutes left! Help them!* I don't know what to do, so I wave and shout like a man on a desert island attracting the attention of a passing freighter. "Here! I'm here!"

It turns out a rock awards is the wrong place to wave and shout. A hundred TV and paparazzi cameras and mics are immediately raised in my direction, making a sound like the clatter of weapons and shields being raised just prior to a hillside charge in Braveheart. And then just as suddenly they are dropped. *He is not famous!*

"Hi, guys, it's me, Michael. Remember Milan?" I say when the Gallaghers finally free themselves and reach me.

"Course I fucking remember," says Noel. "You're not going to try and hypnotise me and ask me to explore my childhood, are you?"

"No," I say, "but I'll be looking after you today."

"Mega," says Liam. "You can start with a bottle of decent champagne."

We enter the ballroom. An attendant offers him a bowl of nibbles. He flicks a peanut up in the air. It arcs through the air and bounces of my forehead. "Goal!" he shouts.

I laugh a hollow laugh. I feel muted hysteria at the back of my throat.

We circle the tables and mingle. I smile and nod where appropriate and, sometimes, where it's not appropriate: a pale young woman catches my eye. I think I know her.

I smile and give a discreet wave. She ignores me. I cannot take my eyes off her.

"You awright boss? You look like you've seen a fucking ghost," says Liam

"Who's that girl?" I ask him.

"You're not on the pull now," he says, "you're working. We need more nuts."

"That's Natalie, Ian Curtis's daughter," says Noel. "She's here with New Order."

"Fuck!" I say.

"Are you okay?" asks Noel.

When I was in Mental Elf, we tried to cover Joy Division's "Transmission". Pete Bannerman could imitate the guitar, but he couldn't do Curtis's guttural vocal.

"That bloke's energy comes from somewhere scary," Pete had said.

It's all too much. The suit. The memory. The sight of Natalie Curtis spins me off axis. While the Gallaghers accept industry back-slaps and man-hugs, I text Nicola at work: "I am going mad. Help!"

I stare at my phone screen. I need an instantaneous response. It doesn't come. "For fuck's sake! Help me!" I say to my phone.

Gareth breezes past and commands, "Stop texting. Oasis are about to win."

The ballroom falls silent as a gold envelope is ripped open. A gasp. A whoop. Oasis triumph with the coveted Best Album award for *Don't Believe the Truth*.

My phone pings. Message from Nicola: "Weird text! Can't talk. Day centre kitchen on fire. Have a drink?"

I slip away to the bar. But it's no ordinary bar. It's

sponsored by a Russian vodka company. They are working to a strict "the more rock stars who get shit-faced = better promotion for us" formula. Young staff in Cossack hats are pouring not just doubles or trebles but effectively offering to replace your whole blood supply with vodka. They hand me a jug. I sip slowly. I feel my confident music industry persona returning.

One of the Russians approaches me. "Excusing myself to you. Is possible you achieve for me a signature of Liam Gallagher."

"Sorry, no autographs," I say.

"But are you not his servant?"

"No, I'm not his fucking servant," I bristle. "Go away, I'm trying to work in the music industry."

It's rude, for sure, and a little overly literal. But I have to think literally about what I am trying to do here or I am literally fucked.

The pretty Cossack uses a combination eyeball bulge/nostril flare gesture to indicate to her colleagues I should not be served any more sponsor's vodka.

"Sorry," I say, "I am not drunk. I am mental."

WATCHING THE AWARDS unfold from the bar, it's as though a firewall between the past and present has collapsed. Ghosts and memories waft around me. Peter Bannerman. My dad. My sister Charlotte in her punk clothes. The membrane between present day industry professional and half-Bolivian teenager in the suburbs has ruptured. There is a leakage of internal narrative. In fact, chin slumped low, I begin talking to the lapels of my dad's suit.

"Dad, I'm wearing your suit while looking after

Oasis, who you would probably have wanted arrested," I mumble.

"Pete, if you'd accepted the new electronic sound, Mental Elf might have made it."

"Sis, after punk failed, you said it was time to grow up. But I haven't. In fact, I'm at a music awards, talking to Dad's suit."

It is while I am muttering into my lapels that I see Gareth pressing his earpiece into the side of his head and frowning darkly, like an American secret service agent receiving news that an assassin has broken through the presidential cordon. He canters over to me at speed.

"Okay, we have a problem," he says looking directly into my eyes.

"I've only had half a jug. I can still talk."

"What?"

"I can still talk, bro'!" I say clapping him enthusiastically on the shoulder.

"We need a photo of Oasis holding their award," he says, "but they've lost it. Someone says Liam drop-kicked it under table nine."

"Don't worry," I slur and, crouching on all fours, begin a hands and knees under-table migration north east across the ballroom. It's strangely calming under the table at a major rock awards. I feel less stressed among ankles. I think it's because celebrity only works from the neck up. Down here, they are just people again.

But it doesn't last. I soon find the award lying on its side near Björk's handbag. As I exit from under the tablecloth the little Icelandic singer gives a puffin-squawk of surprise.

I take it to the makeshift photo studio where winners

are being photographed and interviewed. The Gallaghers are already there, drinking award compère Jonathan Ross's personal supply of champagne. They offer me some.

"No thanks, guys," I say.

"Don't call us *guys*," says Liam Gallagher. "We're not fucking *guys*. We're *geezers*. Now stop running round like a fucking Butlins redcoat and 'ave a drink."

They give me a glass of champagne. I gulp it down. It doesn't mix well with vodka. I don't think I can do a showbiz "How d'ya feel?" awards interview. I start to feel like I did back in Milan. But I have to try. Oasis have won the biggest award of the day, and they are the standard-bearers for a particularly belligerent working-class creed. Right now, they represent proper rock 'n' roll.

We talk a bit about the rock artists they currently have a problem with. The new crop, like Keane, James Blunt and Coldplay who pose no cultural threat, come in for particular attention. When they discuss rival bands, it's like tossing pork chops over the fence into the lion enclosure at the zoo. They attack. There is a thrilling blur of violence, and afterwards there only remains a splash of blood and a remnant of tendon.

"Keane look like estate agents," says Noel.

"Coldplay are a bunch of Morris dancers," sneers Liam.

"Who," demands Noel, poking me in the chest, "who among that lot poses a threat?"

I say that I don't know. "Pete Doherty maybe?" I suggest finally.

"As it happens, I like The Libertines," says Noel, "but that guy needs to sort himself out."

"Gear 'ead," snarls Liam. "End of."

While Oasis assess the current vigour of rock, a wave of drunken sadness washes over me. I notice Ian Curtis's daughter Natalie is now sitting alone, tentatively probing her lunch. I feel like I did in Toronto with the Rolling Stones again.

Here is the ballroom of winners, icons clutching their gongs. But what about the ones who aren't here? The ones who didn't make it?

"You've lost a few members of the band over the years," I say to Noel, "does that weigh heavy?"

"Don't take things so serious, man," says Noel. "You're always so uptight. Chill out."

"But Guigsy, what happened to him? And Scott too?" (Over the years Oasis have proved something of a mental health no-go area. Original bass player Paul 'Guigsy' McGuigan left the band following a rumoured breakdown. His replacement Scott McLeod lasted eight weeks, also citing emotional issues.)

"Not this again. He was on about this in Italy, wasn't he?" says Liam. "What is up with you, you daft cunt?"

"I'm actually not feeling too great," I say. "In fact, I'm having a bit of a tough time at the moment."

"Who's upset you?" says Liam throwing an arm round me. "I'll give 'em a slap."

"It's no one," I say. "Just me."

# 3
# Panic!

"Daddy, we saw you on the TV! You got hit in the face with a peanut!"

The next morning Ronnie runs into my bedroom and clambers over my prone bulk under the duvet, eager for reports from the awards. But I do not reciprocate his enthusiasm. I sit up, look past his wriggling body at the suit hanging off a chair. My stomach gives a nauseous lurch. *You were having a drunken conversation with that suit last night!*

For a split second, I fear it might say something or come alive. However, it is no longer the ghost's apparel I was talking to. It's just a suit again.

I cast my eyes round the inside of my head, looking for any signs of the imposter, the maniac who made me piss on my shoes and talk shit yesterday. I am half expecting him to leap out in front of me, as though hiding behind ordinary brain mechanisms, and launch into a diatribe: *You disgraced yourself in a toilet with one of the Bee Gees!* But he doesn't. I am okay.

"So, Daddy, why did that man flick peanuts at you?" Ronnie asks me.

I am annoyed. Of all the moments from the day that the

TV cameras should capture, why did it have to be the one when I was being bombarded by bar snacks?

"It was a game," I say.

Nicola enters with two cups of tea. "Leave Daddy alone now. He's got to go to work and write about the awards," she says.

Ronnie leaves the room to prepare for school.

"Good time? We saw you on TV last night," Nicola says checking he has gone. "You looked ... busy." The way she pauses slightly before saying "busy" translates to me as "You looked mental." However, when I look at her closely I see I have misjudged her tone. She is not being sly or implying anything. I am being paranoid.

"It was okay. Not the best," I say levelly.

"You sent me a really weird text," she says. "What was that about?"

"Nothing. I was drunk."

"Look, I hope you don't mind, but your shoes smelled funny," she says. "I think the cat might have pissed on them, so I've put them outside."

OVER BREAKFAST, I decide the awards meltdown was a blip. I am fine. I will head for work and, immersing myself in the communal post-awards hangover, I will write my report. Then I will collect the van from the NCP car park and drive home. Yes, I feel like shit, but there is important rock bureaucracy to attend to. The awards' huffs and spats, rows and walk-outs are the very fabric of rock 'n' roll. Someone said they saw James Blunt with his nose to the bathroom marble as though making a forensic study of hotel's cleaning standards. Someone else said they saw Damon Albarn take a phone number from Björk. These micro changes in the culture must be analysed and reported. Hence the post-awards issue of the magazine is always very popular and, despite my mental jitters, I am determined to play my part.

I say goodbye to Nicola and Ronnie and enter the mass transportation system at Brixton tube station alongside a phalanx of suited drones.

As I exit the tube at Oxford Circus, fighting hangover nausea, I look at the other office workers and realise that I have much to be grateful for. I am not a drone. I am a rock writer, one of the few jobs in which impaired mental faculties can be interpreted as enhancing my credentials.

*I work in the music business! Any one of these indentured corporate zombies would kill to drink as I drank, touch who I touched, see what I saw!*

On Oxford Street I feel like I might vomit. However, I can rationalise this: *Of course I'm wasted! I rock!*

It's early. I decide I have time to burn off my hangover with a walk, a detour through central London's key rock heritage sites. I amble past the original site of the Marquee Club on Wardour Street. I stop and imagine the queue outside on 24 January 1967. What a night! Most of the Big Six were out here on the pavement! Not as rock stars, as mere punters! The Beatles and the Rolling Stones and Pete Townshend and Jimmy Page were queuing to see the new kid in town – Jimi Hendrix! I turn south past Adam Ant's graffiti on Denmark Street and then past the old Astoria. I remember seeing Richey Edwards from the Manic Street Preachers perform here for the last time in 1994. I saunter through Soho and glance up at the first-floor room of the Bricklayers Arms where Brian Jones named his band the Rollin' Stones (in a suspicious grammatic cop-out, a "g" was added later). Circling back past the former Speakeasy club, I imagine the evening in 1977 when another great sea-change in rock crystallised in violence. The road crew of hippy rockers Procol Harum fought a pitched battle with the Sex Pistols out on the street. Finally, I detour to Heddon Street, off Regent Street, and stand in the spot where Bowie was photographed on the cover of the Ziggy Stardust album.

Suited drones, slot-mouths to their phones, whir by on the pavement like figurines on a Swiss clock. I exhale richly. I am at peace. *At least I'm not a corporate slave! Rock 'n' roll has made me a free man!*

And then I turn towards the Q offices, confident that, writing my report about the awards, I am adding to the ongoing narrative of rock history, albeit in a tiny, incremental way. *I am a gatekeeper of the culture!*

I round the corner onto Winsley Street and enter the lobby. The lift arrives with a soft ping. The doors open. I step forwards but, eyes bulging and nostrils flared, I refuse like a horse at a jump. I cannot get into the lift.

Inside are anglers, bikers, skateboarders, dieters, pensioners, crossword puzzlers, paraplegics, horse men and women, trout enthusiasts, model-makers, knitwear maniacs, kung fu artists: the writers and editors servicing the hundreds of magazines housed in the EMAP building, a tinted glass penis-shaped word factory.

At the back of the lift are my people: goths, punks, beatniks, rappers and nerds who work on the music magazines. They shuffle up to make space and press the Hold Doors button in a most accommodating way. But my feet will not travel forwards. I just cannot go in. I am overwhelmed by waves of anxiety about crossing the threshold. I feel like I am back at the awards again. Except here there is nothing to feel anxious or nervous about. My people look at me and I look at them. Then they look back at me harder. *Why isn't this guy getting into the lift?*

I step back, give myself a pat-down and pace about the lobby. Then, making the internationally recognised "I'll wait for the next one" face, I hand in my laminate at the desk and exit the building. I go for a walk along Oxford Street to calm down.

But I cannot calm down on Oxford Street. I am carried away on a rill of shoppers and office workers. Arms pressed to my sides, I bob in the sea of humanity like a fisherman's float, eddying south to Soho then north past the glass complexes that ingest suited knowledge workers through their revolving doors.

I am flotsam. I am obstructive jetsam. A hundred tiny shoulder collisions with city folk tell me it's time to get off the streets.

I hole up in a McDonald's looking aimless and downbeat. Complex socio-economic factors dictate that a central London McDonald's on a weekday morning is an established hangout for the aimless bum. I find a booth. My head feels so heavy that when I lean it against the tiled wall of my booth I immediately fall asleep. Well, not asleep exactly. I am sucked into a black hole of lethargy. There are dreams waiting for me, just below the surface of consciousness.

I have always thought of my dream-life as a free cable channel showcasing cheesy comedy and occasionally low-budget porn.

But these flicks are different. They are insane. In one

dream, Ronnie is in my dad's suit, playing air guitar and giving me the middle finger. In another, members of Mental Elf call out to me from the open doors of a speeding tour bus. I am chasing alongside on foot while their heavily jewelled, cigarette-yellowed fingers stretch out to help me clamber aboard. But I cannot reach them. The bus speeds away.

"Come back!" I shout and wake myself up.

I am back in the booth. Now I have company. A tramp sits opposite staring back. Even with his high threshold of weird, he looks sceptical. Then with a flourish he disappears behind a tabloid newspaper. I try to concentrate on the pages I can see to stave off waves of anxiety. But there will be no solace here: I can see pictures from the *Q* Awards on the showbiz page. Noel Gallagher with a human hand gently guiding his back into the ballroom. *I know that hand! That hand belongs to me!*

"That's my fucking hand!" I say to the tramp. He looks at me and then leaves the booth.

Panic crowds in. *Tramps are rejecting me!* I swallow hard, leave McDonald's and run to the NCP car park. I must get home.

"MICHAEL WHAT ARE you doing out here? Is everything okay?"

I am sitting outside the house in the van. I hear Nicola's voice but stare through the windscreen silent and immobile. On the original cover of one of my favourite singles, Gary Numan's 1979 hit "Cars", he sits gripping an imaginary steering wheel with his eyes rolled back into his head. I imagine this is what I look like.

"Michael, speak to me!" cries Nicola.

I do not speak. I hear music coming from inside the open front door of the house. I want the music to stop.

"Stop the music!" I shout finally, cupping my ears to block it out.

Nicola looks frightened. "I was just listening to one of *my* CDs for a change. Sorry," she says.

"Turn it off. *Please*," I say.

"Michael, what's happened?"

"I'm not sure. I think I am having a breakdown. I think I am going mad."

"Come on, you're just tired and hungover that's all."

"No," I insist. "I am mad."

"Why have you got your hands over your ears?"

"The music. Stop the music."

Nicola runs inside to turn off the stereo. This is a complete inversion of our family values. It is almost always Nicola who craves silence while attending to an emergency call from the day centre concerning a fire or hostage situation. Our world is upside down.

"Tell me. What's happened?" she implores once I am inside.

"I couldn't get into the office," I say, studying myself in the hallway mirror. The mirror is a piece of rock kitsch. It is etched with a silhouette of Elvis Presley so that when you look into it, you are standing next to the King as he hip-swivels to "Jailhouse Rock". But I look past Elvis in his prison drab and see an ashen faced ghoul staring back.

"Maybe everyone is still hungover from the awards," offers Nicola.

"No. The office was open. I just couldn't go in."

"Do you need a Nurofen?"

"I'm not hungover. I am mentally ill."

I feel stupid saying it. If I was truly mentally ill, I wouldn't be able to say "I am mentally ill." Nicola deals with mentally ill people all day, and she has told me they don't say it. They re-enact the crucifixion or run into the TV room ducking and shouting because they earnestly believe they are taking part in the D-Day landings. In one of Nicola's most interesting cases, a middle-aged man believed himself to be 1970s ITV sports presenter Dickie Davis. The one thing they don't say is, "I think I am mentally ill."

"Of *course* you're not mentally ill," Nicola says to me. But actually she does look a bit worried. I suddenly imagine that a mental healthcare professional saying "Of course you're not mentally ill" is the sign that something is definitely up.

"Go upstairs, drop your bag, and I'll bring you a tea," Nicola advises.

RONNIE'S BEDROOM DOUBLES as my office and storage facility. In one corner is his little bed, in the other my desk and assorted memorabilia. I spend a lot of time here. It's where I feel safe, where I can slough off the family persona and be me. It's also another shrine where even more hallowed pop artefacts are stored. These artefacts are too important for the bathroom. They are mementoes of my career with Mental Elf: a guitar, a box of notebooks containing lyrics, some effects pedals and promotional flyers.

The office/bedroom is also where I listen to music. I can really make a pig of myself with rock music. Sometimes I can put away three or four rock albums in a sitting. And I don't mean just listening to them. There are air guitar solos, high volume sing-alongs, and often drum soloing on my desk. Occasionally, if the mood is right, there are uncontrollable crying jags.

Music affects me deeply. This is reasonable for a rock writer. At least you'd think so. And yet, if I were to pinpoint the part of my relationship with Nicola which causes most conflict, it wouldn't be that I go away on glamorous trips, or that there are occasional money issues, debates over child care or squabbles over the social responsibility component of my job. It would be *how* I listen to music.

Mostly I listen to it on my own. I listen to it on headphones in the house while cooking or doing Ronnie's bath time, sometimes even while helping with homework.

"Do you think you might be jeopardising a proper emotional connection with Ronnie, parenting in headphones?" Nicola sometimes asks.

"WHAT?!" I shout. Then I will take the headphones off and make Nicola repeat the question.

"Kids like to see their parents happy. It's proven," I answer.

"Yes, if you share it. But when he sees you making cymbal sounds and getting phlegm down your chest, he is not sharing it, he is a spectator."

"I don't think he notices or cares."

"Wrong. Ronnie asks me, 'Why does Daddy like the men in his head more than me?'"

And so that has become a firm house rule: no parenting in headphones.

There is another problem in our relationship. Under the influence of rock, I become a different person. I cease to be Michael. I disappear into music, sometimes to the point where I have no idea who I am.

Once, when I was going to interview Sting, I took this as an excuse for an all-day Police binge. I planned to listen to all their albums, even some of Sting's solo stuff. Nicola was at work, but it was half-term so Ronnie was home. I put on a *Bob the Builder* DVD for him downstairs and went up to my office to gather my binge materials. I got out my CDs, made a tray of toast and a pot of coffee and put on my state-of-the-art Sennheiser cans.

Then I got lost inside the Police's "Bring on the Night" and was there from 10am until after lunch. To me, it's not a song but a sonic cathedral. From the brooding intro to the sudden onrush of doleful figured guitar and onto Sting's rendering – in a baleful falsetto – of the gloomy angsty lyric, it has an intricate architecture the rock writer can enter and explore.

When I have tried to explain this to Nicola, using pre-cisely this language, she nods plausibly but I sometimes suspect there is a cartoon thought-bubble above her head which contains a single word: "Wanker".

I might have stayed lost inside "Bring on the Night" all day. But something happened which ruined everything. A touch, a simple human touch detonated me like a bomb. Unbeknownst to me, while I was immersed in "Bring on the Night" a fire alarm had gone off downstairs in the kitchen. Ronnie had paused his *Bob the Builder* DVD and called up the stairs to me. I didn't respond. Ronnie panicked, picked up the phone and called his mother at work.

"I think Daddy's dead," he said.

Nicola comforted him and told him to call me again from the foot of the stairs. He did. I still didn't respond. And so he came upstairs, opened the door to the office/bedroom, crept up behind me with index finger extended tremulously like ET and touched the back of my neck.

When someone is lost in music, you should never creep up behind them and touch the downy hairs on the back of their neck with an extended finger. Like a tasered bullock panicking in its abattoir stall, I leapt up and tried to charge through my office wall. I smashed my knees into the underside of my desk and then, with a Wookie roar, tipped coffee and then a tower of CDs and paperwork all over myself. Shocked and scorched, I ran in a tight circle, fists bunched in terror, dragging my computer to the floor by its cable. Ronnie burst into tears.

"Why did you TOUCH me?" I yelled.

"Daddy, why don't you LISTEN to me?! The kitchen is on FIRE!"

I went downstairs to disable the alarm. There was no actual fire. A residual stump of toast crust was slow burning in the toaster giving off a pungent smoke plume.

When I'd quelled the smoke alarm, I calmed Ronnie down. Squatting on haunches and facing him with a benign fatherly smile I tried to explain where I had been. "I was lost in music. You should never touch Daddy's neck when he's lost in music."

Even though I spent the rest of the day coaching him that the incident was no big deal, actually quite funny but probably didn't merit a mention to his mother, he immediately recounted every detail to her as soon as she got home. This gave rise to another parenting ground rule: no listening to one song more than 100 times in a row.

"No song is that good," Nicola says. But I know that isn't true.

TODAY, HOWEVER, I am not going up to my office or into the campervan to immerse myself in rock. I want silence. I want calm. I sit in my office chair and run a damage assessment. My mouth is dry. My body aches. And when I rub my right eye, it makes a grotesque rubbery squelching sound in its socket, audible to people around me.

"Jesus is that your eyeball?!" Nicola exclaims when she joins me in the office with a drink and I "play" my eyeball to her.

"Okay, I'm calling a doctor," she says.

Nicola insists on an emergency appointment, and we attend the surgery together. I am tetchy and nervous in the waiting room. I can see tabloid newspapers on the waiting room coffee table as well as a few music magazines.

"Do you want a paper to read?" Nicola offers absent-mindedly.

"Is my hand in any of them?" I ask, flexing my tense back.

"What do you mean is your *hand* in any of them?"

"I don't want to see my hand in the media," I say nervously.

"What's got into you?" she asks, annoyed. "I know you're feeling stressed, but for God's sake try and keep a sense of proportion."

I explain about the tramp and my hand in the paper. We have a hushed argument over whether I am really mentally unwell or just being neurotic and ridiculous. I sulk and insist that I will see the doctor alone.

The consultation is a disaster. Confronted by the severe, budget-sensitive gaze of a healthcare professional my powers of persuasion desert me.

"Listen to this," I say, as the doctor looks on sceptically. But when I try to rub my eye socket to make the squelchy noise, it doesn't sound half as loud as it did before.

"Setting your eye noises aside for one moment, what else seems to be troubling you?" the doctor asks patiently.

I don't like the way the doctor furrows his brow and says "troubling you". Also, he has well-tended fingernails and boring hair. I resent such professional stiffs.

*If it wasn't for me fighting the cultural wars,* I think, *you'd still be playing the Bay City Rollers at your GP Christmas party!* But I am not mad enough to say it.

"I can't get my head right," I croak gravely. "I can't control my thoughts."

He looks at me as though I have told him I am having trouble completing a difficult jigsaw.

"We all have off days," he says eventually.

"No. I am going mad," I say, "I can feel it."

The doctor looks at me with practised incredulity, as though people thinking they know what is wrong with them is one of the most annoying parts of his job. For him, "the mind" is not a set of essential human cognitive functions, but an annoying, obsolete decision-making apparatus, still frustratingly available to civilians who really ought to stop fiddling around with their own perceptions and let the professionals and/or machines tell them when they are ill.

"I see no evidence for that," he says.

"Don't you think I ought to talk to someone?" I ask.

"The waiting list for counselling is six months," he shrugs. "Why don't you take a day off and watch TV or listen to some music?"

# 4
# Sister of Mercy

"Why are you sad, Daddy?" asks Ronnie.

I do not respond. I sit in silence at the dinner table, a brooding King Kong, staring across a skyline of high-rise sauce bottles.

"Why is Daddy sad?" he asks Nicola.

"We all get sad," she replies gently.

"Put on Nirvana," says Ronnie.

"No," says Nicola. "Your dad doesn't want music now. Especially not Nirvana."

We eat in silence, and then Ronnie goes to bed. Afterwards, I sit in my chair staring dumbly into the middle distance. Nicola circles, frowning, as though in a museum examining a sculpture of questionable quality. Finally, she squats in front of me and looks directly into my eyes.

"Why don't you call a friend? There must be other rock writers who've had a wobble like this," she says with an imploring grip of my hand.

I think about the word "wobble". I like it. It's a cosy euphemism which makes everything I am experiencing feel a bit more manageable. But then I think about it some more and it frightens me. People in the care professions often use a cosy euphemism when the reality is starker. When my dad went into hospital with cancer he seemed fine for ages, and then the doc rang sounding unusually meditative.

"You father is now very poorly," he announced. I drove in with a bag of grapes and a DVD. I sat there watching *Mutiny on the Bounty*. By the time Fletcher Christian had got the rebels into the rowing boat my dad was a fucking corpse!

"When you refer to this *wobble*," I ask Nicola tentatively. "Do you actually mean I am dying?"

Nicola doesn't respond but instead insists I reach out to the rock writer community. She even passes me the phone.

"Do it. You'll feel better. It's a crazy industry, and I bet you're not the only one to have a meltdo— a blip."

I dial the number of Gary Samson, an award-winning American punk expert. I like Gary. I've been on a few trips with him. You've never seen anyone go at an all-you-can-eat hotel buffet like Gary Samson. And because he has brutal neck tattoos and terrible teeth, like the half-fallen tombstones in an ancient graveyard, no one stops him. He gets all the bacon and eggs. He rocks. Well, he did. Last year he suffered some sort of mental disturbance and took a job as a check-out operative at an out-of-town Sainsbury's. After half a lifetime of listening to heavily amplified guitar, I've heard *Q* writers say the electronic bleep of a bar-coded product passing over a scanner is all he can cope with now.

Gary doesn't answer the phone. His outgoing voicemail message is pretty uncompromising though: "I no longer work as part of the record industry, so please do not call this number again if you are connected with all that shit," he says. "But I am open to other offers."

Instead I ring Rex Trauma. It's not his real name. I think it's Rex Jones. Anyway, Rex is the guitarist in a punk band called Cot Death. As a rock writer, I can be friends with the guitarist in a band called Cot Death because it's clear they are never going to make it. My ethics will never be compromised.

But I am still not sure Rex is the right person to consult about psychic disturbance. He is pretty cynical. Once, when I told him that Lemmy from Motörhead was cutting his alcohol intake down to two bottles of Jack Daniels a day on doctor's orders, Rex said he was a "pussy". Nevertheless, he answers the phone and listens carefully to my ailments.

"Listen, mate, this is between you and me, right?" he says finally. "I went through a bit of a dark patch myself last year."

"Sorry to hear that," I say. "How come?"

"Tinnitus, bruv," he says.

There is no more terrifying medical prognosis for the rock writer. Tinnitus is a persistent and debilitating ringing in the ear. Like listening to the bloke from Scissor Sisters, but forever.

"Shit. What did you do?"

"I had to stop listening to Sham 69, Buzzcocks, Pistols. Gone. Just like that."

"That's brutal, Rex," I say.

"Yeah, I got very depressed. In fact, I became fucking suicidal."

"I can't get into lifts *or* listen to music. I'm fucked, aren't I?" I say desperately.

"You looking for a ... way out?" Rex asks confidentially.

"Yes, yes, I am," I say tentatively. Rex doesn't mess

about. In my head I am picturing a car, a cliff or a sawn-off shotgun.

"Durutti Column," he prescribes finally. "Really nice calming tunes. And then gradually ease yourself back in via Siouxsie and the Banshees."

I say thank you to Rex and put down the phone. I am sorry that he has been having a hard time. Mental health problems are often hidden in plain sight among our closest friends. But I don't know if listening to soft-end punk is a potent enough remedy for my situation.

"I need drugs," I say to Nicola. "Can't you get me some?"

"You should try one more thing first," she says with finality. "And I don't want you to fight me on this."

"Fine, what is it? *Please*, just tell me what to do."

"I think it's time to ring your sister."

IT's A TOUGH one. In one way, Nicola is offering sound advice. Charlotte could be the right person to ring because she might offer valuable mental health insights. She too was a diehard, half-Bolivian rock 'n' roller from Croydon.

In fact, Charlotte is the reason I am a music journalist. When we were very young and pop music took hold, Charlotte was my guide. She had a Saturday job. She had money. Every weekend she brought home a new music magazine or record. I stole her James Brown and punk records to show my friends, and when I was old enough I assumed her tastes as my own.

"I'm not stupid, I know you take my stuff," she used to say. "Why don't you get your own personality?"

On the other hand, Charlotte might be the wrong person to ring because she has now rejected rock 'n' roll. She flipped out, abandoned college, left home – leaving behind family, records, everything – and went to live in Brighton.

"You can keep all that crap. I've grown out of it," she said a bit haughtily the day she left. "I want Van Morrison and Tears for Fears, but you can have the rest. One day, if you're lucky, you'll grow out of it too."

But I have not given up. I have stayed with rock 'n' roll, while Charlotte and my peers have gone on to become professionals who buy only one Coldplay album a year, absent-mindedly tossed into a supermarket trolley with the pulled pork. I still buy lots of albums. That is why Ronnie has to share a bedroom with my collection. I have a thousand plus recordings. I am particularly strong on late 70s and early 80s post-punk, with a collection of limited edition Gary Numan vinyl in a corner where a desk or chest of drawers could easily be.

That is why I do not want to ring Charlotte. She certainly wasn't very helpful when I rang her from the airport about the Rolling Stones. These days, she does a lot of therapy and, in terms of pop music, only listens to 80s synth duo Tears for Fears. Their debut album *The Hurting* was imbued with ideas gleaned from therapy (sample lyric: "Shout! Shout! Let it all out!"), the first and perhaps last pop group to explore the intersection of psychoanalysis with synthesisers.

In Brighton she lives extremely frugally with Bob, a gruff Geordie taxi driver with a lot of facial hair. Bob is a giant. Well, officially, he's one inch shy of being an actual giant, but the first time I set eyes on him it seemed pointless dwelling on such niceties. Charlotte and I were on the London Road exiting a record shop I'd made her go into. Bob was at the wheel of his cab driving past.

"That's my boyfriend Bob!" she cried. I looked up to see what looked like a bear driving a car with a human hostage in the back.

Bob too came to Brighton following a troubled youth and some problems with drugs and alcohol back in Newcastle. He and my sister met at a primal therapy session. This is an intense form of self-re-evaluation, during which people can supposedly re-experience the most formative life events: their own birth, and even their time in the womb.

"Last night I swear I re-experienced coming out me mam's chuff," Bob once told me with the saucer-eyed glee of someone who's just come down a giant water chute at Alton Towers.

I don't like the way therapy has taken over Bob and Charlotte's lives. When I last visited, I noticed they had amassed a store of building materials in their back yard: wooden posts, plasterboard, rolled rubber sheeting. Bob did some building work on the side to augment his cab driving income, and so at first I assumed the equipment pertained to some modest freelance construction project.

"Actually, we're building our own primal therapy suite," Charlotte explained.

"I want to be able to come off the cabs and just scream the fucking place down," Bob added, pulling a comedy Munch face.

"Why does it have to be a rubber room for screaming?" I asked.

"Because we need to be able to punch, kick and break things too. I want to go fucking crazy," Charlotte added clenching her little fish teeth and bunching her small white fists.

*Thank God I'm not as screwed up as that! Thank God for rock 'n' roll!* That's what I had thought. But now I am not so sure.

⚡

"HI, CHARLOTTE, IT's Michael."

"Wow. My brother. My brother who never rings me unless it's to show off about some stupid rock star interview."

"I'm not calling about rock stars, I promise."

"Which means it must be the only other reason you ever call: you've got a problem."

"Sorry. Look, I've got a problem," I admit. I tell her my symptoms. Inappropriate behaviour with Oasis at an Awards ceremony. Refusing at the lift doors. And now, a generalised anxiety and mania.

"So, you've been acting like a dick with Oasis?"

"No!"

"What then?"

"I tried to give them counselling and then hid under a table when I was supposed to be looking for their award."

"Jesus Christ," she says in a concerned murmur.

I find her reaction annoying and unhelpful. We fight again. However, we always fight a lot. We were siblings forced to compete vigorously for sparse parental attention. This short spat is about the merits of Oasis and modern rock. I get nasty.

"Just because you've grown out of rock and graduated to CDs of whale song doesn't make you more mature," I say.

"Fuck off. Why did you even call me?"

I am worried enough about my situation to apologise. I share further details of my recent meltdown. I tell her I wore our dead dad's suit to the awards.

"You're too fat for that suit. You must have looked insane," she points out, echoing the general party line.

I find this fucking annoying.

"I'm not really looking for style advice. I need mental health insight," I say testily.

"Obviously there was something deeper going on," she soothes, trying to be a bit more therapeutic.

"I'd say. After a few drinks I was talking to the suit."

"What do you mean, *talking* to it?"

"Sort of narrating the experience into the lapels. As though Dad's ghost was inhabiting it."

There is a silence which I interpret as meaning that, in therapeutic terms, this is definitely not good. In fact, Charlotte sighs heavily. I know this sigh. It means "For fuck's sake".

"It's that shallow, meaningless industry you work in," she opines. "Pop stars are overpaid wankers. That's what punk was all about exposing."

Back in the day Charlotte was a punk. She bought gel sandals and put on weird make-up to see Generation X at a club called The Greyhound in Croydon. I was envious and later stole the record and the ticket stub for my rock memorabilia collection. She also once saw Sex Pistols' Sid Vicious in Bromley near Croydon and wrote a poem about him called "All Hail the Punk Hero: Pale as Instant Mash Potato".

But she gave up on the transformative power of rock and turned instead to therapy, shamanic dance, astrology and mung beans. This regularly causes friction between us, and I am always braced for particular difficulties when she raises the subject of Ronnie.

"I hope you don't mind me speaking freely, but, even if you are determined to waste your time chasing rock stars, be aware of the damage you are inflicting on your own son."

"Damaging Ronnie? How?"

"His first name is Tom! But you call him Ronnie so he can be like a rock star!"

"Ronnie is his middle name!"

"Well, the Ronnie persona is affecting his behaviour!"

While I hold the phone away from me and swear at the ceiling, Charlotte backs up this bruising charge with some observations regarding her last visit.

"Ronnie answered the door playing air guitar and sticking his tongue out at me. When I said 'Enough!' he gave me the finger. Is that how you want your son to grow up?"

"You're his aunty, surely you can indulge him a little?" I say.

"You're letting him run riot because of the upbringing you had."

Charlotte believes that, since moving to Brighton, she has come to terms with our dysfunctional Croydon childhood. It is her considered sisterly opinion that I am overcompensating with rock. "Do something more grown-up," she advises. "Why don't you write a book?"

We expand the sibling row to take in the writing of books as a signifier of maturity. I say that there is nothing fundamentally mature about being an author. People who say "Why don't you write a book?" as a way of indicating maturity are invariably conjuring up an image of an erudite, 18th-century nobleman with mutton-chop sideburns, distilling his life's knowledge onto parchment with a quill, while sitting in an orchard.

"Writing a book would be more mature than what you do now," she insists.

"You can write a book and still be immature," I counter and cite, as an example, the advanced copy of a rock memoir I have received called *Get Your Cock Out*. As a second example, I cite Mötley Crüe drummer Tommy Lee's autobiography *Tommyland* which challenges literary conventions regarding perspective and moral context by being co-narrated by his penis.

"No, *that* is immature," Charlotte retorts, "Bringing those books up as an example. I cannot talk to you."

"No, *that's* immature. Baling out of a conversation with your kid brother when he needs help," I snarl back.

I am angry because Charlotte has rumbled me. Some months back I did embark on a book. And it did have a faintly mordant Victorian air to it: it was entitled *On the Evolution of Rock by Natural Selection*. I was attempting a complete taxonomy of all pop music – like Charles Darwin but instead of beetles and thrushes, my focus was rock stars. I wanted to enumerate the founding species and the myriad resultant sub species with their defining nihilistic and counter-cultural content. The more negative and rebellious, the better.

I had got as far as K before abandoning the taxonomy. Kylie Minogue was listed thus:

*Bimbo Blondus Australianus. A showbiz blonde in the crotch-flashing, air-kissing tradition. Irrelevant to the revolution.*

Talking to my sister, this now feels like feckless immaturity. I feel vulnerable.

"I just need to be able to get into the lift at work," I say. "Help me. I'm having panic attacks!"

"Okay. But only if you agree to take this seriously and talk to someone."

"Okay," I grumble. "I agree."

"You need to do at least six months' therapy for it to work," she insists flicking through a telephone book for contact numbers.

"I know, I get it," I say submissively. But, to me, going into therapy sounds suspiciously like entering the Hotel California, i.e. you can check out anytime you like, but a definitive departure is problematic due to unspecified reasons relating to bad karma. I am absolutely determined I will have this thing licked in a fortnight. *I am not a self-indulgent hippy! Two weeks!*

Charlotte enumerates the various schools of therapy, estimates the cost and speculates whether a male or female therapist would suit me best. Then she makes me transcribe the various treatments on offer: short-term counselling, long-term therapy, body-centred transactional analysis, life goal attainment. Nobody seems to offer anything as focussed as a man's fear of getting into a lift.

I fade her out and visualise something more to my liking. I see myself making a pit-stop at the mental health equivalent of Kwik Fit where a boilersuited technician strolls across the forecourt towards me wiping his hands on a rag.

"She's running a little hot," I say, indicating my personality. "But she's got plenty of miles left in her. I just need basic psychic functions restored."

He waves me up onto a ramp, shines a couple of halogens onto my underside, welds shut the confidence leak, re-boots the panic/don't panic circuitry, plugs my fear outlets – with gum if necessary – and sends me on my way.

But it's as though Charlotte can see this cheery fantasy being formulated in my head. "Panic is just the presenting symptom of much deeper issues. *Do the work*," she persists.

"Okay, okay. I am committed," I say.

I am lying. I am not going to deal with my upbringing. Being in it was bad enough. I don't need a scenic tour of the low lights. I ring off and go downstairs.

Nicola has done some useful preliminary work regarding getting Ronnie out of my face. She has told him that Daddy is not feeling very well and that he would appreciate some peace and quiet and maybe a Get Well Soon card.

Ronnie has worked diligently to this end, using felt tips. I take the card and look at it. On the front I am pictured in bed wearing headphones while the house burns down.

"Thank you, son," I say. Then I open it and read the scrawled dedication:

"Don't be sad, Daddy, you rock!"

# 5
# Mental Health's Backstage Area

Usually, I consider the telephone handset to be an instrument of rock. Mine has superstar numbers logged in its speed dial. Most days, I shut the office door, put my feet on the desk, crack open a beer and dial. An icon answers. Then I become the other person, the louche-voiced, gum-chewing rock writer. I know where I am with all stripes of rocker madness. I know exactly what to say. It was on this very handset that I asked Ozzy Osbourne what a live bat actually tasted like.

"Funny you should ask that, Michael," he intoned in a hang-dog Midlands burr. "It tastes a bit like chicken."

But today, the handset looks daunting. That is because I am not going to ring a rock star and ask about the crazy things they did with a Mars bar, a shark or a Rolls Royce. I am going to ring a therapist and enquire about the crazy things I am doing, and thinking of doing, instead.

I am frightened. What will I say? How will I explain an ailment so nebulous, so vague?

*Do you know who Oasis is? Well, the other day I chaperoned them at an awards ceremony, where a contained industry persona was called for. Instead I behaved like a dick.*

or

*I cannot get into a lift.*

or

*My eye squelches noisily when I rub it.*

But I soon discover I am jumping the gun. The world of therapy moves very slowly. In fact, the world of therapy moves a bit like someone depressed, someone who has lost the will to live. I first ring one of the major organisations based in Hampstead, north London because Nicola once told me Hampstead is the home of therapy – the leafy enclave where speccy, tweedy Freud lived out his final days, but famous to me as the place where several members of the Big Six live.

In a passionless tone, the receptionist says she will send me some forms. "On receipt of these forms, a properly trained therapist will call you back within a couple of weeks."

"*Weeks?*" I squeal.

"Yes. Minimum. Our therapists are very busy."

"It doesn't sound like you are really geared up for panic!" I respond, tetchily.

I put the phone down and consult Nicola. When I say "consult", I suppose what I really mean is "blame". "Why is your industry so slow?" I demand. "And why does everyone sound so fucking miserable?"

"It's not a drive-thru service," she points out. "Therapy

is a considered process. A good therapist might not have availability for ages."

I didn't really want to speak to a therapist, but now I know I can't have one, the thought chills me. And then it makes me angry.

"For fuck's sake!" I cry.

I can't help myself. I hold Nicola responsible for the dire state of psychotherapeutic customer relations. When she steps into my world of rock, she is treated well. Free tickets. Chilled beer backstage. Occasionally even some banter from a rock star. In 2002 Q sent me to do a cover story about Coldplay. Nicola and I met Chris Martin at a show. He was charming, handing her a beer from his own personal supply and then engaged her in chat about the Egyptian Pharaoh Tutankhamun (he did Ancient World Studies at UCL, and Nicola once cared for a client who, when his anti-psychotic meds were wrongly administered, believed himself to be an Egyptian pharaoh). Why can't Nicola fix it for me to get in to mental health's backstage area? Where is my VIP pass to good feelings?

"Not everything is run like the music industry," she says. "This is the real world."

It turns out, she is right. In mental health there is no guest list, expense account or goodie bag. It's grimly democratic. The last thing I expected the mental health industry to be was so depressing.

I decide to try more of Charlotte's numbers, embracing the dodgy looking ones which, for one reason or another, scared me away when I first looked at them. The British Association of Psychotherapy was okay because it seemed entirely reasonable that British psychotherapists should form an association in order to compare notes (and occasionally scratch marks on the face).

But I hadn't rung the Institute of Therapy because the word "institute" sounded too much like "institution", and I imagined myself in a secure strip-lit room weaving baskets, waiting for a trolley of meds. Then, after staring at them on the page for a few minutes, the words resolved themselves into the acronym TIT. I know that in therapy one's early relationship with one's mother is crucial, but TIT just seemed over the top. Come to think of it, the British Association of Psychotherapy's acronym, BAP, had no less a matriarchal resonance.

Nevertheless, I now dial the number of TIT because it is the last one I have. Panic rises. But this time, panic mingled with aggression.

"Hello, the Institute of Therapy," says a woman with a strong Germanic accent. The voice is low, business-like and assured, with top notes of entrenched Teutonic dominance. I am feeling scattered and flimsy and therefore ready to submit. But I do not want her to pass me over to a secretary or send me some forms, so, before she can say anything else, I launch at her, like a cop throwing himself shoulder-first at a door.

"Hello, no, I don't want an appointment in six months' time, and I don't want to weave baskets after electric shock therapy. I just want to speak to someone who can help me right *now*," I blurt out.

"Okay," says the voice. "This is clear to me."

"So, can you put me through?"

"I am a therapist," she explains. "My name is Mrs Henckel."

I can't believe it. I have a live shrink on the phone at last. Immediately I am subject to regressive tendencies. I feel I can at last let it all hang out. The boil of aggregated neuroses bursts.

"*Thank* you!" I say. "Thank fucking Christ for that."

Mrs Henckel asks very deliberately what seems to be the matter. I burble my desperate plight once more – "Oasis, lift doors, etc."

She responds with measured empathy, "This experience of panic sounds very frightening." She sounds kind, understanding and experienced.

"It is very scary, I don't want to feel like this anymore."

"No. No, you don't. I can hear that in your voice."

I am so relieved at this simple kindness, my eyes well up with tears. "I am really frightened," I say.

"Do you have any ideas as to what has triggered this state of affairs?"

I have a lump in my throat, and I struggle to speak. "I think it has something to do with—"

There is a sudden stifled commotion outside the office door. I can hear Nicola trying to quell Ronnie in a frantic whisper. "No, don't you *dare*, you naughty boy!" she hisses.

"But I want to!" he replies and crashes through the door gurning and air-guitaring in his onesie. He gives me a tiny middle finger.

I hold the phone away from my ear. I look at his little pink tongue lolling grotesquely.

"I think ..." I say into the phone, "I think it has something to do with rock 'n' roll."

# 6
# Mrs Henckel

I knew rock 'n' roll was an important art form as a nine year
old, when I heard the baroque lunacy of Queen's "Bohemian
Rhapsody" leaking from a transistor radio for the first time
("Scaramouche! Scaramouche, will you do the fandango!").
I felt a more visceral connection with it than with my Lego,
crayons or school recorder, the forms of self-expression nine
year olds were then encouraged to embrace. But I didn't
imagine that being a rock star was a *job*. I didn't know
rock 'n' roll was dangerous and transformative. I assumed
"Bohemian Rhapsody" was something that Queen did for
fun, and that Freddie Mercury and the boys enjoyed sparkly
eye make-up and little fur boleros in the same way that I
liked dressing up as a fireman or, with the encouragement
of my dad, a rear admiral. I thought that, after they'd had
their fun, the members of Queen must go back to being
postmen or insurance clerks in the same way that I went
back to being a recalcitrant suburban child.

But proper rock stars are *not* pretending, as I learnt years
later when I began meeting them. Great music emanates
from strange minds. As a cultural pathfinder, a rock star is
mentally wired differently.

Once, I was granted a rare interview with the soul singer Al Green. Before we settled down to talk, he asked me, out of politeness, to say hello to his friend. I was happy to, except that I couldn't see anyone else with us in the room.

"Where is your friend?" I asked, looking about gamely.

"He's right here," Green said, gesturing to the hotel sofa, coffee table and mini bar.

I swallowed hard.

"Don't you see him? *Feel* him?" Green asked.

"Not really," I mumbled.

Al Green began laughing. "Jesus!" he cackled in a most disconcerting way. "Jesus is here with us! Can't you hear him and feel him? Let him hear you say hello, Michael! Jeeeeeesuuuuuus is heeere!!"

Once, I met Happy Mondays singer Shaun Ryder. The interview progressed well, until I admitted I found it hard to believe he'd seen a flying saucer over Manchester when he was twelve years old. He became agitated.

"One day, mate, when it's proven that they are here, living among us, you'll have to tell your grandkids that you are an extra-terrestrial denier, and they'll think you are *pathetic*," he growled.

And one time, I was doing an interview with Ian Brown of the Stone Roses, and he told me that when he was sent to jail for threatening to cut a flight attendant's hands off on a journey from Paris to Manchester in 1998, he used his time away to think of ways to improve the world.

"One of the ways would be to find the hidden Nazi gold that's never been recovered and give it to the Rastas. The Rastas, man, they should be our government."

Another time, I went to meet former Clash frontman

Joe Strummer in a West London café. The café was near the Westway, the brutalist concrete flyover which also served as a key piece of punk iconography. I navigated the mean West London streets, admired the local Clash graffiti, and reminded myself of the band's past glories. On arrival, Joe Strummer's publicist met me outside the café and ran through the usual control-freak interview caveats.

"Joe will under no circumstances discuss the legacy of punk," he said.

"Sure," I sighed and entered the café.

Inside, I let Joe Strummer ramble freely about his new band The Mescaleros for five minutes. I nodded with wild enthusiasm. Then, when I couldn't take it anymore, I put down my pen and said: "Let's talk about the legacy of punk."

It's tough being a punk icon. Much is expected of you. The huge pressure can manifest itself in bad mental health. At least that's how I interpreted Joe Strummer throwing the salt cellar across the café table and fixing me with a malign glare.

"I can't breathe for the likes of people like you weighing me down with the legacy of punk," he said. "What people don't understand is that I cannot live their dreams for them. Punk was about not following the leader. But I try and tell people this, and all they say is, 'Yes boss, if you say so,' and it drives me nuts."

I felt sorry for Joe Strummer. The job was getting to him. Rock stars are worshipped for their knowledge of, their intimacy with the hidden self, the dark side. But all too often the fans aren't happy with access to the inner kingdom of wisdom. They don't grasp the self-knowledge that is being offered. They just want to worship the king.

"Every time someone asks me for an autograph, I feel like telling them to fuck off," Strummer said. "It proves they don't get me at all."

I nodded gravely in agreement. Then I stole the teaspoon with which he had been absent-mindedly stirring his drink, and picked up the salt cellar he had swept off the table in rage and left.

I have seen a lot of rock stars go mad with the stresses and contradictions of the job. However, as a rock writer, I have always managed to stay outside the mental danger zone. Wearing the padded suit of objectivity and, where necessary, the protective visor of ironic detachment, I have remained safe. Despite handling much hazardous rock 'n' roll material, I have not been harmed. I thought I was cool. I thought I was okay.

I was wrong.

It is a monumental effort to get to Kentish Town without freaking out. Nicola offers to take the morning off and drive me. I decline. I have a plan.

"I'll get the tube," I say.

Although the bus and the walk to the tube station are a trial of exquisite neurotic agitation, (bumping into people, reacting to loud traffic noises with an audible yelp), the tube itself proves a great demotic arena. I freak out at tannoy announcements and cringe in fear at the thunder of the serpent trains writhing into the platform. But at least down here in the clamour I can scream.

"I am going fucking mentaaaalllll!" I roar down in the tube station. It helps.

For the rest of the journey, I knead my fists anxiously and flee my own reflection in the darkened carriage window: a ghoul, a husk with myxomatotic eyes. I reflect on my new predicament. How long will it take to feel better? Will I have a few sessions and feel fine, or will I need an open-ended mental refurb and perhaps even my own rubber room, like Charlotte and Bob?

The economics are daunting. If she agrees to take me on, Mrs Henckel has recommended at least two sessions a week. That's £70–80 a week, plus travel costs. It's almost another mortgage, and you don't even get a house at the end of it. However, the reality is, I don't need a new house. I need a new head. I certainly won't be able to live in this one much longer.

I get off the tube at Kentish Town. Mrs Henckel lives ten minutes' walk away. I slope through the local streets head bowed, now and then turning to check for pursuers. Why? Because Kentish Town and neighbouring Camden are places steeped in rock. I have been hereabouts to interview tens, perhaps hundreds, of rock 'n' roll acts. Many rock writers live near here too.

I do not want to be spotted, for it will soon become clear I am not undertaking an interesting rock 'n' roll errand. I am not heading to do an interview, browse the nearby record shops or buy drugs. I am going to see a shrink. As such, I am in a strange bind. In rock there is a premium on the mentalist. If you have a scintilla of madness, you amplify it. You don't go and fix it. Only a pussy wants to be normal.

I make my way along Mrs Henckel's street, and when I have identified her house I look both ways and then dart down the path. I am relieved to see there is no brass plaque bearing her name or profession. I ring the bell firmly and then spend a moment composing my face in a manner which says, *I may have low-grade mental health problems which I expect you to fix, but let's not make too big a deal of it here on the doorstep, okay?* I know that's a lot for one face to say, but I think I have achieved my goal.

Behind the door I hear a dog bark, followed by stern chiding in German (*"Helmut!"*). I am immediately overcome by such panic that my "not too big a deal" face dissolves into a rictus of terror.

I calculate my chances of running away unseen. Mrs Henckel's house is at the end of a long road adjoined by a broad expanse of parkland. There is no natural cover for an escape on foot. Running across a park, I would look completely mental. But then I decide I could run across the park calling out a dog's name, pretending to chase a run-away pet. This strategy appeals, but almost immediately I see a problem: what if people in the park offer to help? Then I would have to admit there was no dog, and that I was running across a park shouting "Elvis!" for no reason whatsoever other than it was the only name I could think of for a pet I do not have.

Frantic thoughts crowd in: *Shut up! You are mental!* Having these thoughts is just exhausting. I revert to Plan A. I must see a therapist.

Mrs Henckel opens her front door. She is stern and doughty looking, wearing a sensible skirt and flat shoes. I cannot connect her with the empathic voice on the phone. I smile but feebly, mentally. I am hoping she will offer a "Don't worry, everyone feels that way the first time" smile, but she doesn't. She looks embattled, pissed off. She holds the door only slightly ajar, gesturing for me to slip through.

"Come in quickly or the dog will escape," she says.

Considering one of my key presenting symptoms is an inability to pass through doors, this greeting strikes me as particularly insensitive and unhelpful. But then I see she is fending off a terrier with her right foot. The dog eyes me and gives off a low grumble.

I bring a dozen paranoiac angles to bear on the situation. Why doesn't Mrs Henckel smile empathically? Why does she have a terrier that is aggressive to guests? Do very few people come to the house, suggesting she isn't a very successful therapist? Her recycling box is full of empty wine bottles, also suggesting she is not a very good therapist. The window frames on the front of the house require attention, suggesting she has not prioritised home improvement over wine and is therefore not a very good therapist.

I am mentally exhausted and I have not said a word or walked over the threshold yet.

I enter, and we walk down the hallway. Mrs Henckel is playing the dog along the floor with the side of her foot like a footballer dribbling tentatively down the wing. She turns to me and says: "Would you prefer I get rid of the dog? He often sits in sessions with me and is very quiet."

I surprise myself by barking: "Get rid of it."

The dog's dark eyes are on me as it is hauled away. I attribute thoughts to him: *I may not be in the room, but I'll still be listening to your pitiful tale. And by a complex network of late night howling, every dog in London will soon know what a fuck-up you are.*

I imagine Mrs Henckel is pissed off too because I have

asked her to get rid of her dog. I feel guilty. I feel angry. I am about to say "Okay, bring the stupid dog in with you", but she disappears with the dog into the kitchen at the end of the hall.

"Go through," she says, punting the animal further along into the kitchen.

I could still run, I think to myself. While she takes the dog out back I could quietly work the latch and just slink away. More paranoid thoughts support this plan. *There is no brass plaque because she is not really a therapist. In fact, she has never had anyone in this house before. I have seen Misery and now I am going to die.*

There are German exhortations in the kitchen and a single bark. Desperate thoughts crowd in. *There is nothing wrong with you. Leave now and save £35!*

I am at the front door when Mrs Henckel reappears and catches me dithering in the gloom.

"Nice painting," I say, pretending to consider a picture in the hallway. I'm sure she can see my nose is way too near the painting for me to be actually appreciating it. I look like I am smelling it, but she is good enough to indulge me.

"Yes, it's by a former client of mine," she says.

And then I step back and properly look at it for the first time. I see that it is a picture of child in a jar.

*I will do one session and seem keen but then never come to this fucking madhouse ever again!* I think as we enter her consulting room. It is dark inside, full of cloying gloom. *If Joy Division had ever gone into interior design, this is the sort of thing they would have come up with!*

Two chairs of varying quality face each other. The springs of the therapee's chair are shot, a situation I immediately ascribe to fat people. I have often thought that depressed people comfort themselves with carbs and are thus over-weight. Is that why therapy is so expensive? Because depressed people use up so much furniture?

By contrast, Mrs Henckel's chair opposite is in good nick. I take vague comfort from this. Perhaps it means she is a good therapist. She does not overeat or pick at threads of the upholstery. I am surprised at how strident my own internal demands are: I don't want a therapist who eats loads of biscuits or who in other ways cannot handle herself.

I notice a file resting on the arm of her chair. It bears a Post-it note with "Michael" and the time of our meeting written on it. I am vaguely touched that Mrs Henckel has used up some stationery on my behalf. The file looks empty. Wanly, I wonder how fat I will make it. Perhaps I will fill several files? I feel bad about planning to run away.

But then on the wall behind her chair I see another painting, even more terrifying than the one in the hallway. It depicts two cloaked, stooping figures making their way across a blasted, apocalyptic landscape. One person has stumbled and is being helped up by the other.

*This is not a painting. This is a business card. This is what you are signing up for!*

Other than this macabre daub and the compromised furniture, the room says very little. No memorabilia. No personality. It is painted magnolia, even the radiator, and there is a highly unimaginative potted plant in one cor-ner. Charlotte warned me. Magnolia décor is standard in therapist consulting rooms. They are decorated blandly to forestall client distraction. Who started that? Freud? Is magnolia the colour of the adequately functioning person's mind? *I will not make a very good rock journalist if I have my psyche painted magnolia!*

"So, sit, and we shall begin?" asks Mrs Henckel.

We look at each other properly for the first time. I am disappointed. One of the first things I decide is that I do not want to have sex with Mrs Henckel. This is important. Charlotte told me it can be helpful if you develop a crush on your therapist because then it makes the sessions interesting.

"Oh my God, I wanted to have sex with my therapist for years, and that delicious sexual frisson unlocked some powerful Oedipal issues for me," she confided with off-putting sauciness.

But Mrs Henckel doesn't look like the sort of woman who welcomes a sexual frisson. She is solid-looking and emanates pheromones of rigour. Her skirt and tights could be from any post-war era. I find myself imagining her in her bedroom earlier that morning choosing her clothes from a chest of drawers. *I am a no-nonsense therapist. I don't have time for the fripperies of modern fashion, and I don't care if no one wants to fuck me!* Those are the sartorial motives I attribute to her.

"It is good to meet you at last," she says. "I hope your journey was not too onerous."

She says "onerous" in a self-conscious way, like a foreigner assiduously working new vocabulary into their English, having that morning decided "Today I'm going to use the word onerous." *I don't like her. She'll be too busy practising new English vocabulary to think seriously about my problems.*

My instinct is to survive the session assuming the

qualities of an upright fridge-freezer. When she comes eagerly foraging for goodies with her analytical gaze, I will allow my door to be opened and the light to go on. But after that, I will let the internal light go off. I will just stay still, emitting a low fridge hum of impatience.

"The journey was fine," I lie.

I see there's a box of tissues by my side with one sticking up, tousling like a flame. I try to imagine what the client before me was crying about. Perhaps no one loves them. Perhaps someone loves them but they no longer love that person back. *I merely freaked out at an awards ceremony and failed to enter a lift. My problems are not serious. I will not be needing any tissues!*

Mrs Henckel glances over the notes of our phone call. Her brow furrows as she revises them fully. Then she looks up at me and, with a demure throat-clearing, indicates: *You have the talking stick. Begin.*

I look at her and then I look at the macabre painting above her. Suddenly, I see that Mrs Henckel is the inspiration for the upright cloaked figure. She has the same inscrutable face. She has the same small eyes.

*That makes me the stumbler.*

# 7
# Serving the True Believers

"Why do you think you are here?"

"I told you on the phone."

"Yes, you did. But let's go over it again."

"I felt anxious meeting Oasis."

"Yes. And what else?"

"The magazine I work for is on the fifth floor. I can't get into the lift."

"And why do you think that is?"

I feel a twinge of annoyance. Like I said, I want a quick-fix. If I knew why I couldn't get into the lift, I wouldn't be blowing £35 of the family holiday fund talking about it. But I don't complain because Charlotte has explained the rules of the therapeutic process to me with considerable sisterly vim.

"Don't wind them up or be a smart-arse," she advised me. *"Do the work!"*

And so I accept the question. In fact, I *have* thought about my situation. I have also revised key Freudian terms because I assume that in therapy, macabre psychosexual impulses lurk behind almost every problem: you want to bang your mother, you want to kill your father, etc. I lean forward on the edge of my seat, jiggle my hands about with an earnest presentational flourish and say: "I'm guessing the *Q* office block is some sort of a big penis."

Mrs Henckel looks at me quizzically. Something in the slightly cocked angle of her head encourages me to develop this idea further.

"I am a sperm who wants to ride up the shaft to the magazine. The magazine is my mother's vagina. I want to fertilise my mother with my record reviews. I want to get the magazine pregnant."

Mrs Henckel puts down her pad and pen. Her head drops and her chin sinks into her chest as though she is assessing these ideas. And then she sort of nods, which I interpret as deep approbation. After that I think she is crying, perhaps because these insights are so poignant. But then I realise that none of these is true. She is chuckling to herself. She has lost it.

"Really? Is this really what you believe to be happening?"

"It's my best guess."

"I don't think you want to ride up your father's penis. Or make the magazine pregnant with your writing."

And although there is disappointment that my self-diagnosis is so wrong, there is also relief. *Relax! There's really no problem here at all!*

"Panic is often the result of stress. I think merely that you are overloaded. Like, say, a computer running too many programs."

"So, I'm ... Not OK Computer."

"What? What is this?" asks Mrs Henckel.

"I am a rock writer," I explain. "*OK Computer* is a key album."

"I have no idea of such matters," she replies.

"But it's a really important album by Radiohead. You must know about *OK Computer*!"

"I don't. How does this impact on your present situation?"

"The problem is I don't know how to be around musicians any more. I can't get inside their heads."

"Musicians, you say?"

"Yes. Well, bands."

"Like a brass band?"

"No. Bands. Pop bands. Rock bands."

Mrs Henckel offers a querying gaze. "Why do you need, as you say, to get inside their heads?" she asks.

"Rock stars are modern priest-gods. They are seers to be listened to and followed."

"This is not something I know very much about," says Mrs Henckel.

And so, for ten minutes, I find myself explaining the post-war counterculture, the emergence of teenagers and the birth of rock music. Then I do a couple of minutes on Bill Haley and the Comets through to Radiohead with a final micro-presentation on Oasis.

"Come on, rock music," I say. "You must have had *some* rock music when you were growing up."

Mrs Henckel looks at me as though I have just made up the 20th century. "Mine was a rather a strict, classical upbringing," she demurs.

"You've never heard of Kraftwerk?" I say, hoping to forge common ground with a phenomenon undeniably Teutonic and rigorous but nonetheless pop-orientated.

"I have not attended so much to these matters," she shrugs.

However, there is one useful revelation. Under duress, she admits that not all her CDs are worthy classical piano sonatas or sonorous orchestral dirges. She owns a Van Morrison album. She gestures upwards to the shelving where the great porridge of Morrison's visage glowers from her adorable little CD collection. It numbers just two: *Astral Weeks* and a collection by Schubert. We agree that Van Morrison counts as a pop music.

"And it's my job to hang out with rock stars like Van Morrison, but the problem is ... I've slipped a couple of notches in terms of handling myself coolly in the industry."

Mrs Henckel looks puzzled. She looks like she couldn't give the tiniest shit about behavioural protocols in the music industry.

"Tell me about your family," she says with an insinuating edge to her voice. I am well aware that for every therapist "the family" is a sophisticated matrix of power relations wherein so many personal mental issues are rooted. But not for me. My family are two loved ones who live with me among a peerless collection of rock memorabilia.

"It's a family," I shrug. "Me, my girlfriend and our son."

"No. The family you grew up in," she says, "Tell me about them."

"Dysfunctional," I say. I like the word "dysfunctional". It's a hard-working word. It covers a multitude of things and is sort of non-negotiable and irrefutable, like "deceased". To my mind, you really shouldn't have to elaborate further. People who elaborate further, trying to unpack the endless nuances of what "dysfunctional" actually means, end up like my sister: eking out an impoverished existence in a shitty Brighton flat in order to finance endless rounds of therapy.

But Mrs Henckel doesn't agree. "Why dysfunctional?"

"Well, my mum is from Bolivia, and my dad was from Purley in Croydon. That's the nub of it."

"Tell me about your mother being from Bolivia."

"What about it?"

"Did she bring you up in the culture of that country?"

"No."

"Not at all? You followed none of the customs or spoke the language?"

"We had a siesta in the afternoons. That was it."

"Nothing else?"

"No. If anything, we raised our mother in this culture."

"Who did?"

"The children."

"What do you mean by this?"

"Me and my sister. We brought my mother up. She needed a lot of help fitting in to England."

"She wanted to be English?"

"Yes."

"And how did you set about achieving this?"

"Rock 'n' roll," I announce triumphantly.

There is a silence while Mrs Henckel digests this information.

"Like I said, dysfunctional, but if we can cut to the real issues here," I continue, because I do not want to talk about my family and spend the rest of my life in therapy, "the problem here is my relationship with rock."

Mrs Henckel doesn't look very happy about this. Nevertheless, she shifts in her chair to signal heightened seriousness. "And so, then, you are a musician yourself?"

"No. Yes. No."

"Which is it?"

"No. But I was in a band once. A band where you didn't need to be a musician."

"What sort of band is this?"

"A punk band."

"And what is this 'punk'?"

"It's a band where you are against things – even the ability to play an instrument."

And now, in spite of myself, I am subject to a half-moment of misty recollection and so I can't help adding: "We were called Mental Elf."

Mrs Henckel's eyes narrow darkly. "This band was called *Mental Health*?"

"No. Mental Elf. But you are quite right to see the joke because it does *sound* like 'Mental Health', doesn't it?"

"Is this amusing to you?"

"Give me a break. I was seventeen," I say. "Didn't you do anything stupid when you were seventeen?"

I look closely at Mrs Henckel and it is abundantly clear that she didn't.

"This name. Do you think this is significant?"

"The band was named after our science teacher. She was petite and highly strung. If I drummed on the desk during a lesson, she'd go mental – send me out of the room, give me a detention. Hence, Mental Elf."

"I see," Mrs Henckel says, although I have never heard this affirmation sound less convincing.

"Punk. That's what punk was about. Subverting the status quo."

"And this punk, so to say, is a department of rock?"

"Yes."

"I am wondering whether you are immersed in what I believe is commonly termed the famous 'rock and roll lifestyle'?"

There is a long silence. In good English, which is none-theless somehow rendered judgemental by her strong German accent, Mrs Henckel continues: "I expect there has been much taking of the drugs and sleeping with the babes ..."

I angrily refute the suggestion. "No. I am a critic. I am objectively positioned above all that. I might have a toke once in a while to be friendly but ..."

"And you are not enjoying multiple sexual partners?"

"No."

Mrs Henckel nods sagely with a noticeable flicker of the eyelids. I take this as being good. I imagine a sheet of multi-choice psychoanalytical tick boxes where all the cor-rect answers are skewed towards teeth-gritted abstinence, and I have got them right. Even so, I feel hot and scruti-nised. Watching her scribble notes, wearing her forbidding woolly tights, and sat beneath her one Van Morrison CD and an unnecessarily dour rendering of the apocalypse, I am wondering whether I shouldn't clap my hands together, tell her I feel much better already, and be on my way.

But Mrs Henckel presses on. "Please, what is the nexus of interest with these rock stars?"

"What does that mean?"

"Why are they so important to you, these people who perform songs?"

"These people are ciphers. They articulate the dark side of modern existence."

"The zeitgeist. I see. Fascinating. Most interesting."

"I can't really imagine what it must be like growing up without rock stars," I say and immediately realise I am staring at her CDs contemptuously.

"And so your job is to follow them and report on their lifestyles?"

"Yes."

"So, tell me please, in detail, what happens when you undertake a typical rock 'n' roll journey such as you mention."

This is fine. I don't mind this. I will happily take Mrs Henckel for a vicarious walk on the wild side. I can easily draw upon the heavy store of rock anecdotes I use when the neighbours come round.

"The rock writer is a kind of auditing apparatus," I begin. "I must place myself in close proximity to the rock star, like a Geiger counter."

"Really? What it is it you are detecting?"

It's a good question. It's a very, very good question, but I've run away with the simile, so I do not readily have an answer. "Dangerous levels of arsehole?" I offer finally.

"I do not follow this."

"Rock stars have a duty to live by the code. They must be cool, seditionist and interesting. And they must resist the temptation to become dull, cynical businesspeople."

"And you enforce this code?"

"Yes. Yes, I do."

"How?"

"Hold a mirror up to them. See if a dickhead stares back."

"Can you give me an example?"

By way of supporting evidence, I offer the following

examples: once I went to Amsterdam to interview Sting. The self-proclaimed eco-warrior had just accepted a large fee for appearing in an advert for Jaguar cars and had performed at the opening of a Japanese tourist resort, the construction of which had required flattening a forest. We sat down to lunch. His meal arrived.

At the very moment I was going to suggest that he might be considered a hypocrite, I reached across, took a handful of his chips and ate them.

"Why?" asks Mrs Henckel.

"To see how he'd cope."

"With an incursion into his meal?"

"Yes. Just the chips though. I didn't touch his fish."

"What happened?"

"He offered me as many as I wanted."

"Oh."

"And so, I went to the next level."

"Which was ...?"

"To discuss his environmental credentials while address- ing him as Gordon. I said: 'So, Gordon ... with a definite ironic stress on the Gor.'"

"Why?"

"Because that's his real name. He's not really called Sting, which sounds cool and casual; he's called Gordon. And stressing the 'Gor' in Gordon is all part of breaking down the rock star persona and reaching the person inside."

"And what did this Gordon say to that?"

"He said he was quite happy there was no contradiction between his activism and business interests and then laid into his haddock."

Item two: in 2000, I entered the Dorchester Hotel in

London to interview Janet Jackson. Waiting in the anteroom pre-interview, sniffing the Jo Malone candles, a member of her management warned me Janet would terminate the interview if I asked any questions about her brother Michael.

"And what happened?"

"I entered the hotel bedroom, complimented her body-guard on the rigour of his workout regime and began the interview. Three questions in, I asked her what it was like growing up with a knobhead of a brother like Michael."

"And how did this Mrs Jackson respond?"

"She asked me what a knobhead was."

"And then what?"

"She said Michael sometimes called her fat when they were kids, but all brothers occasionally act like dicks. She seemed fine. But then a week later I got a letter from her PR calling me a 'disgrace'."

Item three: I went to interview members of The Strokes at a London TV studio. I was kept waiting because guitarist Nick Valensi was recording a promotional spot for a brandy company. I got bored and disillusioned waiting for a rock star to complete his brand ambassador duties, so, sitting alone in his dressing room, I decided to try on a pair of his trousers.

"And?"

"They fitted quite nicely, so I kept them."

"What happened?"

"When I came out onto the set, Nick Valensi mouthed to a member of his crew, 'Hey! Those are my trousers!'"

"And what did these episodes tell you?"

"Gordon has evolved into Sting the Businessman, Janet Jackson is quite chilled out but her PR isn't, and even when

Nick Valensi is making a whole new wad of cash, he is still precious about his trousers."

"And this is your job?" asks Mrs Henckel.

"Yes. I am the scourge of movers, the bane of shakers. I identify those who are true to the spirit of rock."

Mrs Henckel looks very interested in my work. For the first time in ages, I do not feel anxious or low or freaked out. I feel good.

"When you first rang me, you sounded troubled."

"I am."

"And yet you sound like a completely different person when you discuss your work."

"Do I?"

"Yes."

"Well, I feel like a different person when I am a rock writer."

"Can you describe for me how and when this personality change takes place?"

"That's difficult," I say, "but I suppose, for me, the transition occurs on the plane."

"What plane?"

"A Q assignment takes on a familiar trajectory," I begin. "First, the features editor sends me a *Mission Impossible*-style email containing a date, a venue and a superstar's name. Could be Bono. Could be McCartney. Then I await courier delivery of a plane ticket to a desirable foreign location where the interview will take place. This is mandatory. The far-flung location plays a crucial role in depicting the rock star's distant, unobtainable life."

I watch Mrs Henckel probe her inner cheek with the end of her tongue in what I take to be a "Fancy that!?" way.

I plough on. "Then I receive an advance CD of the new album."

This doesn't get the flicker of mild awe I expect, so I add: "This is exclusive, encrypted material." Mrs Henckel offers a vaguely impressed moue that emboldens me.

"I pack a tape recorder, a spare tape recorder, some swimming trunks, one clean pair of underpants and a t-shirt."

"Nothing else?"

"I already have multiple currencies stashed in my wallet from my many global assignments," I say, feeling the heat in my cheeks. I think I sound like James Bond.

Silence. Mrs Henckel's eyes bore into me.

"I also take photos of my kid," I add. "I love my little boy."

Mrs Henckel smiles. It feels like a small victory. "What happens next?"

"On the flight, I will watch a movie. If they have *Terminator 2*, I will always watch that because the T-800's interpersonal skills always struck me as an inspirational template for rock interviewers. In a sense, the Terminator is also an interviewer, asking tough questions of humanity, albeit with a pump-action shotgun and a metal face. Then, I will drink about three of those little bottles of wine and think of my interview questions."

Mrs Henckel stops me. "And how would you character-ise your mental state during this time?"

I think she's trying to break up my flow with a distract-ing psychotherapeutic sub agenda and so I say, quite tersely: "I'm thinking about the job in hand. Nothing else."

"Go on."

"I land and de-plane. At Immigration, the grumpy, small-minded official often asks, 'Couldn't an American be doing this job?' and I reply with what I imagine to be a rollicking Henry VIII laugh, 'No, they couldn't!' And I mean it."

"You seem to have considerable pride in your work," says Mrs Henckel with the beginnings of scepticism, which I decide to ignore. I am on fire.

"Then I cab out to the rock star lair. A mansion, a hotel room, a recording studio or a concert venue. The PR greets me at the stage door, hands me a call sheet and, as we stride to the interview location, invariably garbles a few words about subjects which are 'strictly off-limits' and which, if mentioned, will result in the interview being terminated. And then – you'll like this – I feel a surge of pride because when she shows me the questions I *mustn't* ask, they are exactly the questions I have in my pad, questions I now know that I *must* ask. I am in perfect telepathy with the superstar's paranoia. I know these are definitely the right questions."

"This is the alternative work persona I mentioned before. Perhaps there is a power dynamic in play at this—"

"Let me finish. I then look at how the PR is dressed. If she is in evening finery, this suggests she will soon be heading out to the opera with her boyfriend. If so, how long will she hang around, observing the interview, eating from the artisanal cheese selection or texting friends, before she gets bored and leaves?"

"Why is this important?"

"Because this is when the embargoed question will be asked – the grenade question."

"The grenade question? What is this?"

"The one that terrifies them. You just drop it on the floor and wait for them to react."

"But have you not promised you will not ask them this question?"

"Yes."

"You break the promise?"

"Yes."

"And you have no particular feelings at this time?"

"Is 'I don't care' a feeling?"

"No. But what happens next?"

"I finally meet the superstar. They enter the room and we shake hands. They are always smaller than you imagine. Always. Sometimes I fight the impulse to say: *Jesus, don't you look like your dad?! Now run along and tell him I'm here!*"

Mrs Henckel stops me again: "And is the size of the pop star impor—"

I have shut my eyes, pursed my lips and raised my palm to silence her. "Never mind," she says with a sigh. "What happens in the interview?"

"I will say I have enjoyed the advance CD of the new album. But I will only say that if I *have* enjoyed the advance CD of the new album. If I am confused by the new album and, mid-flight, have switched it off to watch more movies, drink more wine or play Space Invaders on my seat-back screen, I might say the tracks are 'interesting' or 'challenging'. Or if it's awful, I might say: 'Hmmm yeah, I really must talk to you about the new album,' much like a doctor would say to a patient 'I really must talk to you about these images' after noticing a troubling shadow on a brain scan."

Mrs Henckel doesn't laugh, but I am enjoying myself

and so continue. "Finally, if it is Robbie Williams, and it's a foregone conclusion that the music is terrible, there is a third way. I will say: 'Once again you've done what you do best' and we both understand this is a platitudinous code for:

*You have produced a selection of chicken-nuggets-for-the-ears, which suburban zombies who don't really like music will enjoy. As provider of entry-level entertainment experiences for morons, once again you've done what you do best.*

"You seem to enjoy your role as a critic very much."

"I do. I feel I am serving my people."

"You mean your editor?"

"No. My people. The 100,000 Q readers. *They* are my family. These are the guardians, the true believers in rock 'n' roll."

"And you serve them?"

"Yes. One-hundred thousand readers is the same as a whole Wembley Stadium full of fans. Sometimes, before an interview, I actually imagine them, the readership, in their seats at my imaginary Wembley, waiting expectantly for the show."

Mrs Henckel looks perplexed, as though she could do with a little peek at a training manual for treating rampant egomania. Maybe I have gone a little too fast because her eyes are boring into me. She looks shocked. And this shocks me. Why should she be shocked? In a way, we do the same job. We ask questions, we lay bare the soul. Except, her findings go in a confidential file, while mine appear in a glossy magazine with an advert for antiperspirant on the facing page.

"I see," she says finally, and then she closes her pad.

I am expecting her to ask: "Who was your favourite star ever to interview?" and "Have you ever met Van Morrison?" And then, when I have answered these questions, I really want to address my anxiety and panic, although, to be honest, it really does seem to have abated somewhat over the last few minutes.

But she doesn't ask about my favourite interviewee. She simply uncrosses her legs, stands up and says: "Are you adamant that you will not discuss your family?"

"Yeah, because they're not the problem."

"I think you have given yourself much to think about," she replies and opens the door of her consulting room.

I slump back deep into the chair and say: "Have I?"

"Yes," she confirms. "Call me if you experience another crisis, but that is the end of your time."

# 8
# Nicely Does It

I sulk all the way home. What exactly have I given myself to think about, apart from: *Was it worth spunking all that money up the wall schooling a po-faced shrink in the ways of rock 'n' roll?* As I approach the house, I feel guilty. I have spent £35 of holiday money on personality augmentation. But I do not have £35 worth of progress to show for it. I should at least be smiling.

When I reach the house, I find Nicola and Ronnie having fun with a paint set. As I enter, Nicola lowers the music on the stereo. Ronnie ceases his daubs. They stare at me as though a stranger of uncertain temperament has entered the room.

Nicola has a hunted look about her. I sense questions in the air. Finally, she sends Ronnie off to play in another room and breaks the silence. "How did it go?"

"Fine," I say. "No, weird actually. I have given myself a lot to think about, apparently. I just can't think what it is."

We sit down and have a cup of tea. I relate details of the session, lingering on my assertion that there have been not been multiple sex partners or drug-taking.

"Perhaps you regret that?" Nicola asks airily. I should have known it was a mistake to be frank about the contents of my therapy session. She is worn out from work. She is feeling vulnerable, and everything I say will be seen as a coded criticism of our relationship.

"No. No, I don't. But she made me feel like perhaps I *should* have."

"How did she *make* you feel that?"

"By implying that my job, my lifestyle, should entail, and I'm quoting directly here, 'taking of ze drugs and sleeping with ze babes.'"

Nicola doesn't laugh at my fake German accent. She just thinks I am talking in a stupid voice because I am hiding something.

"Therapists don't make you feel anything. That thought occurred to *you*. You own it."

"Come on, don't get paranoid. We didn't talk about anything like that."

"Did you discuss our sex life?"

"No!"

"Did you discuss our relationship?"

"No, not really."

"You didn't discuss us at all?"

"No."

"You just talked about music, I suppose?"

"Yes. Kind of. Most of the time."

It's not a good enough answer. I can feel Nicola's gaze upon me, like search lights roving over a runaway POW, hiding behind a tree in a forest.

"You told her about Michael Bublé didn't you?" she says suddenly.

"I didn't, actually," I say breezily.

"You did. It's fine. But I can tell you did."

"I mentioned quite a few pop stars, but I didn't mention Michael Bublé."

"I'm sorry if you feel I am not cool enough for you."

"Did you not hear what I said?"

"It's fine. I feel slightly betrayed, but it's fine."

"But I didn't mention him! *I swear!*"

There are hot button issues in any relationship. Michael Bublé is one such for us. He is a Canadian pop star who strikes at the very heart of the nice/nihilist debate. Our reactions to him have come to represent a major schism in how we think.

EARLY IN 2004, *Q* sent me to interview Bublé. He had high hopes of making it in the UK, and I flew into Manila in the Philippines where he was already a superstar.

"Come and join me," he said, a cheeky face of mischief beckoning from a blacked-out limo. I travelled through the bustling city in his motorcade, feeling vaguely presidential as I chatted through the open window with our police outriders. I watched him being mobbed at in-store signings. I chillaxed in his luxury suite and even autographed some albums for competition winners on his behalf.

I found him an affable man, who was enjoying his stardom but maintained a down-to-earth bonhomie. For example, he enjoyed playing pranks and, while I was having a backstage massage, he quietly took the place of the masseuse who had been pummelling my lower back. That's when his untrained hand touched my testicles. It was an accident but also a mark of his burgeoning international profile that he was forced to issue a clarifying statement to the Canadian press after I wrote about the incident. But when he wasn't larking about and talking about music, he was a man of serious intent.

"The UK is where I want to be taken seriously," he said." The musical heritage of that place ... I really hope it happens for me there."

The trip ended in a Manila strip club called Rascals on Burgos Street. Bublé ordered some drinks. Young girls in bikinis shimmied and pandered to him as we sipped cocktails. A couple of them even offered to marry him. But Bublé was a consummate smoothie. He declined their marriage invitations, and hoped they stayed warm in their swimwear and got home safe.

"I never pay for touchy touchy, man," he told me outside the club. "If money changed hands, I couldn't get it up."

The only number he took was mine. "Next time I'm in London, I'll look you up. We can have a beer," he said.

When I got home, I was sent an advance copy of his new album, the collection of songs intended to break him in the UK market. I put it on. Bublé's croon filled the room.

"This is lovely. Who's this?" Nicola asked from the kitchen. I didn't answer.

"I said, who is this?" she reiterated, sashaying into the living room and executing a dainty spin while holding two glasses of wine.

By now I was sitting on the sofa in the aircraft brace position. "This isn't an album, it's a cry for help," I mumbled. "I just cannot believe anyone would want to make music as hollow and cheesy and horrible as this."

"Don't be silly, dance with me," Nicola said. "You spend

all your time trying to work out if music is cool or not, but you never dance. Dance!"

I got up, ejected the CD from the tray and took it outside. "You fly in the face of everything that rock 'n' roll is trying to achieve," I said to it before frisbee'ing it over our back wall onto the South Circular.

"What are you *doing*?!" cried Nicola from the back door. "Are you insane?!"

A month later, Michael Bublé is in the charts and on TV. He has done it: he has become a UK star. One evening the phone rings downstairs. I hear Nicola answer it. There is a shriek and an "Oh My God".

"Really?!" she says. "Can we?!" She is talking in rapid, breathless speech, the sort I associate with two scenarios: a) when I'm driving, realise we are lost, and so begin cornering like a maniac; and b) the approach of orgasm.

Red faced with excitement, Nicola runs upstairs and bursts into my office pressing the handset to her breast. "You'll never guess what," she announces in a violent whisper. "It's Michael Bublé on the phone!"

I look at Nicola in terror, which she mistakes for dawning excitement.

"Yeah, Michael Bublé! He wants to meet for a drink!"

I consider my rebuttal options: I can be busy. I can be ill. I can be dead.

"Can you do this weekend, Michael?" Nicola says suddenly into the phone.

*Maybe you could go for a quick one, let Nicola get an autograph and then get out.* But I think about the airborne CD glinting on its journey over the wall: the unctuous Sinatra karaoke was demonic in its insincerity. *He's a nice guy, but hold firm! You cannot be seen to endorse the crooning of Satan!*

"Saturday?" Nicola says excitedly, holding the phone up to me. "He says Saturday is good!"

"Put down that phone," I say in a low, broken voice.

"What? What did you say?" Nicola asks, cupping the phone in exasperation.

"Put. Down. The. Phone."

Nicola looks like a wolf whose cubs have been threatened. "Sorry, Mr Bublé," she says to the handset defiantly, "we're just juggling dates."

Cupping the phone again, she mouths, "It's *Michael Bublé*! Are you out of your mind?"

In a hissed rage, I explain my position as best I can: "Look, he's a nice guy. But I can't go."

"Why can't you just be nice?"

"Give me the phone," I say.

"Tell him my friend Vicky loves him." Vicky works with Nicola in mental health, and she also listens to Michael Bublé. I don't see how it can be fair for one human to go through life carrying two such burdens. I take the phone.

"Hello?" says Michael Bublé in a small faraway voice. "Is that you Michael?"

I gently replace the phone on the cradle. *Click. Brrrrr.* He's gone.

"Why did you do that, you utter *arsehole*?"

"Because," I say, "it's the right thing to do."

"Listen. I work in a tough environment every bloody day, dealing with other people's shit and getting paid a pittance for it, and so when someone nice comes along, someone who happens to be a successful pop star, and invites me out for a drink, my answer is yes. *Yes bloody please!*"

"There's more to this job than being nice," I say.

"No, actually there isn't. And there isn't actually much more to life than being nice and enjoying a bit of music that doesn't hurt anyone."

"That's just too easy."

"There's something wrong with you," she says darkly.

And so, Michael Bublé becomes a fault line in our relationship. We try not to talk about the Michael Bublé incident, and Nicola gets particularly angry when I get drunk and mention it in front of guests. "It is your gender's greatest cultural weakness," I say, sloshed and subversive. "It is women's deep-rooted desire to be crooned at seductively by men with big gloopy eyes and symmetrical faces that has allowed simpering mannequins like Bublé and Take That and Justin Bieber to succeed."

TODAY, I CAN see that I need to tread more carefully. I have been to see a therapist and Nicola is clearly feeling vulnerable about the contents of this first session.

"All we really discussed was I had a funny turn with Oasis and I panicked entering a lift. That's all. We didn't cover Michael Bublé or our sex life. And we never will. I'm done with therapy."

"Well, fine, but I'm not asking you to do that," she says.

But I am satisfied that, in one 50-minute session, I have taken psychotherapy as far as I can. I don't need a complete psychological refurb. In fact, Mrs Henckel has done her job well. She has fucked me off to such an extent I now have a clear focus for my angst: Mrs Henckel. If I externalise my anger and frustration, I am not depressed. When I hate her, I feel okay. I feel alive. I am even able to thank her for this. *You have shown me, by way of your sober woolly tights, your morbid paintings and your uptight Germanic rigour, how much my life actually rocks! Thanks, I'll take it from here.*

All I need is to focus on the positives. These are as follows: I am good at my job; I serve the 100,000; I *represent*.

"Basically, what I take away from Mrs Henckel is that therapy is a crock of shit," I say. "I am feeling much better. I need to get back to work."

# 9
# Hell vs Heaven (Slipknot vs U2)

There is news on that score. While I was visiting Mrs Henckel, Nicola took a message from Ben Mitchell.

"He says there's an important meeting for all writers with Chesney Hawkes tomorrow at eleven," she says.

"Really?" I say. "Everyone? Must be serious."

"But why a meeting with a cheesy one-hit wonder from the 1980s?" Nicola asks. "Chesney Hawkes sang that god-awful 'The One and Only', didn't he?"

"Actually, when he says Chesney he means—" I begin, but Nicola cuts me off. "The weird thing is, your editor Paul then rang and said that there was a big meeting scheduled for eleven tomorrow too."

My blood runs cold. "Please, God, tell me you didn't say—"

"Yes, I told him he'd better reschedule because everyone would be busy meeting Chesney Hawkes."

I put my face in my hands.

"What's wrong with you now?" asks Nicola. "I was trying to *help*."

"That's Paul's bloody nickname!" I bleat helplessly. "He just looks like Chesney Hawkes. It's the same meeting!"

"No need to shout. It's not my fault you lot choose these stupid nicknames."

Nicola is right. But I am still angry. "I just wish you hadn't mentioned Chesney Hawkes, that's all. Ever heard of boundaries?" I snap, using the new therapeutic lingo I have picked up.

THE NEXT MORNING, I head for the Q offices. My heart pounds as I stand in the lobby and the lift doors open. I swallow hard and throw myself in.

"Phew!" I say to myself, landing at the back of the lift. "I did it!"

I look up. A hairy biker from *Motorcycle News* eyes me carefully. But I don't care. I am back in the game.

In the magazine boardroom, the cream of the UK's rock writer crop is gathered around a table. Here are clammy-fingered collectors in cagoules, Oxbridge chin-strokers in chinos, and seditious, septum-damaged psychos from the suburbs. Lots of writers are from the North, and Scottish people are over-represented. But I am a half-Bolivian, which gives me unimpeachable outsider credentials. Among the younger writers I notice some are wearing rock badges on their lapels. I feel a pang of envy. Nicola stopped me wearing badges when I turned 40.

Paul Rees breaks some bad news. Readership figures have taken a hit. Once as plentiful as penguins crammed onto an Antarctic rock, the 100,000 are dwindling. The internet is giving rise to a dangerous new phenomenon: amateur keyboard warriors forming their own opinions and sharing them online, for *free*!

"Our key strength is still access. No one gets closer to

the artists than *Q*. We just have to be sure we get that *detail*," advises Rob Fearn.

"Yeah, we just need to get closer, get *deeper*," a voice says from a seat along from me. I can only see their bunched fist on the table. There are murmurs of approbation. The room crackles with the energy of rock writers meaning it.

"And we need to introduce rock 'n' roll to an uninitiated audience," adds someone else.

"What about an arrogant German cow?" I say absent-mindedly, staring out of the window. I am picturing Mrs Henckel receiving my best anecdotes with disdain.

"I think the mag works best when we confront people, take them *on*," asserts an earnest young writer at the back of the room.

"Like Slipknot," Ben says, jabbing me in the ribs with an elbow. "That was a good one."

I feel a little chill inside. Since writing for *Q*, I have been centrally involved in its search for rock's dark materials. I have proudly audited many bands for rock authenticity. But when I went to interview Slipknot, I saw something which shocked me to my core.

IN 2002, *Q* sent me to interview Slipknot – five American maniacs in black boiler suits and masks who perform a growly black metal dirge as part of a rock panto of unspeakable horror. They were considered the most dangerous and dysfunctional band in the world.

They had a new album called *Iowa*, an unusually prosaic title for a band who were known to puke on stage, and even throw animal parts at their fans, whom they called "maggots". But they had used it in the reverse sense of how a local tourist office might title a brochure "Iowa": they weren't extolling the virtues of their home state or advising the best place to play golf or eat lobster. Song titles like "Disasterpiece" and "New Abortion" made it clear that Iowa is a place of massive adolescent dysfunction, where the temptation to terminate a pregnancy or commit suicide was almost irresistible.

My research told me that Iowa is part of the great American Corn Belt, a vast acreage of land devoted to industrialised farming, which keeps corn and also pork-based foodstuffs within America's sausage-fingered grasp. But that's all there is there in Iowa. Pigs and corn. Someone told me that, when you wake up on a Iowa morning, instead of the rejuvenating chirrup of birdsong, you hear the dispiriting murmur of hog-grunt.

It came as no surprise to me that rock had filled this yawning cultural vacuum. Rock germinates wherever there is nothing to do. I know this. I also grew up in the suburbs: Croydon in south London. I saluted Slipknot for enfranchising young people in America's hinterland.

On the plane, I put on my headphones and, stoked by my free Merlot miniatures, I let the guttural rock screed wash over me. Slipknot sounded so angry it was almost as though their instruments – the guitars and drums and even the microphone used to amplify Corey Taylor's voice – were inconvenient obstacles, getting in the way of them venting pure spleen. I felt that their new song "People = Shit" was a fine and noble distillation of male grudge. Over my in-flight doughnut, I decided that here Slipknot articulated inchoate menace better than any band since the American quartet who set the gold standard of nihilism: Anal Cunt. Yes, I felt Slipknot were definitely throwing down the gauntlet to AC's superb "I Sold Your Dog to a Chinese Restaurant" and fast closing in on the purging darkness of their startling anti-parent diatribe, "Your Kid Committed Suicide Because You Suck".

However, as a rock writer I try not to squander superlatives. After a second listen, I didn't think "People = Shit" was quite the equal of classic AC epic fan-taunt "You Quit Doing Heroin, You Pussy". As the cabin staff distributed little choc ices, I reached a further important critical conclusion: although bleak and nihilistic, Slipknot might be considered "soft" in the way that a song like "Disasterpiece" seemed to proffer a hint of comfort to their fans. It was certainly not as starkly confrontational as AC who, for me, forever re-calibrated the often dishonest, exploitative rock star/rock fan dynamic in their rallying anthem: "You're A Fucking Cunt".

However, Slipknot were clearly onto something, and I looked forward to meeting them. Carefully grading and ordering these fresh critical insights, I re-played "New Abortion" once more and poked at a tiny chicken dinner with a foldable fork. Even when my neighbour asked the cabin attendant if he and his son could be re-seated, I didn't care and continued listening and gently head-banging as they clambered over me. I arrived in Minneapolis genuinely excited by Slipknot. Assisted by the in-flight drinks trolley, I was convinced I had found a band who could articulate psychic agony for a new suburban generation.

The Immigration guy asked what I was doing in America.

"Interviewing a rock band," I said.

"Anyone I've heard of?" he asked, mildly interested as he flapped through the multi-stamped record of my high-rolling life.

"Slipknot," I said. "'People = Shit'?" Then I lifted up an earphone to allow a little of Slipknot's hysterical bawling to leak out.

"You have an enjoyable trip," he murmured, wearily throwing my passport back to me.

I never take it personally when law enforcement officials are unable to take my work seriously. *Sometimes rock 'n' roll makes you an outsider! You just have to handle it.*

I APPROACHED THE stadium where Slipknot were rehearsing. I could hear the distant rumble of the band's rhythm section from the car park. I noted that singer Corey Taylor seemed to have created completely new vocal modalities. He growled like a hungry bear retching on a paw-full of dodgy berries. The band supported him with opaque sludge-rock. The overall effect was like listening to a guy undergoing a tracheotomy while major road works are in progress around him.

At the security gate, I met a manager who chaperoned me through a network of backstage stadium tunnels. She read from notes in a pad.

"So, I just wanna warn you, there are certain question areas you guys love to dwell on, but which the band are sick of discussing and so which, if addressed, may lead to termination of the interview."

The most sensitive question area concerned Slipknot's Nazi-style armbands. This, I noted with no little satisfaction, was my grenade question.

"Sure," I said, "I don't want any trouble."

Suddenly, turning a subterranean corner, I found myself among the nihilists. Slipknot's founder and percussionist, Clown, was welding iron stage props. He raised his flip-up mask and gave me an aggressive head-to-toe look-over, which felt more like an airport pat-down than a greeting. But then again, I liked this. This was weird. This was rock 'n' roll. You don't get this with Coldplay.

"Wassup, England?" he growled eventually.

Clown led me to a hang-out area that looked like a frat-house living room midway through a hell-raising weekend. Beer flowed. Restorative fast food was everywhere. A sports channel showed helmeted gladiators throwing a football, to roars from a vast crowd. "Own that motherfucker!" "Fuck yeah, break his legs!" The big game was in its final quarter.

"Sit down and have a beer, bro," ordered bassist Paul Gray. In Slipknot, Gray was known as The Pig. This raised immediate questions of etiquette. I didn't know whether to reply: "Thanks, The Pig." Or perhaps "Oink oink!" And so I just said "Thanks."

I know that solid research is the way into a band's heart, and so I told The Pig I had enjoyed his work with two previous bands, Anal Blast and Body Pit. He seemed chuffed I knew them. In fact, Slipknot, when not in their vom-flecked masks, seemed like ordinary guys, regular Mid-Western shit-kickers whom you might expect to find fixing agricultural machinery or shooting tins off a wall with assault rifles.

But it's Clown, who plays his percussion with a steel baseball bat, that leads their transformation into the scariest band in the world.

"Turn it off. We gotta talk to this *journo* from Ing-lun," Clown growled from the doorway.

The TV went off. They made a space for me among the pizza boxes on the sofa. I got out my tape recorder and we began. There was a preamble of farting and grumbling, but slowly they worked up some thoughts about how Slipknot speak for America's lost youth. Singer Corey Taylor said that if he wasn't in Slipknot he'd probably be a mass murderer. He said their fans identify with this inner darkness and reciprocate in highly imaginative ways. For example, when Clown dragged a severed cow's head onstage at their last show, a fan responded by launching the head of a pig at him. "Awesome. The maggots put so much thought into stuff like that," he marvelled.

I enjoyed listening to their nihilistic stories. Nihilism – the rejection of all values and beliefs – can actually be incredibly liberating if undertaken as a group exercise. Once you and a friend abandon all hope and reach the nadir, experiencing the sheer bleakness of life can feel as cathartic as sunshine. Sunshine which is made of shit, though. I remember this from my teenage years in Croydon: extreme nihilism was the binding agent of young friendship, like a good rosé at a suburban barbecue. Rosé made of piss, obviously.

Slipknot were real doyens of doom. It felt good talking to guys who could bring me up-to-date on the current standing of the abyss. They made not giving a shit look a lot of fun. I drank it all in and chewed carelessly on a pizza slice. When I got a bit of topping on my face, I didn't even wipe it off.

Pig asked me if I had enjoyed my initial meeting with Clown.

"Stupid old bastard," I responded gamely.

While we chatted, a member of management went to collect a package that had arrived at the arena's reception area. In her absence, I decided to explore my chief area of concern regarding Slipknot's negativity.

"So, you guys like to dress up as Nazis?" I asked, as soon as she was out of earshot. Nihilism is one thing, but tipping over into Nazism is not cool.

"Do not call us Nazis," the one with the pointy proboscis they called Dicknose said.

"Yeah, fuck you," concurred the one with metal spikes coming out of his head. "That's negative."

But there wasn't a complete consensus. Clown put down his drink and waded in. "Wait a minute. If Adolf Hitler was here now, I would probably offer him a soda," he said. "I'd at least hear him out."

"Yeah," said spikehead changing tack. "We'd at least *listen*."

After a few minutes, the manager came back with the package. She needed Clown to check its contents and sign a docket. He opened the box. We all watched in silence and awe as Clown, grunting with effort, yanked at something half-buried in a shallow grave of protective polystyrene chips.

*Jesus Christ!* It was something even more revolting than a severed pig's head or surfing on vomit.

"Oh fuck, awesome!" marvelled Dicknose, looking at the monstrosity: a prototype Slipknot lunchbox with the band's masked characters depicted on a wipe-clean cover.

"Yeah, this works," Clown said, signing the docket.

I couldn't take my eyes off the lunchbox. It struck me

as the most depressing thing I had ever seen in my life. The moment confirmed a suspicion I had often held: you cannot trust Americans with nihilism. They might start off grouchy and miserable but will always find a way to monetise the experience into a burger franchise or a workout video. Americans are just too upbeat and showbiz to mean it. As they ambled off to resume rehearsing "People = Shit" I was convinced: they do not know how to handle the dark side.

＞

As THE Q team sets about finessing a strategy to boost sales, my mind wanders. I think about Clown and The Pig. We need rock 'n' roll's culture of resistance but not in the form of themed wipe-clean lunchboxes. I find myself thinking about Mrs Henckel. How is it even *possible* to get through life with only two CDs, one by Schubert and one by Van Morrison? And yet, she has. In fact, her notebook is probably filled with exactly the obverse question: how is it possible to get through life listening to rock 'n' roll? As the meeting drags on, I peer through the window and survey the teeming London streets, steeped in rock history. Two conflicting thoughts swirl through my mind: *Get closer, get deeper!* and *What is ze nexus of interest in zees rock stars?*

The meeting ends and I slouch my way along Q's main corridor, lined with framed magazine covers, each declaring some sort of negative mental health episode – "I nearly went mad!" "Inside their heart of darkness!" I get a fizzy drink from the vending machine. It thumps into the collection tray and I pick it up. I notice Beyoncé is a brand ambassador for the drink. She glowers at me meaningfully from the can.

I press my thumb firmly into her face, making a dent in her forehead. *You sell fizzy drinks! Ergo, you do not rock!*

I notice features editor Rob Fearn watching me carefully from further along the hallway. As I take a slug of drink from Beyoncé's face, he calls me over.

"I've got a job for you," he says.

I sip my drink in a gnarled way. I want to look tough and ready, although I feel spooked and confused by my own thoughts.

"I want you to fly to New York and have a go at Bono."

In 2005, Bono is the biggest rock star in the world. In fact, he has taken the rock star portfolio places that no artist ever has before. Not The Beatles. Not Elvis. No one. Sure, those guys met the US president and the Pope, and maybe had a photo taken. But Bono wields real power that goes way beyond showbiz. He has stood alongside the US president on the White House lawn to endorse a $5 billion aid package for Africa. He has negotiated debt relief for 23 poor countries. And, as of 2005, he is the singer in the biggest band in the world.

But still, this is *Q*. However great his achievements, the legacy must be protected. Did he really give President Bush a signed Bible? Is he driving rock's tour bus somewhere good, or merely hijacking it for his own ends? *He must be given a proper examination on behalf of the true believers of rock!*

However, I still feel ragged and conflicted from my abortive session with Mrs Henckel. I am really not sure I am up to it. On the other hand, even though he is not included in my Big Six – the actual founders of modern music – Bono is still a big deal. I decide I cannot let Mrs Henckel get to me. I must go.

"Is everything okay?" asks Nicola when I get home.

"Yes, we just need to get closer, *deeper*," I say.

"What the hell does *that* mean?"

"More like an aggressive pig but ... but ... no lunch-boxes," I say distractedly. Sometimes when I try to define rock 'n' roll, I don't seem able to find the words to articulate it. For a rock writer, that's obviously not good news.

Nicola frowns at me. I tell her I am going to New York to interview Bono.

"I think you should think carefully whether you're ready to do this," she says. "I'm worried about you."

"It's Bono!"

"But didn't your therapist suggest you think more carefully about what you are doing?"

"Who cares about her? I'm fine."

However, just in case, before I fly I decide to make the most of the fact that Nicola works in the mental health industry. She is on Prozac and she regularly takes 60 milligrams to get her through the stresses of her day. She has also recently upped her meds due to the fact that the day centre is soon to undergo an inspection and also because of the added stress of living with a man (me) who is tetchy, anxious, illogical and depressed. So I reason: if Nicola is depressed about me being depressed, then I must be at least twice as depressed as she is, and thus require a double dose of whatever antidepressant she's taking. I start popping pills from the blister pack.

"It takes about a month for those to kick in," Nicola says from the doorway, watching me wolf them down from an open palm, swearing at the ones that slip down my open shirt or fall to the floor.

"Really?" I mumble, looking up with a mouthful. I don't care. I am taking action.

When Nicola has gone, I stamp on the pills that have fallen to the floor so Ronnie doesn't eat them. Satisfied this is diligent parenting, I begin to pack my bag. Slamming balled socks, clean underwear and a sheaf of Bono research into my holdall for my international assignment, I get back an old feeling. A good feeling. *I am a rock writer. A curator of a proud legacy. I am being flown 8,000 miles to aim my unerring critical ray at the world's biggest rock star. Forget Mrs Henckel. I ask the questions around here!*

EARLY THE NEXT morning, Nicola and Ronnie regard me with an unnerving intensity as I climb into the campervan and gun the engine. I have brought my copy of U2's *The Unforgettable Fire* and begin blasting it through the speakers.

"Everything okay?" I ask, examining their stares. The shadow of your own madness is invisible to you, like a storm cloud chasing you across a field on a sunny summer day. You may not see it, but others, from a distance, do.

"Be careful out there," shouts Nicola above the racket of my campervan pulling away.

I drive to Heathrow, dump the van in the twilight of the multi-storey short-stay car park and head for check-in. I do not see U2's PR. I decide to check in alone.

"Could you give me an aisle seat?" I say to the check-in attendant in her bonnet and scarf. I like the aisle. It's near the booze at the back of the plane.

"I am sure I could," she says, tapping vexedly at her

computer keyboard, "if you come back in 24 hours when your flight actually leaves." She points to the date on my ticket with a pen.

I swallow hard. *Since when can you not read a fucking calendar?!* I head back to the van.

After shouting and kicking my bag around for a bit, I decide not to go home humiliated but to stay and wait it out in the short-stay car park. It's only 24 hours. The van is my home away from home. It is always stocked with a few tins of food and some beer.

I make a meal on the mini hob and listen to some music in the eerie daytime darkness of the third floor. I feel both conspicuous and moronic. However, I satisfy myself that it won't be long until spending the night in a multi-storey car park becomes funny, and I will be able to tell it as an amusing rock anecdote. But, before long, there is a voice within me. An unamused voice. A serious voice. *What is the ze purpose of ze rock 'n' roll dream?* I have only seen Mrs Henckel once, but here she is. My new conscience. My critic.

I need to get away from her. I enter the airport terminal and displace her invasive presence with tannoy announcements and piped music. There is an awful lot of *X Factor* balladeering and terrible soft rock in the charts at the moment. Usually, I would avoid it. Today it is a comfort.

I spend a couple of hours splashing on the tester colognes in Duty Free, trying on the ties at Tie Rack and the sunglasses at Sunglass Hut. By the end, I look and smell like my dad circa 1971.

I have a memory. When I was a kid, after years of nomadic living in Iran and Bolivia, my family arrived in England to live. We walked through this very Arrivals concourse and my mother said: "I hope England is like they say ... a country for the young ones." It makes me want to see if there are any planes arriving from Bolivia and, if so, if any of the passengers look like they have come to start a new life here, lured by rock 'n' roll. I go to Arrivals. I don't see anyone who looks like a seeker starting a new life under the aegis of rock 'n' roll. Just businessmen.

I take a seat in a café instead, drink coffee and watch the blazered pilots striding through the terminal in their fancy caps and epaulettes. Their pert little moustaches remind me of my dad. He had a pert moustache too. Pete Bannerman once said it made him look like Freddie Mercury or one of the Village People. In fact, he said it out loud, and my dad said "What was that?", so I told Pete to shut up.

"Don't be so uptight," he said.

I feel a bit sad watching the pilots at the gate stroke their little moustaches in a downward motion with finger and thumb like my dad did. However, it feels important that I am noticing these little things and making connections, and so I ring Charlotte and tell her I am at Heathrow airport watching pilots.

"Why are you spending a day at Heathrow?

"I got the flight wrong."

"So go home."

"But I'm here, remembering when we arrived in England."

"Jesus, what's wrong with you?" she demands.

"What's wrong with *you*? I thought you'd be pleased. I'm starting to *do the work*."

"Well, I suppose it's a start. But you know damn well your issues go much deeper than that."

We have an almighty row about how much deeper my issues go.

"At least I don't need my own fucking rubber room!" I scream down the phone, and make my point forcefully by hammering a concrete pillar with my fist outside of Gap.

"Calm down," says Charlotte. "Why are you getting so angry?"

"It really fucks me off when I've made a start on something, and some moron says 'Well, I suppose it's a *start.*'"

"Grow up!" she says and hangs up.

I go back to the van. It's dark and I feel alone, so I play loud music and swear into the rear-view mirror. Then I turn it off and begin to cry because I am a rock writer in a short-stay car park in the night-time and not a pilot in a smart suit with gold braiding, epaulettes and a moustache. I ring Nicola to say goodnight.

"I'm glad you rang. I was a bit worried about you," she says. "Are you at the hotel yet?"

"Yes, the hotel is lovely," I say staring out at the blackened concrete void.

THE NEXT MORNING, I wake to the sound of the day's first jets. I examine my reflection in the rear-view mirror. I am okay. I have survived the night. Today is the correct date of my assignment, therefore I am due an all-expenses-paid airport breakfast. I bump and twist through the churn of Departures' transient community, following the fumes of coffee and bacon. I decide to shrug off yesterday's mental blip and begin my journey in a new, positive frame of mind.

*Fuck nay-saying sisters and thoughtful therapists, in fact, fuck all sceptics and doom mongers. Come on, dude, you're a rock writer! And you're going to meet Bono!*

On the flight I revise Bono's incredible global standing and drink lots of beer. As I scan the stats, I am full of contempt for Mrs H's pathetic CD collection housed in her little Hampstead bunker. *Did Schubert ever cancel Third World debt?! No!*

The rest of the flight I spend in a self-satisfied rage with Mrs Henckel. Why did I ever go and see her in the first place? How could something as vital and elemental as rock 'n' roll be explained away by a worthy German shrink with two CDs and an aggressive dog? In fact, I am so convinced that Mrs Henckel has led a stifled, cosseted existence that, when I have landed and checked in at Manhattan's palatial Rihga Royal Hotel, I throw a few more mini bar refreshments down my neck and decide to ring and tell her. *She said to ring in a crisis! Well, it's critical she knows what a high-flying badass rock writer I am!*

My call goes straight to her machine but, to be honest, the automated voice is barely distinguishable from her professional one. "Please leave a message and I shall attend to your needs forthwith."

"Hello, it's Michael Odell. I came to see you recently, and you were quite disparaging about my interest in rock, brazenly questioning the legitimacy of ... 'ze rock 'n' roll dream'. However, now that I am here in the fuck-off Rihga Royal Hotel with Bono, I find my faith in the transformative power of rock is very much in evidence, and if you want me to tell you about it I will."

Afterwards, I pace around my suite drinking more miniatures and uttering the occasional "fuck you". Then I fall asleep on the aircraft carrier-sized bed and slip into a weird dream where Mrs Henckel is sitting by a fireside reading my file.

"I find this new client absolutely fascinating," she says in the dream. "He has opened my eyes to new cultural possibilities. I am learning so much from him about zis phenomenon rock 'n' roll!"

When I wake up I drink half a bottle of wine and ring her again. "By the way, I'm having a great time," I say. "Tomorrow I'm going on their private jet."

I have almost finished my screed when I hear a click and then a non-automated human voice full of indignation. "Hello, who is this?"

"Mrs Henckel, it's me. Michael Odell. I was just leaving you a message."

"People only usually ring me at such an hour during a crisis. Is this a crisis?"

"No, no trouble here," I say, glancing around happily at my step-up bath, thick curtains and Access All Areas laminate for tonight's U2 show at Madison Square Garden. "I just wanted to let you know how good things are for me right now."

"Not a crisis then?"

"Fuck no! I have the total fucking opposite of a crisis going on here right now! What is the word for the opposite of a crisis?"

"This I could not tell you," she says.

"Maybe that proves you're a bit downbeat and negative in your approach to life, huh? You should learn what the opposite of a crisis is shouldn't you?"

I wait patiently for her rejoinder.

"Shouldn't you?" I repeat with a horrible yodel to my voice. Then I realise Mrs Henckel isn't on the line anymore.

I WATCH U2 at Madison Square Garden. Afterwards, I mingle in the star-studded backstage party. I jostle Josh Hartnett. I rub shoulders with Rachel Weisz. I still haven't actually met Bono, and I am hugely gratified when I spot him wading through the high-celeb-content mêlée in my direction. *I really wish Mrs Henckel could see me now!*

"Good trip?" Bono asks, jiggling his drink, making a ring-a-roses with the ice inside.

"Yeah," I say manfully. "No hassle."

Congress between rock writer and icon is in play. I must show no weakness. I cannot tell him I spent the previous night weeping alone in a short-stay car park. And I will not tell him that there have been considerable other complications: the voice of an irascible therapist interrupting my regular internal dialogue, like a badly tuned radio allowing a sombre discussion programme to break through into a rock music broadcast.

I jiggle my drink too and chew some gum. We chat a little rock talk. Arcade Fire have made a good album. Pete Doherty has been in trouble but, if he could just get his act together, might prove a flag-bearer for rock values. Finally, I tell Bono I live near the Half Moon pub in Herne Hill, south London, where U2 played in the summer of 1980.

"Were you there?"

"No, but my mate Pete Bannerman was," I say seeking reflected glory. "He loved it."

I can't bear to admit that the reason I wasn't there is because I was revising for O levels. Pete Bannerman said I was a sell-out swot for missing the gig in favour of scholastic endeavour. "Do you know what being in a band actually means?" he had said. I decide not to tell Bono any of this because, even though he wields great geo-political power, it's not the sort of debt he can cancel. A debt to rock.

A girl approaches as we talk. She touches Bono gently on the arm. "Hello, I am Kal Khalique," she says. "We danced at Live Aid, remember?"

Live Aid, the Ethiopian famine relief extravaganza organised by Bob Geldof in 1985, was the show that made U2. In front of a global TV audience of a billion, Bono plucked a fifteen-year-old girl he saw struggling out of the vast Wembley Stadium crowd and danced with her while his band performed the song "Bad". Afterwards, the rest of U2 were furious with him. Because of his spontaneous dance, they didn't have time to play their single "Pride (In the Name of Love)". But U2 became international superstars anyway.

She is meeting Bono again for the first time since that day. It is a beautiful moment. I feel like ringing Mrs Henckel. *Rock has healed more souls than a billion hours of talking shit in a frayed armchair!*

I leave Kal and Bono to chat. I feel good. But being a rock writer is not about feeling good. It is about urging our icons to be better rock stars. It is about protecting the legacy. I circulate and trawl the party for gossip. Among the sock-puppet PR operatives regurgitating amazing U2 tour stats and trying to read my notepad upside down, I find another journalist. She tells me that, back in London, Sinead O'Connor has done an interview with *Q*'s sister magazine *Mojo*, in which she expresses her anger at Bono mixing rock with politics. She has said it is a wonder Bono can still speak because "his mouth is so full of American politician cock". However, Sinead, later thinking better of it, has managed to have the quote removed from the interview pre-publication.

I store it away. Tomorrow it will be my grenade question.

THE NEXT MORNING, I go to Bono's apartment on Manhattan's Upper West Side. His car is waiting to drive us to La Guardia airport, where the U2 jet is due to take us to their next show in Philadelphia. Bono emerges from under the building's awning, sipping coffee. He ignores his driver Samson's entreaties to get in the car.

"Let's take a walk," he says to me. We cross five lanes of traffic. Bono is still holding a hot mug of coffee as we enter Central Park.

"Where are we going?" I ask.

"See a friend."

People in the park start to recognise the short man in a hoodie. They whoop and cheer and follow. We arrive at a candlelit nook, the John Lennon memorial at Strawberry Fields.

"Happy birthday, mate," Bono says, sloshing his coffee mug upwards in salute. "Sorry I didn't bring any flowers."

"Yeah, happy birthday, John," I say quietly and then tell the misty-eyed Irishman that we'd better go. The crowd has swollen. We are late for the plane.

We get on the U2 jet at La Guardia. It's an Airbus, and I can't help wondering why U2 need such a big plane and what might be on it. Equipment? Drugs? Groupies? Shrink-wrapped stacks of cash on pallets? I don't see any of those things. But there is something even more incredible.

*Jesus Christ, is that a fucking priest?!* Yes, U2 travel with their own personal man of the cloth, Father Jack Heaslip. In a way, I am grateful because I have always been a nervous flier, and so his presence convinces me that today at least I am not going to die. After all, if there *is* a God, he'd have to be an utter fucker to kill me, Bono and his priest, having already behaved so badly towards the music industry in his dealings with Buddy Holly.

Band members Larry Mullen, Adam Clayton and the Edge sit at a table, eating nuts and playing cards. I am directed down the plane to sit next to Bono. He is busy signing a stack of boxed Apple iPods, presumably for friends or competition winners.

The interview begins. My first job is to explore how the U2 singer actually got from being Paul Hewson to Bono, the most influential rock star in the world. He tells me about when his mum Iris died when he was fourteen (she collapsed with a cerebral aneurysm at her own father's funeral) and how, after he prayed "very intensely", he met the other members of U2 at school in Dublin and his future wife Ali.

"When I was sixteen, my head was exploding. I just felt my life wasn't going anywhere. I didn't fit in. I couldn't get a job. I didn't know how I'd do my exams, and I didn't know if I could even concentrate at college. In those days, I remember a prayer that came up from inside of me. I said, 'I don't know what I'm going to do with my life, but if there's a God out there, and I believe there is, and you want me to do something, then I'm ready. I don't have any plans for myself, and I'm available for work.' Pretty much within a few months of that epiphany I joined U2 and started going out with Ali ...

"Now, had my destiny been, if the God in heaven had said, 'I want you to be a fireman and run up very dangerous buildings and save people's pets,' I'd like to hope I'd have gone at it with the same gusto. So, I couldn't let go of my faith. But what's more interesting is that I don't think God will let go of me."

It's difficult to argue with a man of such deep faith. I am not backed by a divine power. I am backed by Rob Fearn and an editor who looks like Chesney Hawkes. But also, I guess, by the 100,000. I swallow hard. The plane banks right. I drop the grenade.

"Sinead O'Connor has said, 'I'm surprised Bono can still talk, his mouth is so full of American politician cock.'"

Bono mulls this over calmly, like an announcement from the cockpit that the aircraft has run out of nuts. An annoyance but nothing to get too upset about. "Hmmm. In this game, people will always throw custard pies ... I can take the custard pies," he says. "Believe me it's hard to do this job if you don't like the taste of custard." He goes on to make a cogent case for mobilising both left and right wing politicians to support debt relief and AIDS charities.

I feel bad. I am on his plane. I am being served free drinks and treated like a king. After a while, Bono leans in a bit. In his wraparound Armani shades, led by a vigorous nose, I feel I am about to be pecked by a highly opinionated eagle.

"The question you have to ask sometimes is about intention: even if I look like a twat sometimes, am I trying to do the right thing? And if one is standing on the sidelines, shouldn't one at least try and do *something*? I never claimed to be cool, but I do make a claim for rock 'n' roll being able to somehow lift people up."

For the rest of the flight, I can't stop thinking about Slipknot, their masks, puke and lunchboxes, and then Bono at Live Aid, his speeches on the White House lawn and the millions of people he has helped. Do I want my rock stars to lift me up or take me down? I no longer know. As soon as we land, I call Mrs Henckel and book another session for when I am back in London.

# 10
# In the Event of an Emergency

"The telephone message you left for me at the start of your trip was extraordinary," says Mrs Henckel.

"I thought you might want to know about my world," I shrug.

"By the end it seems you had doubts."

"Maybe," I admit.

"I think you want to tell me something. So, tell me about this trip."

I hold nothing back. I explain that I misread the itinerary and so spent a day at Heathrow, moseying first in Tie Rack, then Sunglass Hut, before watching for Bolivian immigrants at Arrivals and arguing with my sister.

"And why do you think you found yourself in this predicament?" Her face is fiercely analytical.

"I told you I got the day of the U2 trip wrong."

"Who are U2?"

"Oh, come on! *Achtung Baby*!"

"Excuse me?"

"*Achtung Baby*! It's German!" I feel myself getting angry. Why have I chosen such a dumb therapist? There are a frustrating couple of minutes in which I have to explain pop music's growth from 1950s teens in bobby socks, rocking around a clock, to U2, a cultural force able to leverage change at a governmental level.

"The reason this is never going to work is because I have to explain everything to you, which drives me up the fucking wall," I grumble.

Mrs Henckel gives me a grave look. "Say this again."

"I said, how is this supposed to work if I have to spend my whole time explaining things to you?!"

She has a strange look. Not hurt – it's a look signalling dawning insight. "Does this frustration feel familiar to you?"

"No, it doesn't."

"Let's focus on going to the airport early."

"I got the day wrong."

"... and spent it watching for Bolivians."

"I didn't see any."

"What are your associations with this?"

"Being a six-year-old boy. When my family arrived in England, I ran to the baggage carousel at the airport so that no one stole our cases. I didn't want my mum to be unhappy."

"I think that is important."

"Really? I don't think it is very important. No one likes luggage to get stolen."

"You said you didn't want your mother to be unhappy. This is important."

"What is important is that you stop talking in riddles."

Mrs Henckel looks at me in the infuriating way that therapists do when they can see things you can't.

"What?!" I say.

"This airport incident. I think we might explore this further."

"I don't want to."

"Why do you want me to understand rock music?"

"I don't know. But I had this dream where I wanted to teach you things."

Suddenly I sound like a suitor making a clumsy declaration in a romcom – a strange, terrible romcom, where the female love interest doesn't reciprocate but instead seeks endless clarification with questions like, "Why were you watching for Bolivians at Arrivals?" or "What are your associations with Tie Rack?"

"Why do you find it so frustrating when my English falters?"

"I don't know!"

"You told me in the first session that you spent your youth explaining pop music."

"Yes."

"... to a foreigner who didn't understand it?"

"No! What? To my ..."

"Yes?"

"To my mother."

"Yes, to your mother who didn't understand this country. And you tried to change things for her, using the uplifting power of this rock 'n' roll, yes? And now perhaps you see how you have re-created this scenario with me?"

I sit and fret the arms of the chair, working a loose seam on which some other poor unhappy soul has wreaked havoc. I feel sure Mrs Henckel's eyes bored into them during dark epiphanies just as they do to me now.

"And so now you are seeing a pattern, yes?" she coaxes.

I nod. I get it. My eyes are glassy with tears. I have been outmanoeuvred and humbled. "Can you help me?" I ask.

"Tell me about your mother and your family. In as much detail as you can."

"Must I? Really?"

"I think so," says Mrs Henckel sounding very serious. "I sense very strongly this is what you came here for."

⟩

IT IS THE early 70s. My family has recently relocated from Tehran in Iran to the London borough of Croydon. My dad has left the Navy and is now a pilot. We move around a lot, usually to places where there is oil because he flies geologists and executives from the oil industry anywhere the precious resource might be found. First it was Pakistan, then Bolivia and then Iran.

Of course, there is no oil in Croydon. Under pressure from my mother, he has finally found work flying passenger planes at nearby Gatwick airport. Even so, there is tension, a hissed discord.

"You've no place telling the children they'll be able to see Big Ben from their bedroom window," my dad says. "We're moving to *Croydon*."

"But you said London," my mum responds. "London is where the life is and where you said you were taking me."

Me, my mum and my sister have high expectations of London. It's true we expect to see Big Ben or Buckingham Palace, but when we arrive we can only see cement mixers and burly Irish hod carriers labouring under pigeon skies. We are not "in" London as such. This is Croydon, an outlying borough and, what's more, we have moved to a part of it which is still under construction. The Ridge Langley estate is a cluster of starter homes marketed as a vibrant new community in one of the world's great cities. But even the builders finishing off the garage blocks don't hide their disdain.

"Dad, what does 'the arse-end of nowhere' mean?" I ask the day we arrive.

"Why? Who is using that sort of filthy language?" my dad growls.

"One of the builders said it," I explain. "He said it's where we live."

"Typical bog Irish talk," my dad says. "He was probably talking about *his* house!"

My mother is not very happy with our new surroundings either, and for her the stakes are higher still: after leaving Bolivia and migrating round the world with my father, she is keen to sample life in Britain's capital city.

"This is not London," she sighs, gazing out at a sea of cement and builder butt-crack. "I do not like this place."

But for me and Charlotte there are possibilities. The construction company has finished work and sold the inner ring of three bedroom houses, and it becomes an instant community. All the families arrive together, like change-over day at a holiday camp. There are a lot of families with young children. I soon find a boy to play with. Andrew Fieldman isn't like the smartly dressed Iranian boys I remember parading along the streets in shiny shoes and little suits. He is pale and undernourished-looking with scabbed knees. He is starting a fire down at the garages. "I'm an IRA bomber!" he enthuses. "Bet you can't catch me!"

After I manage to detain him and pretend to "kneecap" him, just like he says they do on the news, we get chatting. He even lets me set off one of his "bombs": a crisp bag filled with paraffin he has taken from a lamp his dad uses in the all too common power-cuts. Afterwards, I bring him home for tea.

"My dad says you are a dago," Andrew informs me airily over Rich Tea biscuits, confident this is a quite respectable racial denomination. It's a difficult moment. I explain I am half-Bolivian, and he seems to accept this. But my mum is in the background listening. She doesn't like my new English friend.

"We are not your so-called dagoes. Your father is the fucking ignorant peasant," my mum says. I am embarrassed. My mum can't speak English very well and has started picking up new language from Croydon's Surrey Street Market. She hasn't yet fully mastered the power and register of the trader's salty argot, which can make her sound ruder than she intends to be.

My dad takes my mum aside. "You mustn't use language like that," he says. "Also, this boy's father is not *the* ignorant peasant. He is *an* ignorant peasant."

I hate being half-Bolivian. I want to fit in. I want Andrew Fieldman and my other new friends Barry Stevens and Gavin Barnford to accept me, but it's hard going. This being the 70s, over those initial weeks of bonding we spend a lot of time drinking Tizer, collecting toy soldiers and re-enacting the Second World War in which, they remind me, Bolivia played no part. "My dad says the only thing Bolivia did in the war was hide Nazi war criminals," Andrew says darkly when my mum is in the kitchen.

Worse, Gavin says his dad saw Bolivia in a film called *Butch Cassidy and the Sundance Kid*. Butch and Sundance are on the run from American law enforcement and have heard that Bolivia is a beautiful sunny place with endless opportunities. "And then they get there, and it's a dump with pigs snuffling through piles of rubbish," Gavin says accusingly.

On another occasion, my parents have a sudden and explosive disagreement about the cultural direction I will follow and, not entirely disconnected from this, about what my name is. Gavin and Andrew knock at the front door. Gavin has a tiny transistor radio pressed to his ear with Slade's "Mama We're All Crazy Now" leaking from it in a tinny squall.

"Do they even have any pop music in Bolivia?" Gavin asks me in our hallway.

"Yeah, do they have Slade?" goads Andrew.

I don't know what to say. I do not notice my mum behind me until she chimes in. "Of course we do!" she says. "We have everything you have but even better!"

"Turn that bloody row off!" my dad orders from behind his newspaper in the living room. "Who said you could have a radio on in here?"

"Mick did," says Gavin.

"Mick? Who's Mick? There's no Mick here," my dad replies.

I step forward from behind Gavin. "I am Mick," I say timidly.

"What?"

"Me. I am Mick."

In the short weeks we have been in Ridge Langley, I

have re-invented myself as Mick. I'm not sure it really suits a half-Bolivian in Croydon, but I am prepared to firm up the connection with my new friends in any way necessary.

My dad looks angry. "Your name is not Mick, it's Michael," he says. He turns to Gavin, "He's *Michael*."

My mum hears the commotion on the way back to the kitchen and turns to re-enter the fray. "Why are you calling him Michael?" she snarls at my dad. "His name is Julio!" My mum pronounces it lavishly, like Tom Waits clearing his throat: *Hoolio!*

"He's *Michael*," my dad shouts.

For some reason my parents can't agree what my name is. My dad is called Michael and, as far as he is concerned, I am called Michael too. But my mum insists I am called Julio, the name of her Bolivian father. She has even given me a little silver-effect bracelet with my Bolivian name inscribed on it. I wear it when I am alone sometimes but never with my new Croydon friends. They have simple nicknames that are easy to shout across a park, like Gavva, Bazza and Adda. You can't do that with Julio. I keep it under wraps. I am a part-time Bolivian.

My mum closes the argument with a final "He's Julio!" and then tells my new friends, "Now you little – how does one say? – toerags must to have to go away. Julio needs his siesta!"

My new friends think it's hilarious my parents cannot agree what to call me and that I am not allowed out because I have to have a siesta. I go upstairs and lie on my rickety pull-down bed. I bid Death come take me. I can never now be accepted as a normal English boy.

The siesta thing is a killer for me. It's insane. People in

hot countries have a siesta because the midday temperatures and humidity make work impossible. That is simply not the case in Croydon. Also, it almost guarantees I will not sustain new friendships: on weekends and in the school holidays, while the new clique roves round the estate, cementing their new bonds by playing "IRA games", I must roll disconsolately on to my bunk bed and shelter from an imaginary Bolivian sun.

"Sweet dreams, Julio!" they shout from a safe distance up the path. "Enjoy the *siesta*!"

Downstairs I hear a row detonate. "They're calling him *Mick*. Who are these people?"

"Rough ones. You have brought us to live here among the rough ones."

"They are not to be called rough ones."

"Toerags then."

"No. You mustn't use language like that."

"This is not London. This is a land of *pendejos*."

"For God's sake, speak English."

"It means tosser," my mum says, arms folded belligerently.

"You've got to try," my dad says. "You've got to make an effort to fit in."

"In Bolivia I was someone," she says, "You have brought me here to live among beggars."

WHEN MY MOTHER was 21, she was a beauty queen back in her hometown Cochabamba, Bolivia. They gave her a sash, a scroll and a cheque. She often shows us two photos of the glory days: one of her sitting with these accoutrements on a makeshift throne. The other celebrating at home with her pet monkey Fico sitting on her shoulder. My mum looks happy. The monkey is gobbling a piece of fruit.

Soon afterwards, she met my dad, who was flying geologists around, promising, new, oil-rich territories. She was lured to England by romance and pop music. Even in Bolivia, you could pick up English-language music radio stations and hear fuzzy, tinny dispatches from the youth uprising in London. She liked the sound of the Swinging Sixties, but her dreams are not being fulfilled in Croydon. "Where is the action?" she would say. "Where are the young-at-heart ones?"

One night, shortly after my parents have this spat about the "land of the beggars", Charlotte wakes me up in her Donny Osmond nightie with dread in her eyes. Ashen faced, she tells me our mum is downstairs, crying alone in the darkness.

We creep down stairs together to investigate. Peering round the stairwell into the living room, there she is: pacing around in the darkness with a cigarette in her hand. Her eyes are black pits of smudged mascara. She has been sobbing. She has been drinking. She looks wild and desperate. "Believe me, I would never knowingly have come to this land of rain and cold English fish!" she rants to no one.

We ask her if she is alright. Barely acknowledging our presence, she whispers, "This is not a place for me. This is not the London of my dreams."

While she mumbles drunkenly, her voided eyes staring into space, Charlotte and I turn on each other. "It's *your* fault," she says. "You are being so difficult about having a siesta. And why don't you let her call you Julio?!"

"I don't want to be Julio! It's a *stupid* name!"

"What are we going to do then?"

"We need to get her a monkey."

"You are just so dumb. This is Croydon. Where are we going to get a *monkey*?"

Our mother has passed out on the sofa. Charlotte strokes the hair at her temple while I quietly pick up the glowing stump of her cigarette from the ash tray and smoke it.

"What are you *doing*?" Charlotte cries.

"I'm putting it out!" I say.

"How is that going to help?!" cries Charlotte. "Why can't you be sensible for once? Why don't you grow up?!"

In the proceeding days and weeks, our mother's moods are erratic. She shouts strange expletives at us, but we do not speak Spanish, so it's hard to know what she is saying. "*Flaca desgraciada!*" "*Cochino!*" Crucial bits of parenting are delivered to us in these splenetic outbursts. We are curious.

"I know who we can ask," says Charlotte. There is one other Bolivian/English family that my parents know living in London, Sophia and Roger. Roger is my dad's old friend from flying school, an English pilot who took a gig flying in Bolivia at the same time as him. My mum and dad met each other, then introduced Roger to Sophia, who subsequently also married and moved to London.

Charlotte and I have never been able to avoid comparison with this family. Sophia and Roger and their two kids, Guillermo and Carmen, are attempting the exact same exercise in cultural assimilation as us. The difference is: they are succeeding. They have given their kids Spanish names and taught them to speak the language. Sophia has learnt good English, hosts dinner parties and has found an access point into the host culture via the local golf club. She has a handicap of four. Also, she doesn't swear. Somehow, I feel both proud and despairing that my mother has not similarly claimed a place in her new world.

The next time we go to visit Sophia and Roger, Charlotte writes down some of the strange Spanish words my mum uses on a piece of paper and slips it into her dress pocket. While our mum and Sophia are gossiping in Spanish in the kitchen and my dad and Roger are guffawing heartily in the lounge, she approaches young Carmen, who is wearing priggish braids and frilled ankle socks while dawdling on the swing in their large Chiswick garden. Carmen stops swinging. She looks at the piece of paper, puts a hand over her mouth and laughs.

"Oh. My. God. Where did you get these?" she exclaims.

"Our mum. They are our names. What do they mean?"

"I can't say these things. They're rude," says Carmen.

"Say them," growls Charlotte.

"Well, it seems you're a skinny complaining cow," Carmen says tentatively, reading from the list.

I start to laugh.

"And you're a fat pig," she continues turning to me.

I burst into tears.

"What else?" demands Charlotte.

Carmen clears her throat. "Croydon is a place of ... well, a shithole."

Charlotte shrugs and seems to accept this.

"What about my other nickname?" I ask. "What's *crio de mierda*?"

Carmen runs a finger across the list and frowns. "You are ... a stupid little cry-baby."

"Actually 'de mierda' means 'of shit'," adds a boy's voice

IN THE EVENT OF AN EMERGENCY

behind us. Her brother Guillermo has appeared with a football jammed under his arm. "So, that's literally 'baby of shit'." He chuckles and shakes his head in disbelief.

"Unbelievable," he adds laughing to himself.

"Well, you're a stuck-up Spanish cunt!" I snap. I've heard my mother use the word, although I am not certain what it means.

"I'm telling!" says Guillermo throwing his ball down.

"Shut up, Michael!" Charlotte says.

My nostrils flare and I swallow hard to avoid more tears.

"You've actually done quite well," Charlotte says in an attempt to mollify me. "Really, cry-baby is not very bad at all."

I brighten a little. We pause.

"Okay, what else? What's that name she uses for Gavin?" Charlotte demands.

"*Campesino gordo con el radio*," says Carmen reading the list and struggling for a translation, "... means well-fed dweller of the country regions who likes music."

"Cut to the chase," says Guillermo. "He's a fat peasant with a radio."


ON THE WAY home, Charlotte and I hold a frantic whispered discussion in the back of the car. "Do you think there is something wrong with Mum?"

"I don't think she likes us."

"I don't think she likes *anything*."

There is more troubling news. Late that night, Charlotte overhears a heated conversation from our parents' bedroom. Strangulated recriminations in crisp English diction from my dad. Counter-accusations in faltering Spanglish and liberal use of "*pendejo*" from my mum.

"You can't behave like this," he says. "You're not making an effort to fit in. Why not play golf with Sophia?"

"I came here to see the London of the young ones," she retorts, "not to be an English housewife hitting a ball with a metal pole."

She wants to leave England. She wants to go home.

We know our mother is depressed. We don't call it that, but we sense something is wrong. And we want to help. We do not want our mum to return to Bolivia.

"For a start, she can call us and our friends whatever names she likes," says Charlotte. "We'll just have to take it."

"Even baby of shit?" I whisper tentatively.

"Yes," she replies, "they're just words."

Secondly, we have to make the "young people's England" available to her. I have noticed that whenever Gavin comes over with his little transistor radio, she often asks him to turn it up or to identify who is singing. "Music. She likes music. We have to play her the latest hits," I say.

Pop music makes our mother happy. She smiles to herself, and there's a bop to her walk when the radio is on at home. I have heard her singing along to The Beatles. I have seen her tap out a beat on the rim of the sink to Roxy Music, Slade, T. Rex and Queen.

"Your mum's cool, you know," Gavin concedes one day. "My mum never listens to my sort of music."

And so, when my dad is away flying, Charlotte gets out her records. Our mother comes sailing out of the kitchen with a cigarette in her hand and starts dancing in front of the bulky, coffin-shaped radio cabinet. Sometimes, when we are supposed to be doing our homework, she tells us not to be so boring and cranks the music up.

"Don't be too stuck in the English way," she counsels, twirling to the Rolling Stones while drying up a saucepan. "You have to enjoy life too."

While my dad despises pop music, fears its transgender experiments, satanic flirtations, narcissistic pouting and insurrectionist fervour, my mother sees in it a new world.

And then one day on one of her trips to buy fruit and veg at Surrey Street Market my mum hears a trader singing along to a song called "Starman" on the radio. She likes "Starman". She asks who it's by. "It's that bender, Bowie," he tells her.

"Play me the song of Bender Bowie, will you?" my mum asks when she gets home. At first, we laugh. But it also dawns on us that Bowie might have a particular resonance for her. Not only is he a local hero but "Starman" is a song about an alien experiencing cultural assimilation issues.

"I think we should show her what David Bowie looks like," Charlotte says. And so, the next time Bowie is on TV, we haul her out of the kitchen and sit her in front of him performing in a sparkly jumpsuit and feather boa. Charlotte finds my mum her cigarettes, lights one for her and places it in her mouth. She absorbs the androgynous figure on the TV screen before her.

"What is that?"

"David Bowie. The singer you like."

"David is a boy's name no?"

"Yes."

"This is a boy?"

"Yes."

"But he has no *cojones* ..."

My mum closely examines the fey, jump-suited figure on the TV screen for evidence of sex organs. And then she exhales richly with her verdict: "In my country we would chase this *maricon* through the streets and beat him with a stick."

My mother isn't sure about David Bowie. Really not sure at all. As he parades the stage flirting with his guitarist Mick Ronson, she seems more alienated by English culture than ever before. "Is this what they call in this country ... a poof?"

Charlotte informs our mum that he is based in Beckenham just up the road, an important new pop star that everyone at school is copying.

"What a funny man he is. I suppose he sings quite well. Are there others like him?"

We explain that there are. There are lots more and, if she stays with us in England, we can show them to her.

IN THE GLOOM of Mrs Henckel's consulting room, I fall silent. I have explained that pop music was a way of settling my mother in England. Immigrants have to find a way to engage with the host country's culture. Some assimilate into the working class, others imitate the English middle class. My mother chose youth culture as an entry point, which is by its very nature fluid and accepting of difference.

"It gave her a passport into the culture," says Mrs Henckel.

"Yes, I think it did," I offer in agreement.

It feels good. I have made an important connection. I am no longer merely a demented fanboy compulsively archiving records and stolen rock star knick-knacks. I am beginning to join the dots. I am beginning to understand myself.

"Do you ever feel like that Bolivian boy, Julio, now?" asks Mrs Henckel.

"No," I say, "I am English. I am Michael."

"Really? No hint of this exotic influence at all? You have completely submerged this Bolivian identity?"

"Well, I was interested once, but it ended in disaster," I say.

"How, a disaster?"

"Nicola didn't like what happened to me when I explored Julio," I explain. "I took some bad decisions."

"Let us study this Julio phase in more detail, please," says Mrs Henckel.

# 11
# Me and Julio

When I get home from the session, I find Nicola standing by our gate with Ronnie, chatting to a mum from school. I know the mum. She has mean, darting eyes and a utility haircut, a bit like Enya. She is in the PTA, and when Nicola once let her hold a coffee morning at our house, I became highly suspicious of her. PTA Mum used the bathroom and afterwards didn't ask a single question about my memorabilia. She simply walked out, straightening her tartan skirt and resumed discussing school uniforms. It didn't register at all. What kind of animal behaves like that?

Ronnie is writing in the dirt of a parked van with his finger while Nicola listens intently. PTA Mum is doing all the talking. "I am here to support you in any way I can," she says in a conspiratorial whisper and touches Nicola on the shoulder. I know this conspiratorial whisper. I know this touch on the shoulder. It means Ronnie has done something wrong at school.

PTA Mum sees me approach, clucks something about piano lessons and leaves. Nicola confronts me in the hallway. "Ronnie really wowed the maths class today," she says.

"Really?" I reply, exhaling with relief. "I thought for a minute he'd been naughty. That boy is destined for great things."

I see a moist film developing in Nicola's eyes. Tears of joy and pride I hope. And yet her gaze is so far away.

"Miss Dunwoody asked him to complete a sum," she says in a strained whisper, "and he wrote 'People = Shit' on the whiteboard."

"Oh fuck," I say.

Ronnie spins round from his labours. "Mummy said 'shit' and Daddy said 'f—'"

"No, Ronnie! Stop!" says Nicola. "What Mummy said was a *report* of someone swearing and so it's not as bad as Daddy, who should know better."

"Actually, so was Ronnie's," I point out.

"So, was Ronnie's what?"

"He was reporting our swearing."

"For God's sake, Michael," Nicola says in an enraged whisper. "Our son scribbled abuse on the board in class! You've got to take it seriously!"

We go inside. Ronnie is sent to play in his room while the inquest continues in the kitchen. New emergency household powers are instigated: I must not leave rock 'n' roll materials lying around the house after 3.30pm when Ronnie returns from school. Like passive smoking, exposure to ambient rock 'n' roll nihilism is dangerous for young minds.

"Thing is, you're not really here at the moment, are you?" says Nicola. "It's like living with a ghost."

"I'm trying," I plead. "I promise you, I am trying my hardest."

"I thought you weren't keen on therapy," Nicola says, arms folded in weary accusation.

"I'm not. I mean I wasn't. But Mrs Henckel can see things that I've missed."

"You'll be seeing her for bloody years then," she mumbles.

"What?"

"Nothing."

"You swore."

"Bloody isn't a swear word."

AT DINNERTIME, FLASH-FRYING chicken pieces in a wok with extreme prejudice, Nicola half-heartedly asks about the things that Mrs Henckel has seen that I have missed.

"We're into some tough areas," I say with a self-pitying grimace. "We're really wrestling with the beast now."

Nicola nods sympathetically and begins unpacking Ronnie's lunchbox. It's a Slipknot lunchbox. The record company sent me a promotional sample and, against my better judgement, I let him use it.

"For fuck's sake, let's get rid of this thing," she says. I take the lunchbox. I ball it up with two hands and squash Clown's face down into the bin with menace. *Away nihilism!*

"I think what Ronnie really needs is his own bedroom," Nicola says suddenly. "He's growing up. He shouldn't be sharing it with all your crap."

"My *crap*?" I echo indignantly.

"Sorry, your stuff."

"Well, I'm not sure this is really the moment," I say.

"Why not? Why isn't this the moment?"

"I'm in the middle of some key issues," I say. "I'm in the eye of the storm."

"And what key issues might they be?" says Nicola, her arms folded. "What key issues mean we can't clear out a room for our son?"

I don't like the look in her eye.

"The thing is, therapy is like archaeology. Me and Mrs Henckel have uncovered a valuable site. We mustn't touch anything until we really understand what's going on."

"But you never *tell* me what's going on," she snaps. "Why don't you try explaining it to me for once?"

I swallow hard. I know this is not going to be easy. "Mrs Henckel thinks that, somewhere, perhaps, Julio still lingers," I begin tentatively.

Nicola drops a dish into the sink and puts her face in her hands. "What did you just say?"

"Julio. He's alive."

"Jesus, haven't we been through all this?" she says, eyes shut in exasperation.

"Oh, thanks. Thanks a bundle," I say. I am about to leave the room in a strop, but then I remember I have Mrs Henckel on my side. I have new psychotherapeutic jargon to use.

"Perhaps I sense residual anger issues about me being half-Bolivian?" I suggest.

"I'm not angry with you being half-Bolivian or half-*anything*," Nicola says.

"Then why so dismissive?"

"Because we have enough on our plate already," she says. "Ronnie is struggling and, if you remember, you being half-Bolivian nearly destroyed this family first time round."

149

"Oh, come on," I say, "there's no need to overdramatise."

"Seriously, Michael," Nicola insists, "Julio nearly *finished* us."

⚡

It was a sunny morning in 2002. I was in my office opening my post. A CD and promotional photos of an unknown artist calling herself Shakira fell out of a padded Jiffy envelope and clunked onto the desk.

The press photos showed a petite hardbody with a face like one of the Disney soft toys Ronnie used to have stacked along his headboard as a baby: big eyes, button nose, hair arranged in golden tresses. But Shakira triggered more erotic instincts too; a bare, toned midriff pushed out towards the camera in a belly dancing manoeuvre. Adjacent to her was a jetty harbouring a flotilla of bobbing yachts. The yachts themselves seemed to have triggered this state of pre-coital arousal.

I put on the CD and studied the photos more carefully. Analysing all this material together through the prism of default rock writer disdain, my conclusion was immediate: *Shakira is a cheeseburger for the eyes performing the musical equivalent of bubble wrap!*

Decision made, ordinarily I would have thrown a press pack like this in the bin. All of it: CD, photos, press release. I wouldn't be bothered by the impact on the environment. In fact, I would relish the idea of Shakira's album churning in the jaws of a municipal trash compactor. *Fuck this cynical corporate shit!*

But then I noticed from the press release that she was from South America. I was fascinated by the fact that,

40 years after my mother heard The Beatles on a Bolivian radio, South America was at last producing its own pop stars and sending them to us.

I showed it to my friend Rex Trauma over a beer. When I am in doubt, Rex is always useful at helping me detect genuine rock essence.

"What do you think?"

"I'd definitely give her one," he said absent-mindedly.

"She's Columbian."

"Okay, I'd give her one and then snort her stash," he added with a terrible honking laugh.

"She's Columbian. I'm half-Bolivian," I said. "Have I ever told you that?"

"No."

"Well, I am. I used to be called Julio."

"Julio? That's a hairdresser's name."

"It is if you say it like that. But it's pronounced *Hoolio*," I said, deploying a lot of guttural spit on the first syllable.

"I still prefer Michael."

"I think it's pretty interesting that my mother heard The Beatles in Bolivia as a girl and now South America has its own pop music it wants to sell back to us."

"No, it isn't," Rex insisted scornfully. "Foreign pop music is always shit."

"There might be something in Shakira," I said.

"I wish it was me," Rex chuckled darkly. "Basically, what you're saying is, you fancy her, isn't it?"

"No! I am genuinely interested. I'm going to convince Gareth to put her in the magazine."

"No chance," said Rex. "Pan pipes in the shopping

centre, yes. But no one is going to buy a South American rocker."

I was annoyed Rex didn't get it. I was also annoyed that no one could relate to being a half-Bolivian in the music industry. Still seeking support, I showed Nicola the press photos of Shakira.

"She's such a bimbo," she said.

"No, she's not," I said crossly. "Sexuality is just expressed differently in South America."

"How? How is Shakira doing anything different because she's South American?" Nicola demanded.

"She's in control," I said.

"She's a bimbo!"

I looked again at the photos of Shakira on the jetty. She did seem to be making a fairly mundane point about female sexual arousal being heightened by the prospect of luxury sea-faring. But I was still annoyed.

"She's in control here. There are no men on the jetty. How do you know she's not going to sail the yacht out of the harbour herself and, once she's clear of the lighthouse go down below and give herself a hand-job?"

"She's a bimbo," Nicola repeated, "You just fancy her, that's all."

Walking away, Nicola patted me on the shoulder matily. "It's alright," she said. "Just don't try and justify it by saying you used to be called Julio."

"Racist," I murmured under my breath, but she was already in the living room.

Later that evening, I entered the kitchen with a recipe printed from the internet. I was determined to express my Bolivian identity. Crashing about with pans and occasionally swearing in Spanish, I eventually emerged with some Bolivian empanadas, a snack not dissimilar to a Cornish pasty, but spicier. I served them to Nicola and Ronnie for dinner.

"Be proud. This is your heritage," I told Ronnie. He nodded, while glugging water straight from a jug. I may have overdone the chilli.

"My Bolivian grandfather and uncle were rebels, freedom fighters," I added.

"What exactly did they do again?" Nicola asked.

"They fought for the rights of the common man and got punished for it," I answered grandly. "They were rock 'n' roll before there was even rock 'n' roll."

Nicola nodded solemnly, flapping a hand in front of her open mouth and winked at our son. "Don't worry, I'll do you fish fingers later if you're still hungry," she whispered.

After Ronnie went to bed, Nicola watched TV. I went up into the loft and began rummaging through old bags and boxes. In a battered rhombus of a cardboard box, I found what I was looking for: my old silver effect bracelet with "Julio" inscribed on it. A lost part of me.

At the end of the evening, I entered the bedroom wearing it. I was wearing just my underpants and the bracelet. I let it glint attractively on my wrist.

"Why have you come to bed dressed as an East End gangster?" Nicola smirked cruelly.

I didn't say anything. I got into bed, turned my back to her and admired my shiny wrist jewellery.

"*Buenas noches*," said Nicola.

I refused to reply.

"Come on, don't be grumpy, Julio," she teased.

I pretended to be asleep, but inside I was raging. The slumbering half-Bolivian beast Julio had awoken.

"SHAKIRA WILL SEE you after rehearsal. She would like you to watch," said the burly minder.

Less than a week later I was in Miami. Q agreed with me. Shakira was a South American phenomenon, and Q had reason to investigate. It was one of the few times, in fact the only time, that my search for Bolivian heritage has intersected with British rock 'n' roll publishing.

"As long as this isn't just about you fancying her," Gareth said. "We want a proper story."

"No, she's a genuine cultural pathfinder," I said.

I found myself in a gigantic empty arena watching Shakira writhe, squat and pout to her own songs and also some AC/DC covers. She was wearing a form-hugging black leather outfit. She tossed her hair, grimaced in ecstasy and pushed her groin out over the lip of the stage.

I tried my best to maintain po-faced critical distance. Nevertheless, I soon found myself gently polishing my silver-effect Julio bracelet against a trouser leg in readiness for our meeting. *This is almost a homecoming for Julio!*

Shakira finished with a highly libidinous "Back in Black", pouting sullenly to the vast acreage of the arena's empty seating. I clapped and whooped, my frenzy conspicuous in the echoing hangar. I admired her, and I admired the stage set. Its central motif seemed to be a gigantic Jack Russell terrier snarling at the audience. I asked an assistant its significance.

"Actually, it's a mongoose," she explained. "Shakira is

physically quite small, but sees herself taking on the snakes of the music industry, as well as the bigger, malign forces of the world. This is why the tour is called 'Tour of the Mongoose'."

The aide indicated to Shakira that I had arrived. She nodded and glanced down at me from the stage, one hand on a jutting hip. I tried to compose my rock writer "game face", but I was like a subject meeting his queen.

"Hey, bro'," the aide said, snapping me out of my trance. Then, via a discreet sideways head-flick, she indicated I was to proceed to Shakira's dressing room.

Shakira filled my nostrils before I met her. The ambrosial aroma of pop star.

"Hi, I am Shakira and be very happy to meet you," she said in excellent English, which was nonetheless just off-key enough to be sexy.

Because the Tour of the Mongoose was a gigantic and imminent undertaking, Shakira could not stop for long. Lighting riggers, wardrobe wizards, dancing divas, kings of catering, not to mention her musicians, were hanging around waiting for her on full pay. In fact, her management team requested that, while we talked, wardrobe technicians be allowed to continue tweaking her costume.

"If this doesn't distract you from your speaking," Shakira said to me with doe-eyed consideration.

"Of course, let no man stand in the way of the Tour of the Mongoose," I said, possibly a little lamely.

"I am the mongoose fighting the cobra ... to show that the underdog of the animal kingdom can win against mighty forces," Shakira began.

We had not been talking in her dressing room long

before I decided I liked Shakira. She was so much more than a hottie on a jetty.

"I will – how you say – overcome the cobra of negativity," she announced, and stood to make a mongoose attack stance. But in doing so, her muscular body overcame the constraints of her skin-tight leather trousers. A button on her fly popped, dropped and rolled across the dressing room floor. *I would very much like that button for my memorabilia collection!*

"Excuse me a moment," she said standing up and peering down at the damage.

A wardrobe technician in an adjoining room entered. They discussed the trousers and quickly reached agreement. The trousers were too tight. Shakira looked like she was going to peel them off and then simply carry on answering my questions. If she did, I decided, I would be cool about it. *If she exposes her bush, I will handle the situation with dignity, neither salivating wildly nor po-facedly pretending that this sexual potency isn't awesome.* I can be cool with this, I reasoned, because, as a kid, Charlotte explained the nuances of female sex exploitation among pop stars.

"It's about power," she used to say. "If a woman shows her tits but is somehow in control of them, then it's okay. But if she's just trying to please men, then she's just a stupid cow. And a traitor."

I have used this broad rule of thumb ever since. And so once, when I interviewed Debbie Harry, I questioned her about the sexy skirt she wore on the cover of Blondie's smash-hit album *Parallel Lines*, and she said: "Who cares if guys want to fuck me? As long as they buy the album ... and stay out of my face."

But once, I interviewed Kylie Minogue, and she struck me as a guileless showbiz automaton, offering a glimpse of closely plucked haunch without sufficiently analysing the beneficiary structure of such a gesture.

"Do you feel in control?" I asked her.

"I'm really a simple Aussie girl at heart," she simpered. I stole her hairclip for my memorabilia collection and left, disgusted.

*Which side of the argument is Shakira on?* I waited as she began to wriggle out of her leather skin.

"Could you please wait outside?" her assistant asked, as the moment of crisis arrived.

I stood reluctantly in the corridor listening to the arena's air conditioning ducting. I thought about how air conditioning is a tool of cultural imperialism, imported by softies who can't handle the climate. I thought about my mum, her monkey and Bolivia. *The white man took The Beatles and air conditioning to South America! Now they're sending us Shakira!*

I looked down at my Julio name bracelet and felt suddenly gloomy. *All that glorious cultural heritage, and this is all I've got! A bracelet inscribed at Timpson's!*

Shakira peered round from inside her dressing room. "Please, re-enter Michael," she purred.

"Please, call me Julio," I said.

"Your name is Julio?"

I showed her my bracelet. "Yes, half of me is from Bolivia," I said.

"Really?" she marvelled. "When I first saw you, I thought you did not look so typically English."

I liked it when Shakira said that, particularly as she seemed to have pondered my racial background while changing her trousers. More than this, I was elated she could discern elements of Julio.

"Bolivia. You poor guys get negative crap talked about you so much, worse even than my country. Everyone thinks it's a place of narcotics."

"I know," I said. "They don't know real Bolivian culture."

"And you have grown up with it?"

"Of course," I said.

"Like a for instance?" asked Shakira, suddenly very interested.

"Oh, I had regular siestas and special Bolivian pet names."

"That is so cute. Which pet names did you have?"

I swallow hard. I cannot tell Shakira my mother called me "baby of shit". "Fatty," I said, and looked distractedly around the room.

"Tell me. What brought your mother to England?"

"Music. The Beatles, the Stones ..."

"That is very cool. I would like my music to inspire people in such a way," said Shakira.

I felt the first stirrings of a deep love. And I resolved that if ever I got around to resuming my taxonomy of rock 'n' roll, Shakira would merit a massive entry:

*Diva Columbianesis. Deeply hot and intelligent pro-Bolivian South American sex bomb. Could be a game-changer for a continent raised on pan pipes.*

That evening, I accompanied Shakira to the Latin America MTV Awards, where she won an armful of statuettes. The next day she made me a special guest at her video shoot.

The video was being shot on a Miami street, and it aimed, unashamedly, to showcase Shakira's languid sexuality. More than this, it aimed to showcase Shakira's languid sexuality after it has been hosed down by a high intensity water cannon. According to the video concept, she was supposed to be grieving the loss of a heartless lover while singing in the rain. However, there was no rain in Miami, and so they were using a water truck. I watched, awestruck, as Shakira desperately gulped lyrics while the water jet was trained on her. Afterwards, she towelled off and came over to say goodbye.

"You have inspired that I will like to go to Bolivia soon," she said. "Tell me, what is the best city to visit?"

"I'm not really sure," I say. "I have never been."

"So, when you say you grew up immersed in Bolivian culture, where was this?"

"Croydon."

"*Croydon?*"

"It's a suburb of London."

She made a little moue with her mouth. It was challenging, sceptical. "You were given the name Julio, but you've never been to your motherland?" she said eventually, incredulous. "This is a fault."

I said goodbye and slunk back to Miami airport. In the terminal building, I eschewed McDonald's and ate disconsolately from a South American themed food stall. I felt like a pussy not being able to handle the lava-hot spiced potatoes. And I felt like a loser never having visited my mother's homeland. *This a fault! Shakira thinks I'm a dick!*

And then, as I mooched about the terminal waiting for the London flight, I saw LPZ flash up on the Departures board. It stands for La Paz, the capital of Bolivia. I had never actually seen the name of a Bolivian city on a departures board before. I became entranced by it. *You are one step from the motherland!*

I couldn't help myself. I ran to a payphone and crammed money in.

"Nicola listen, I'm having a bit of a moment regarding Julio."

"What? What did you say?"

"I'm finally feeling Julio."

"You're feeling who?"

"Julio!"

"But ... he's you."

"Yes! Exactly."

"What are you trying to tell me, Michael? I mean ... Julio?"

"I've just had this amazing chat with Shakira, and ... it's wrong that I've never been to the motherland. This is a fault!"

"What? What's a fault?"

In the background my flight was being announced.

"... I need to feel him more."

"What?"

"Julio!"

"But what about the—?"

I put down the phone and headed for the ticket desk. Then I shouldered through the scrum of ponchos to my seat on the plane.

I WAS IN Bolivia for five days. I travelled from the capital, La Paz, to my mum's hometown of Cochabamba and back again. I wanted to find out about this brilliant country that my mum always said made Croydon look like "a pigsty". I wanted to discover more about the original Julio, my grandfather, and his brother, my Uncle Jorge. Freedom fighters! Champions of the common man! Rebels!

In a La Paz library, I couldn't find anything about them in books. But the elderly English-speaking librarian was very helpful. She pored over newspaper cuttings and cross-referenced with approximate dates.

"Your grandfather Julio was arrested and sent into exile," she said.

"For subversive rebellious activities, no doubt," I ventured hungrily at her shoulder.

"Hmmm, no I don't think so because it looks like his brother Jorge was ... a cop," she reported, looking up from the papers fanned across her table.

"A *cop*?" I protested. "No, they were rebels. They were freedom fighters."

"Says here he was a cop. Plain as day."

"But a good cop, a rebel cop?" I remonstrated.

"Not what it's telling me here, I'm afraid," she continued, frowning darkly at the old newsprint.

"What does it say?"

"Jorge was the Chief of Police," she said. She swivelled a book of cuttings around so that I could see, and jabbed a finger at a photo. "That's him. That's Jorge."

I looked at the photo. It seemed to show a man in a city square trying to shin up a lamp post, encouraged by a fervent crowd.

"Was he a street performer in his spare time?"

"No," she said shaking her head gravely.

"What the hell?! What is going on here?" I said, looking again. The man was not shinning up a lamp post; he was dangling.

"A mob hung him in the Plaza Murillo. He was not a popular man."

AT THE AIRPORT, I used the last of my Bolivian currency to ring my mother. When she answered, I couldn't even bring myself to say hello.

"He was a cop," I growled.

"Hello? Who *is* this?"

"HE WAS A COP!!" I said louder. "AND THEY HATED HIM SO MUCH, THEY HUNG HIM FROM A LAMP POST!"

"Julio, is that you?"

"I am not Julio. I'm Michael, and he was ... WHY DIDN'T YOU TELL ME?!"

It took a long phone call for my mother to admit she lied about Jorge and Julio. And when I got home to Nicola we had deep issues to resolve too.

"I can't believe you just buggered off without saying anything!" she complained.

"If you were searching for your roots I'd support you!" I pleaded.

"My roots are in Leamington Spa! You went to *Bolivia*!"

Nevertheless, Nicola was relieved. I was home and also, importantly, I seemed to have got Julio out of my system.

That night we made love. In the midst of ecstasy, my mind slipped and I went somewhere else. I said something under my breath in the darkness. Our rhythm stopped. Nicola's voice was no longer whispering intimacies. Her voice became urgent. Staccato.

"What did you just say?"

"I said 'Shhhh'."

"No, you didn't. You said something else."

"You were getting excited. I thought you might wake Ronnie, so I said, 'Shhh ... he'll hear yer.'"

"I'll tell you when I'm excited, and I wasn't."

"You made a noise. I was just trying to be considerate."

Nicola put on the bedside lamp. "You said Shakira, didn't you?"

I admitted that I had done.

"Get away from me, you arsehole!"

I knew it was bad. I knew she had a right to be angry. I promised never to mention Shakira again. And I put my bracelet back in the box in the loft.

"Look, I'm sorry. It's been a crazy couple of weeks," I said, "but I promise: Julio is gone forever."

# 12
# Goodbye to Pain

At the next session, I tell Mrs Henckel what happened between Julio and Shakira. "My relationship will not survive another Bolivian investigation," I say.

Mrs H listens sympathetically to my account. "Very well," she allows. "We must leave the Bolivian dimension alone."

"So ... what next?" I say brightly. "Do you think we're done?"

"No. You must explain how Julio came to embrace the music of the nihilists."

My heart sinks. I feel better, but I want to quit while I'm ahead. Mrs Henckel then picks up her folder, takes out her pad and flicks back several pages to find notes relating to our earliest meetings.

"I would like to further explore your role in this phenomenon you call Mental Elf, which in turn was attached to the musical subsection entitled 'punk rock'," she reads with a sceptical frown.

"Jesus, that's a long story," I say.

"This I believe to lie at the core of your problems," she diagnoses with a beady glare. "I think we are near the heart of things."

"Mrs Henckel says I am approaching the eye of the storm," I tell Nicola when I get home, "but you'll be relieved to hear she's not making me take another look at Julio."

"Good. That's the best news I've had all day," she says, looking up from a pile of paperwork. But she averts her eyes from me quickly. She looks pale and tired.

"What's the matter? I thought you'd be pleased."

"Of course I'm pleased."

"What is it then?"

"We haven't got any money," says Nicola, waving a bill in front of me. "That damp patch in our bedroom is getting bigger, and I want to get it sorted. Also, we owe two months on the electricity bill."

"You know, in the early days of hip hop, when they didn't have electricity for block parties, they used to hack into lamp posts."

"What is your point?"

"We're just so straight the way we, you know, just *pay the bills* when the corporations tell us to."

"Michael, I've noticed a pattern: you always seem to romanticise the early days of hip hop when I ask you about money," she says.

This is a very sore point. Sure, my job means I get to fly on U2's private jet, slide effortlessly into the hand-stitched leather interior of their limo, eat with them in the finest restaurants, and afterwards sip vintage brandy from cut-glass balloons, discussing international debt relief for Bolivia. But I cannot get Bono to ring my bank and cancel my mortgage.

Rock writers do not get paid very much, which is scandalous considering the important and risky work we do.

Our culture is under constant zombie attack, yet, for polic-
ing the front line, the rewards are sparse. What's more, the
financial disconnect between these two worlds has occasionally had grievous social repercussions. Once, I interviewed
Dave Grohl at a club in central London. It went well, and I
left punctually as I'd arranged to meet Nicola outside afterwards. As I greeted her, we bumped into Grohl climbing
into his limo. I introduced them. Grohl was charming and,
shaking his hand, I noticed Nicola turned pink at the ears
like she does when she drinks champagne at Christmas.

"My car's full, but why don't you guys come to our hotel
and have dinner?" Grohl said.

Nicola surreptitiously pinched me on the arm with
excitement. Grohl's limo pulled away, and we ran to hail a
cab. That's when I discovered I only had 50p on me. Two
minutes later, we both watched a cashpoint swallow my
card, declining me funds.

"SOME OF MY memorabilia is quite valuable," I suggest to
Nicola as she ponders the bills.

"You think British Gas will accept a portion of chips that
once belonged to Sting? Or a pair of trousers that one of The
Strokes used to wear?"

Nicola is far better at financial management than I am.

"Then I'll take out a loan," I offer.

"Yes, and please can we make a start on clearing
Ronnie's room," says Nicola.

"I can't."

"Why?"

"I'm not ready yet!"

"Well, *when* then?"

"Can't you see I'm on a journey? I'm nearing the end!"

"I know you're on a bloody journey. I want you to come home!"

"Don't shout at me. I'm in a very vulnerable place."

"*You're* in a vulnerable place?"

"Yes, Mrs Henckel says I am near the core of the problem. If you could just be a bit more understanding ..."

Nicola sighs, looks down at her paperwork again and mumbles darkly. "Someone something somewhere," I hear her say.

"Pardon?" I ask.

"SOMEONE LET A FIRE EXTINGUISHER OFF IN MY FACE TODAY!" she roars, from a very hurt place.

"I'm sorry. That's terrible."

"And you know what?" she says throwing down her pen. "The young man who did it was wearing a Nirvana t-shirt."

"Was he? Good band. The later work is a bit ropey but ..."

"Afterwards, when Vicky was cleaning the foam out of my hair in the office, I thought about you."

"Well, that's very sweet of you."

"I thought about how rock t-shirts are a badge of immaturity. Any guy over 30 in a rock t-shirt is basically saying 'I cannot, or will not, grow up'."

"But I would never, *ever* let a fire extinguisher off in your face!"

I see a flicker of despair in her eyes. "Sometimes I feel as though I really don't know you," she mutters.

"It's funny, I feel like that about myself too sometimes," I say jauntily.

"For God's sake, we are in trouble here, Michael. What are we going to do?"

Later, when Nicola has gone to bed, I slip downstairs and take a look at the bills. I tot up the outstanding debts, adding my invoice from Mrs Henckel. It all comes to £2,112. *That's funny*, I think, *because 2112 is the title of a concept album by Canadian prog band Rush.*

When Pete and our bassist Foetus found out I owned it, they got cross because punks are not supposed to own concept albums by incredibly accomplished musicians. But Rush are a remarkable trio. Singer Geddy Lee has an incredible voice, Alex Lifeson is a towering guitarist, and drummer Neil Peart a percussion titan. Sitting behind his gigantic drum kit, he looks like a man trapped behind a stack of barrels fighting to get out using two pieces of wood. Quietly I love them.

*2112* relates a terrible dystopian tale: rock music has been banned by the Priests of the Temple of Syrinx after it led to the downfall of civilisation. *Maybe they didn't pay their utility bills either!* But then a daring young hero picks up a guitar, strums it and rediscovers rock in the year 2112.

Looking at the number on the piece of paper, it resonates deeply. I briefly imagine Nicola and Mrs Henckel, shrouded in hooded robes, unsmiling as they stand at a pyre burning my CD and record collection. *They are the Priests of the Temple of Syrinx!*

After this brief but highly disturbing fantasy, I look at the number 2112 again. With a pound sign in front of it, it is not a future world where rock is rediscovered by a daring cultural hero. It's just a debt. My mood slides.

I go up into Ronnie's bedroom and look at my memorabilia. Then I take the guitar out of its case, strum it for a while and watch Ronnie in his little bed, sleeping. I soon reach a decision. Mrs Henckel wants me to explore my lurch into rock's dark side. To be exact: *My role in the phenomenon called Mental Elf itself, attached to the musical sub section entitled "punk rock"!*

But I will not do this. Because even though I am not as good with money as Nicola, I do know that for a man £2,112 in debt, spending £35 an hour discussing a failed rock band called Mental Elf constitutes imprudent financial management.

I have gone far enough. We do not have the money, and perhaps some things are better left unsaid. I sleep on it and then ring Mrs Henckel first thing next morning.

"I know I am near the core of my problems," I tell Mrs Henckel, "but I just don't think I am ready to take things further."

"I strongly recommend that you do not cease treatment at this juncture," she says. "I sense you are very close to the truth."

"I can't afford it, and I am making everyone unhappy," I say. "One day maybe, I will go there but not now. This is goodbye."

WEEKS PASS. CHRISTMAS approaches. I think about Mrs Henckel a lot, and often feel irritable, but I put this down to the fact there is cold and rain and a lot of terrible music around. Music that depresses me. Music that makes me angry. Shayne Ward has won the second series of *X Factor*, and his single "That's My Goal" is unavoidable. In the song, he relates how it is his goal to "win your heart and soul". Whenever I hear it, I cannot help thinking: *Sending your sorry ass back to the world of weddings, bar mitzvahs and Butlin's holiday camps: that's my goal!*

It depresses me that pop culture does not work the same as, say, the field of medical research, where you can reasonably expect that, incrementally, things will get a bit better each year. We had The Beatles and glam rock and then punk, new wave and plenty more movements besides, but now, in 2005, we have re-entered the Dark Ages. It shakes my belief in democracy and freedom. Should just anyone be able to buy music? Sometimes I think people should have to pass a knowledge test, showing that they know the price that has been paid for rock, before being issued with a licence to make a purchase.

"I like Keane," Nicola says when another inescapable song, "Somewhere Only We Know", comes on. "Why don't Q put them on the cover?"

I say nothing. We are trying harder to get on. I am supposed to be calming down. But I feel Nicola is testing me. She knows I went to interview Keane in 2004, just before they became massively successful. They were really nice guys. That was partly the problem. We walked on the beach near Birling Gap in Sussex and drank greasy tea at the café. Afterwards, we went back to keyboard player Tim Rice-Oxley's house. I was warming to them when I saw his dad's golf clubs propped up against a fence in the rose garden.

"Do you play?" he asked me jauntily.

I felt deeply conflicted. It was one of those moments when I really confronted how entrenched my expectations of rock stars truly are. I didn't want Keane to offer me a round of golf. I wanted them to offer me heroin or show me the charred remains of sacrifices they had made in the name of devil-worship. I wanted them to frighten me, show some awareness of life's dark side. But Keane didn't. We sat round a polished antique table. Then Tim offered me a slice of Dundee cake.

"I actually think your expectations of rock stars are quite passive aggressive," Nicola said when I got home.

"How do you work that out?"

"As well as writing great songs, you need them to get angry or be dysfunctional on your behalf."

"No, I just don't think offering people Dundee cake is what rock stars *do*," I snapped back.

Now, IT FEELS as though rock's need to be challenging has become a decisive domestic issue. Ronnie says he doesn't want his toy guitar anymore. He wants a real one for Christmas. "I want to play some proper songs," he announces. "I'm bored of just air guitar."

"I can ask at the school if they'll recommend a teacher," says Nicola.

"I think I know one already," I say.

I meet Rex for a drink. I ask if he has an old guitar he wants to sell and if he knows how to give lessons.

"Sure, and of course I'll chuck in a couple of lessons for your boy," he offers.

On the way home from the pub I feel good, but I also sense this is risky. Is asking Rex to teach Ronnie guitar passive aggressive? If he ends up learning tracks from Anal Cunt's seminal album *Everyone Should Be Killed*, would that count as passive aggressive?

By Christmas Eve I am in turmoil. I feel like ringing Mrs Henckel for advice, but that feels like a cop-out. In the end, I dodge the issue. Christmas comes. I hold Rex off. I don't buy Ronnie a proper guitar. I get him something else and say he can have a guitar for his birthday later in the year.

But Ronnie feels rock 'n' roll more viscerally than I give him credit for. In rock, you don't wait for your dad to get you a guitar later in the year. You see a chance. You take it. Early in January I come home from Q and find Ronnie standing in the hall looking pale and nervous.

"Did you have a good day?" he asks.

"Yes, thank you," I say.

"Good enough so that you won't get cross?"

"Why? Why would I get cross?

"I've started on a proper guitar."

"At school?"

"No, at home."

"Why would I be cross?

"I broke it."

"Which guitar?"

"The one in your room. The one you never play."

The skin on my forehead tightens like a drum. I look at Ronnie's stricken little face.

"I took it out of the case and something snapped," he whimpers.

I run up the stairs taking two steps at a time.

"I told you. Never ever touch that guitar!"

I sweep into my office. Nicola is in there trying to fit a new string that she has already bought for it.

"You let him play the guitar!" I remonstrate breathlessly. "How could you!"

Nicola spins round in my chair, her eyes alight with anger. "Okay so he broke a string on your precious guitar!" she exclaims. "But he was just helping me move it!"

"But why, why were you moving it? That's my most precious possession!"

"Good for you! It's not mine! It's a new year, Michael. I'm going to sort this room out once and for all!"

I am so angry I leave the house, sit in the campervan and call Mrs Henckel. "I think I am ready to come back into therapy," I say.

"Are you sure?"

"Yes, if you haven't given my slot to someone else?"

"No, I haven't. Michael, has something happened?"

I explain that the flashpoint was Ronnie and then Nicola interfering with my most precious memorabilia.

"I just think people need to respect other people's stuff!" I cry.

"You sound very angry," she says.

"Isn't that fair enough? How would you feel if someone went into your room and started messing about with your ... your tissues!"

Mrs Henckel leaves a long pause.

"And to whom did this precious guitar belong?"

"Peter Bannerman," I say.

"Remind me, who is this Peter Bannerman exactly?"

"I told you, he was the lead singer in Mental Elf."

"But that's all you have ever told me."

"He was the edgy one," I say. "He was the one who taught me how to believe in rock 'n' roll."

"I think we need to get to the bottom of this once and for all, don't you?"

# 13
# Mental Elf

It is 1978. The Ridge Langley estate no longer resembles the idealistic 50:1 scale architect's model I remember seeing displayed in the show home. I had examined the little plastic figurines while my mum and dad listened to the salesman. There were no Bolivians. Nuclear families strolled hand in hand through the concentric alleyways to the central recreational green. A green perfect for a kick-about but with a "No Ball Games" sign prominently displayed.

But now teenagers maraud the alleyways with spray cans. Andrew Fieldman and Gavin Barnford are older, menacing adolescents. My dad calls them "feckless troublemakers". When they call for me, they are not listening to glam rock anymore. They are listening to punk. And punk in the suburbs is markedly less sophisticated than its cosmopolitan version. It's more nihilistic. Its onus is less on critical thinking than breaking things.

Andrew and Gavin have formed a gang. Since we live on the Ridge Langley Estate, the gang is called the Ridge Langley Boys. They adopt the acronym "RLB" to sound like the IRA, UDA, ANC or any of the other political movements Johnny Rotten name checks on "Anarchy in the UK".

More than ever, I am convinced I cannot make it as a half-Bolivian in Croydon. I must be English. I want to join the gang. However, there are stringent compliance issues.

"You can't let your mum call you Julio anymore," says Andrew Fieldman. "It's embarrassing."

"And you better stop having a bloody siesta after lunch," adds Gavin. "This is Croydon. Punks don't have siestas."

Also, to become a full gang member, an initiation is required. "You have to prove yourself," says Andrew. "Show us you're proper English," adds Gavin.

First, I must sell some stolen footballs. The RLB have broken into nearby Riddlesdown High School and taken a consignment of new sports gear from a storage container. "If we get a coupla quid for each one we'll be laughing," says Andrew.

I accept two footballs, orange ones with Gola branding on them. But as soon as I try to shift them, a marketing problem arises. All my potential customers are in the RLB.

"D'ya wanna buy a moody football?" I ask Gavin, because I have learnt that in south London stolen goods are described as "moody".

"No, course I don't. I've already got three!" he splutters. "And so has everyone else, you dickhead!"

Because there is no viable new customer base, I am offered an alternative means of initiation. The new challenge is more symbolic but also more dangerous. Another new gang member Jason Stevens reports he has been shouted at by a policeman who lives on the estate. I have never seen this policeman, but Jason has. He told him to stop kicking his football against the metal garage doors. This major authority figure must be challenged.

"He's no ordinary copper. He's senior 'cos he's got a peaked cap with all that gold shit on it," says Jason.

"Fuck, that means he's a captain or something!" says his little brother Rob.

"We're still going to ambush him down the garages," announces Gavin.

It is December, and there is snow. Andrew Fieldman formulates the plan. He decides we will wait at the garages and attack the policeman with snowballs as he arrives home from work. When he exits his car, I must make him turn around by shouting "Oi, Old Bill! You've just met the Ridge Langley Boys!" Jason Stevens will throw the first snowball.

"Do this and you're both proper RLB members," Gavin sniffs importantly.

It's dark. Our footsteps make an eerie crump in the snow. From a distance, I hear a car engine straining up the hill. Its wheels spin as it struggles in the deep drifts. The RLB's collective breath makes a cloud, like drifting cannon smoke, as we wait in the white silence behind a low retaining wall. The approaching car revs indignantly on an icy slope. It pitches and skates into view.

"Here he is!" hisses Jason Stevens.

"Remember to shout 'Oi, Old Bill!' so he turns to face us when he gets out!" Gavin whispers to me.

I am hyped, pumped. I am not Bolivian. I am English. This is what English punk boys do.

The car, so laden with snow it looks like a wedding cake, slides to a halt. The police captain gets out to open his garage door. I raise a snowball in my right hand. The word "Oi!" is formed in my mouth.

I pause. I know the car. I know the man. "That's not

the old bill, that's my dad," I sigh and throw my snowball to the ground.

"No, it's the *copper*!" insists Jason Stevens.

"No, it's my dad," I say. "He's not a copper. He's a pilot in uniform."

"But that's the copper who told me off!" insists Jason.

"But he's not a bloody copper!" I say. "He's my DAD!"

No one listens to me. Blood is up and arms are raised. The figure in a peaked cap gets out.

"Oi, Old Bill!" shouts Jason Stevens. My dad turns around and a massive snowball catches him full in the face.

"You little bastards!" he shouts clutching his nose.

There are shouts, shrieks and, amid panicked laughter, the sound of Doc Marten boots scrabbling for grip on the ice.

"What do you think you're doing, you little sods?!" he shouts, as several snowballs find their mark. I have only recently seen the new blockbuster film *Star Wars*. The noise my dad makes as he slips and goes down sounds just like those the Wookie makes.

The RLB disperse up the alley amid adolescent hoots and honks of triumph. I am still behind the wall and, alone, enveloped by eerie wintry silence, I watch my dad get up from the snow and dust himself down. He looks red and flustered, like Captain Mainwaring from *Dad's Army* after Private Pike has said something particularly stupid. I feel sorry for him. He is my dad. But I must save my own life. I run through the snow to another garage block and hide.

An hour later I go home. My dad is on the sofa nursing a graze above his eye.

"Little thugs!" he is telling Charlotte. "They came at me like a pack of wolves!"

The RLB's reign of terror continues all evening. Snow is posted through Mr Hall's letterbox because he once told Andrew Fieldman not to use his "roller skate" on his front path. (It's not a roller skate. It's a new thing from America: a skateboard.) Mrs Dewar, an old lady who lives alone, has snow packed into the exhaust pipe of her Triumph Toledo and "Old Bag" written in the snow on her windscreen. She has committed no offence.

There is an older boy on the estate called Adam. He wears eighteen-hole oxblood Doctor Martens, jeans and braces and a tightly knotted Chelsea scarf. We try to keep away from him. But even he is impressed.

"Any of you interested in the National Front?" he asks us later. "Me and my dad are in wiv 'em. Always looking for young 'uns. You should come up the Shed."

The Shed is where Adam's NF friends hang out at Chelsea FC.

"We'll think about it," we say to make him go away. We may be nihilists but this is wrong. I don't know how we know, but we do. Our punk spirit cannot be channelled into anything so dark, so dumb. And anyway, Jason's dad, Mr Stevens, bumps into Mr Hall, who tells his story of getting ice through his letterbox. Jason Stevens is more frightened of his dad than he is of the RLB. Within a few days, he has named names. Mr Stevens then comes to see my dad. Events are placed in a timeline.

"You were there?!" my dad shouts at me. "You were part of this mob?!"

"Yes, but I thought we were meant to be attacking a

policeman!" I say before quickly realising the lameness of this excuse.

"You are on the road to ruin," my dad rages afterwards. In fact, what he says is, "You. Are. On. The. Road. To. Ruin." using the staccato rhythm of his words as a guide by which to thrash me with his belt.

WITHIN WEEKS OF the RLB's snowball attack, I am at a new school. It's private. My dad got the money from my grandmother on the basis that it was an emergency. The uniform is something to behold: Winton House Grammar has a purple blazer, socks and cap. When I first catch sight of myself wearing it in my mum's full length mirror, I see a condemned man. The RLB attack the boys in purple at the bus stop whenever they get the chance.

"You need to learn values," my dad says. "You seem hell-bent on seeking out bad influences."

I am worried that, wearing a purple cap and blazer, the bad influences will soon seek out me. At the end of my first day, I wait at the bus stop on Addiscombe Road twitching like a gazelle that senses the proximity of a lion.

"Put your blazer and cap in a bag, you twat," says a boy in plain clothes next to me. He holds up a carrier bag with his purple uniform stuffed inside.

"Darren Stitch," he says by way of introduction, "but people I like get to call me Foetus."

*Jesus*, I think, *if a boy lets his friends call him Foetus what do his enemies call him?* I take a covert look at his face. Large head. Wiry body. Asiatic eyes. I would never have made the connection myself, but he does look a bit like a foetus.

Scuffing some ants with the toe of a boot, next to him

is another boy. He too has his school uniform balled up in a supermarket carrier bag. He is wearing a black leather jacket and smoking a cigarette. He looks me up and down with intense, dark eyes.

"Meet Pete," Foetus says. Pete Bannerman flicks some ash to the ground and gives an almost imperceptible shrug of acknowledgement. Foetus offers me a half-smile and a placatory eye-bulge as though to say, *He doesn't say much. Don't take it personally.*

In my local record shop, I've heard an album by an American singer called Jackson Browne. It's full of exquisitely crafted songs about relationships and feelings. I've noticed the people who buy it are at least 30 and often wear ties, so it feels like the soundtrack to the kind of defeated, introspective existence I hope to avoid. But the cover photo of Browne – with his appealing eyes and floppy hair – looks like Pete Bannerman.

"Has anyone ever told you that you look like Jackson Browne?" I say.

Knitting his brow derisorily, Peter Bannerman ignores me, pulls an LP out of his bag and studies the artwork carefully: The Jam's *All Mod Cons*.

The 130 bus pulls up. From the upper deck, there is jeering from an open window. I am carrying a scrunched-up blazer, but I have forgotten to take off my cap. I cannot tell which school they are from. But they have black blazers and stubby ties. Danger.

Peter Bannerman holds the eye of our top deck tormentors and flicks a cigarette butt up at them. "Take off the bloody cap and bring a jacket next time," he says to me. "Otherwise we'll all get our heads kicked in."

We board the bus. The second thing he ever says to me is: "If you grew your hair and lost a bit of weight, you could look like Phil Lynott."

Phil Lynott is the singer with the rock band Thin Lizzy. He is half-Irish and half-Brazilian. My sister likes Thin Lizzy and, because I find nicking the component parts of her emerging cultural identity easier than finding my own, I took her copy of *Jailbreak* to listen to. I thought they were okay, although I had an issue with the lyrics. In the eponymous track, Lynott predicts, with macho foreboding, that there is going to be a jailbreak "somewhere" in the town and every time I hear it I think to myself, "Actually Phil, it's probably going to be at the *jail*, isn't it?" It's a good rock record, but I think the lyrics spoil it. In this sense, I am possibly too pedantic for rock and definitely so when it comes to punk.

When I tell Pete Bannerman and Foetus about my concerns over *Jailbreak,* they exchange meaningful side glances. Then, some understanding having passed between them, they smile at each other.

"I don't think you're supposed to analyse the words like a *swot*," sneers Pete finally. "You're just supposed to be into the fucking music."

He doesn't speak to me for the rest of the journey after that. I have failed a test. I am not cool.

PETE AND FOETUS keep themselves to themselves at school. I only see them at the bus stop. Even then, I only merit a vague acknowledging head-flick, occasionally an open nod. Mostly I stand on their periphery, just out of the range of Pete's flicked fag ash. From here, I listen with interest to him pontificating on which rock stars are the best.

"There's the Big Six," he says, "the legends who made rock music as we know it." He gives the names.

And he has very decided ideas about what rock stars should be like. "There's got to be a sense of danger or it's cheesy, fake," he insists. "They've got to *mean* it." Rock stars have to be angry, rebellious, and even nihilistic, according to Pete. They should be "against the system" and flirt with danger and death. "Like Sid," he says. "He means it." The Sex Pistols' bass player Sid Vicious is an example to us all. He took over from previous bass player Glenn Matlock because he "didn't mean it". In fact, Glenn Matlock is on record as having liked Abba.

"Angry people change the world," Pete says. "Everyone else is just a fucking a passenger."

"Too right," says Foetus and takes a drag on an offered fag. The way he chokes on the inhalation spoils the moment, but Pete soon resumes.

"And you can tell who means it and who doesn't just by looking at someone." Pete's eyes flick to me. I clench my jaw and widen my eyes furiously in a way that I hope denotes "meaning it". Pete looks away.

Anyone at Winton House will tell you – it's not even mumbled gossip but open source info – Pete Bannerman is a "nut-job". He's poor. He's angry. He and another lad, Kev Evans, once took a car for a joyride and flipped it on the Addington Road. The commonly whispered attribution for this waywardness is that his dad is not a pilot or solicitor or manager like everyone else's. Mr Bannerman sells fruit and veg down at Surrey Street Market. He has another son at a different school who is rumoured to be a problem child too. But Pete got into Winton House on a scholarship because he is talented at music.

I want to understand Bannerman and this new doctrine of rock. I want to absolve the shame of being expelled from the Ridge Langley Boys. Also, I could do with some new friends. But with Pete Bannerman and Foetus it is hard to break in.

One afternoon I see them on their way home carrying rucksacks. They look like they are going camping. I pluck up the courage to ask Foetus what's going on.

"Pete is staying with me for a bit," Foetus shrugs. "He hates his family. They just don't get him."

I am envious. I am still alternately Michael and Julio at home, English and Bolivian, with lingering hints of "Mick" on the street. I would like a bolthole to go to when I am feeling alienated. And even though we chat at the bus stop about "bastard parents", I don't get invited to join in.

I don't fit in with the straights. I don't fit in with the rebels. I am a half-Bolivian at a bus stop in Croydon with no friends.

⚡

It is 1979. Britain is changing: Margaret Thatcher has become Prime Minister. Music is changing too. The Sex Pistols have split. Sid Vicious is dead. And so is punk. The music they call new wave has arrived.

Charlotte has bought a new album by The Clash. They started out as punks, but their new album *London Calling* breaks new ground. It is a hybrid of punk, ska and reggae and my new favourite album. I have taken refuge in it. That is to say, I have started listening to it ten or twelve times in one go. The title track is particularly meaningful. During the mid-song breakdown, Joe Strummer emits an eerie wolf call, *Ooh-ahh-OOO!!!!!!* He sounds like an urban wolf. That is how I feel too, stalking the Croydon wilderness, calling out for a friend, trying to locate the pack. Because I am on my own a lot, before long, after a bit of practice, I can do this wolf call. *I too am a lone wolf!*

Occasionally Charlotte can hear me through the paper-thin walls separating our bedrooms. "Look I know you're having a shitty time at the new school and everything but ... it just sounds a bit mental," she cautions.

But I am past caring. One morning we are in a Chemistry lesson. I sit and stare at the board. Mrs Holloway our Chemistry teacher is expounding on the intricacies of covalent bonds. Covalent bonds find it hard to pair up with other molecules because they lack a spare electron. I feel like an element lacking the skill to make interesting compounds. As boredom takes hold, I begin drumming on the lip of the laboratory work bench. I am playing "London Calling" in my head. Mrs Holloway is on tip toes, scratching formulae onto the blackboard. Zoned out, I gently make the unmistakeable wolf call under my breath. "Ooh-ahh-OOO!!!"

The chalk squeal ceases abruptly. Mrs Holloway's forehead tightens. "Who made a noise?"

Silence.

"WHO MADE THAT NOISE?"

Giggles. Looks. Murmurs.

"Me, miss," I say.

"How *dare* you make an animal noise in my class!"

"Sorry, miss."

"Do it again," she orders, "so we can all hear it clearly."

"Ooh–aa-ooh, miss," I mumble solemnly.

"Now, if you can explain why a wolf noise is appropriate in the middle of a chemistry lesson, then let's hear it. Otherwise, you can go to the headmaster."

The headmaster is Mrs Holloway's father. His threshold for tolerating misdemeanours in her class is especially low. I don't want to face him. I think on my feet. I *do* have an explanation. "London Calling" is in my head *because* we are doing Chemistry. I explain that The Clash's song posits a post-apocalyptic London where, due to a "nuclear error", a new ice age approaches and the wheat yield has been compromised. The song's lyricist Joe Strummer predicts dire consequences for human life in our capital city. The wolf noise symbolises a return to a primordial world in the face of failing technology.

"It's actually a song warning against the dark power of science," I say as plausibly as I can.

Mrs Holloway is baffled and she still looks angry.

"It sounds highly improbable to me," she says disparagingly.

"He's actually right, miss," says a voice at the back of the class. "Mick has totally nailed it." Peter Bannerman is on his feet.

"I think we should give the guy a clap for giving us such a brilliant, educational interpretation of 'London Calling'," he says. Then he looks around the class and gives one slow, subversive clap. Everyone begins to applaud. There's even the odd "whoop!"

"I. Will. Have. SILENCE!" cries Mrs Holloway. Then she turns back to the board and begins slashing at it angrily with her chalk. But it's a victory for us. We can feel it. We have won.

Later that day I see Pete and Foetus at the bus stop. We re-live events in the lab.

"Did you make all that stuff up about London Calling?" Bannerman asks me, "Or do you always study song lyrics like a swot?"

And finally, Foetus, seeing Peter Bannerman's approving smile, makes a momentous offer.

"If you can actually drum, maybe you should try out for our band?"

I have read about the heady moment when a great band comes into being in my sister's *NME*. Johnny Rotten was recruited to the Sex Pistols after spontaneously singing along to a jukebox in a clothes shop on Chelsea's Kings Road one Saturday afternoon. Lennon and McCartney got together after a chance meeting at a Liverpool fete. Jagger and Richards met on the London-bound platform of Dartmouth railway station. The offer can come out of a clear blue sky. You just have to be ready. And even if you are not, you just have to have the balls to say that you are. I am at a Croydon bus stop, and this is my chance. Peter Bannerman and Foetus are asking me to join their band on the strength of tapping on a workbench and making a wolf noise during a Chemistry lesson.

"Sure, yes," I say. "I am a drummer." It's a lie. But I want it so much it feels it might be true.

"Come to a party Saturday and we'll talk about it," says Foetus. Foetus has a friend who lives in Beckenham, a suburb neighbouring Croydon made famous by its ethereal pop star resident David Bowie. The friend is having a party. "It's a Bowie party, so dress up," he says. "Meet at mine at 8, and we'll all go together."

I tell my Mum and Dad that a friendly son of a solicitor at my new school has invited me over to play chess. Then I ask Charlotte to put an Aladdin Sane lightning flash across my face in the back garden as I leave.

"It'll be okay until the sweat makes the colours run," she warns.

When I arrive at Foetus's house I ring the bell. No one answers, but the curtains twitch. There is giggling. Finally, the door opens and I am disappointed to find that Foetus is still plain Foetus, and Pete is still just Pete. They have not assumed a rock persona for the evening. There are no other Aladdin Sanes. I am the only one.

"You've passed the test," says Bannerman. "Shows you've got bottle."

When we get to the party, there are a few other Bowies present, and I hold my own as a half-Bolivian Aladdin Sane for the first couple of hours. But the party gets hot and, as predicted, the felt tip mingled with sweat creates a toxic multi-coloured perspiration. At first, he says nothing but then, as the drink takes hold, Bannerman begins to pass judgement.

"You look mental," he says laughing. And then he begins another of his sermons. "Thing is, Aladdin Sane is an alien transgender junkie rock god come to Earth to warn about the apocalypse. There's no way you're going to pull that off with felt tips."

Foetus laughs. Bannerman laughs. I begin wiping the Aladdin Sane thunder flash off my face with one of the host's sofa cushions.

"Aladdin Sane was a real bloke," says one of the other Bowies in our circle. "Bowie based him on this old rocker

Vince Taylor who went mad. Thought he was God. And an alien."

"Well, you're nearly there, Mick," says Bannerman. "You're half-Bolivian!"

There is more laughter and the clank of beer tins as they salute the joke. But I feel a flash of hatred for both Bowie and Pete Bannerman. For the first time, I see how judgemental rock culture really is. You have to walk right, talk right and look right. It's about keeping people out as much as it is inviting them in. I am feeling pissed off and humiliated by the rock 'n' roll project, and we haven't even properly begun. And poor Vince Taylor, whoever he is, obviously found it hard going too.

"Don't take what Pete says personally," advises Foetus when we convene for our first ever rehearsal. "The guy's obsessed, that's all."

Foetus's mum lets him use the front room overlooking a noisy main road for band practice. Pete is on guitar. Foetus plays the bass. At least, I think he does. He has a cheap Fender copy which he plugs into a mini amp and then, as he thumbs the top string, he shuts his eyes in muso ecstasy. But the notes he thumbs don't always seem to fit what Pete Bannerman is doing. However, Pete Bannerman's guitar playing is superb. He has all of the punk and new wave songbook at his fingertips.

"You said you're a drummer, but do you actually have any drums?" Foetus asks.

"No, but I've nearly got enough saved to buy some," I lie.

I sit in a corner of the room and bang on cardboard boxes and a tray filled with cutlery. The truth is, I can probably afford a pair of drumsticks, but that's it. The purchase of a full kit is still some way off. At any other time in rock history, being a drummer without a single drum might get you thrown out of a band. But these times are heady. The spirit of punk is still alive. It's uncool to place too much importance on having proper instruments.

"Punk's not about equipment, it's about your spirit," I say. Pete and Foetus look at each other. They nod uncertainly in approbation. I think I am okay. For now. But there seem to be obstacles to progress everywhere. When we have been rehearsing for ten minutes, Foetus's mother comes in and tells us to keep the noise down.

"The Arab boy hitting that tray is driving me nuts," I hear her hiss darkly outside the room.

"He's not an Arab," I hear Foetus explain, "he's half-Bolivian."

"Who gives him the right to come round here and address you as Foetus?" she says.

"That's my name," he says in a violent whisper. "You just don't get it, do you?"

His mum leaves. Foetus comes back into the front room looking pensive.

"Do you think maybe we could use your house next week?" he asks me.

I tell them him that this is impossible. Just to come to rehearsals I have told my mum and dad I am playing rugby for the school.

"Rugger?" said my dad when I broke the news. "What position have they got you in?"

"Drummer," I said. "I mean runner. Running. With the ball."

On the way back from Foetus's house, I even rub mud on my legs and affect a slight limp before going home. My dad will go insane if he discovers that, really, I bang a tea tray in a punk band.

When Pete goes outside to smoke a cigarette and scuff the dirt with the toe of his boot, I quiz Foetus.

"What about Pete's house?"

"We can't go there," he says. "Ever."

# 14
# American Nihilist

It is the winter of 1980. Mrs Thatcher has been in power for eighteen months. Grim looking men in chalk-stripe suits stride towards Number 10. Pausing for the media and speaking through jumbled, misaligned hippo teeth, they say Britain is "the sick man of Europe". There is talk of strong medicine.

"She'll sort this country out," my dad says, watching Mrs T. walking with her crook-backed stoop towards Number 10. "What we need is a short sharp shock."

Some have already felt it. Pete Bannerman's dad is struggling at the market.

"They're on at me about leaving school and getting a job," Pete says. "I don't want a shitty job. I want to make this band work."

It has been very good year for music. The Jam, The Clash, The Police, Public Image Ltd., Elvis Costello, The Fall, The Specials, The Selecter, UB40 and U2 all have new albums out. Charlotte buys all of them. I pretend they are mine. I note that only one artist, Gary Numan, makes significant use of synthesisers.

Even though we still do not have a full set of equipment,

Pete wants us to write our first original material. As it happens, I have some song titles, but I don't push them forward. It's not my band. I'll wait until I am asked. There is one about my dad's facial hair called "Pert Moustache". There's one about Pete's off-putting hints about a crush on Charlotte called "Siesta with My Sister" and there's another quite self-explanatory track called "Cross-eyed Cockney Tosser".

"You're trying to be funny," Pete says, after looking at my scribbles. "We need to be darker."

HE IS RIGHT. The world does seem very bleak in 1980. Never more so than one morning in December when my mum comes into my bedroom holding a radio to her ear. She is crying. "They have shot John Lennon!" she cries. "He's dead!"

At school assembly, one of the prefects plays "Imagine" on piano in the draughty gym. Mr Clough, our hippy art teacher who used to talk about Lennon as though he knew him ("The thing that impresses me about John …"), has tears in his eyes. At break time, Pete and Foetus sit in silence by the food waste containers called the "pig bins" and discuss the news.

"So, he came out of his apartment to sign an autograph and this geezer shot him," says Pete.

"Mental," says Foetus.

The mood is sombre, but it's not clear what the party line is. Sometimes with punks it's hard to tell. When Elvis Presley died three years previously, some punks celebrated because Elvis was deemed a cheesy showbiz faker from a discredited rock 'n' roll era.

"The lard-arse couldn't get off his own toilet," Andrew Fieldman scoffed. "Fat yank has-been!"

I do not want to appear uncool in the aftermath of another major rock star death. I am not sure what to think about John Lennon. He might also be due a brutal re-assessment.

"Stupid four-eyed hippy," I venture finally. "That's what you get for giving peace a chance. He shoulda bought a gun."

It is immediately obvious I have misjudged the mood. Even Pete Bannerman is shocked.

"God you're so negative sometimes," he says. "Don't you care about anything?"

Pete says Lennon's murderer Mark Chapman had a grudge against rock stars and he should be sent to the electric chair for what he has done.

"He was going to kill others you know," he says knowledgeably. "He had a list."

"OKAY, FINE. YOU write the lyrics since you're such a swot," says Pete Bannerman throwing down a biro in exasperation. I notice his fingers are gnarled and chewed. You get that with guitarists. But also, he's been hefting crates at night with his dad. Added to this, he seems tired and anxious, constantly nibbling at his fingertips.

It's our second rehearsal. The murder of John Lennon has brought increased urgency to our mission. It's as though the death of an icon has created a void. We want to fill it. We are going to write our first single and album. In a day.

But Pete has lost interest in writing lyrics and has reluctantly handed responsibility to me. I have won a prize in

English for writing a poem entitled "Bolivian Oblivion in Croydon". I have also promised to come up with edgier, darker material.

I am relieved of my tea tray and handed a pad and a biro. I am pleased. At last I can present my ideas. The best post-punk bands are writing interesting "story songs". The Police's "Message in a Bottle" and "Roxanne", XTC's "Making Plans for Nigel", Martha and the Muffin's "Echo Beach" and The Vapors' "Turning Japanese" are all good examples. I too will write compelling post-punk tales. However, I will be wary of lyrics with infuriating internal contradictions, like Thin Lizzy's "Jailbreak".

"Fine," I say, an expansive, prima donna-ish sense of entitlement coming to me very naturally, "but I need space to think, to write."

"I've got the perfect place," says Foetus. He leads me out of the front door to his dad's VW campervan sitting outside on the drive. It's a wreck with cracked wing mirrors, rusting seams along the chassis and mildew carpeting the roof. I have long admired this old campervan. Peeking through the windows, I have imagined it as a cool place to hang out. I have even imagined us doing it up and driving off on tour.

Foetus opens the door. The van exhales a gust of stale human pong. It's obvious that someone has been living here. There is a bag and a leather jacket that I recognise lying on the floor: Pete Bannerman's.

"Sometimes Pete sleeps in here, when it's grim at home," Foetus informs me. "Don't tell my mum though."

I enter the van with my pad and biro. Foetus shuts the door. A desultory air freshener valiantly battles the teenage fug. The lower bunk is unmade. Pete's bag is open on the floor. I can see an exercise book peeking from the top with "Death or Glory" scrawled on its cover in biro.

I can't resist taking a look inside. After all, I am the lyricist designate with Mental Elf. I want to see what I am up against.

I pull out the exercise book. It's full of lyrics. Some of them are familiar songs that Pete is learning to sing. "Down in the Tube Station at Midnight" by The Jam. "Holidays in the Sun" by the Sex Pistols. But some are original songs. "Nowhere Fast" is a one-dimensional exercise in punk nihilism. "Bus Stop Blitzkrieg" is a "Down in the Tube Station"-style story detailing an encounter with the RLB.

But there are other scribbles – diary entries, thoughts. "I wonder if those two ever feel like this?" reads one entry. Another simply: "I can't sleep again ... lonely." Elsewhere I am pleased to see my efforts recognised: "Mick did a solo on his tea tray today. Hilarious. What a nutter." More troublingly: "Mick's sister seems cool. Should try and get her in the band."

I turn the page to find beautiful lyrics to a song called "These Days". "I've been losing so long," he writes. I find Pete's words very moving. That's good. I like that. I will have to do better than that.

Outside the van I hear voices. I wrench Pete's bag wide open to stuff his book back inside. The bag rattles loudly. Inside I see a plastic bottle of pills with the label "Master Peter Bannerman: Do Not Exceed Dosage". I shove the book back where it belongs. The van door opens.

"Thought you might want one of these," says Pete, handing me a mug of tea and the stubby remnant of a packet of biscuits, "but hurry up. The music's ready."

The ideas pour out of me. In the van, I write a whole side of an album. I have a penchant for songs with half the title in brackets like the Buzzcocks' "Ever Fallen in Love with Someone (You Shouldn't've)" or the Jacksons' "Shake Your Body (Down to the Ground)". And so, I write my own. The first is called "I Don't Want to Be One of Those Boys (Who Chews Food Loudly Like Their Dad)". And I have been listening to Charlotte crying after her boyfriend Martin McIntyre chucked her, and so I write a sombre punk ballad called "All I Have Left to Remind Me (Are Your Pubes in the Plughole)".

But this is an age when the best rock bands are releasing brilliant singles that, in a gesture of artistic fecundity, aren't even included on albums. Like The Jam's "Going Underground", for example. Punks think it's too cynical to include a great single on an album. That's using music as a promotional tool. You should be able to release great singles on their own.

And so, I have written a handful of singles and B-sides separately. I am a great believer in writing about what you know, and have drawn upon an uncomfortable Biology lesson when Mrs Arrowsmith showed us a film of a young mother eating her fried placenta with onions shortly after giving birth. Viewed through a gruesome punk filter, this has become a song entitled "Flash-Fried Twin Sister".

I have also drawn upon a fraught History lesson, during which Pete was ejected from the classroom. We were studying the Renaissance and Peter accused our teacher Mr Thomson of being "ignorant" because, although knowledgeable on the Renaissance, he proved unable to explain when the original "naissance" had occurred. "When was the naissance, *sir*?" Pete asked with a provocative sneer. Mr Thompson sent him to the Head, but I now have a bold new track called "When Was the Naissance?"

I am pleased with my songs. They are all scabrous and jerky like punk should be. However, I want to stretch myself further. I want to write an anthem, something which captures the post-punk adolescent mind-set, the mood of the times. This means nihilism. Industrial quantities of it.

While I am thinking about how to approach this I overhear Pete and Foetus arguing outside as they share a cigarette. Foetus says waiting for me to write lyrics is boring and that they should go and watch the *Dukes of Hazzard*.

"A lot of bands look back at the years of struggle as the best," Pete says. "This might be as good as it ever gets. We'll probably all end up on the dole anyway."

I am immediately inspired to write the A-side of our debut single "I Peaked as a Foetus". The first verse and the chorus run:

> I worked very hard in my mother's womb
> I grew some hands to hold a spoon
> I grew some legs so I could run
> I was very pleased with what I done
> But now I see I jumped the gun
> [Chorus]
> I think I peaked as a foetus, I peaked as a foetus.
> What if life defeats us, the world excretes us and after
> all my hard work it turns out I peaked as a foetus?

PETER BANNERMAN LIKES my lyrics, and he writes powerful, angular guitar music to go with them. Ergo, I like Peter

Bannerman. We are a writing duo, our surnames forever to be bound together like Jagger/Richards and, yes, Lennon/McCartney.

But my commitment to the band is once again under scrutiny when we discuss two important issues: new haircuts and the use of punk stage names.

First, Pete says he will coiffure us personally. "I can do you a Sting or a Bruce Foxton," he announces, waving around a pair of blunt-looking kitchen scissors. I push him away, explaining my dad will go mad if I go home with an angular choppy haircut.

"I'm taking enough risks as it is," I say.

"Lightweight," he sneers. "Get out. Leave home. Don't let your old man dictate your life and even your hairstyle."

I let him slightly reduce my Bolivian sideburns.

There is further disagreement over proposed stage names. Pete wants us to assume punk monikers according to our astrological star signs.

"'Peter Bannerman' sounds like a local plumber, but if I use my star sign I become ... Pete Virgo," he says. "See? Sounds cool and punk, doesn't it?"

Foetus and I look at each other with dismay. He speaks first. "That makes me Foetus Sagittarius. I sound like a fucking Greek shipping magnate!" he yelps.

"I am *not* going onstage as Mick Cancer," I yell in support, "and that's final!"

It's all such hard work. We even fight a battle choosing a name for the band. I have noticed in Charlotte's NME that, in his grief following Lennon's death, Paul McCartney looks like has put on a bit of weight. I think we should call the band Ball McCartney. It strikes just the right iconoclastic note.

"I'm not going to let you mess up the band with your stupid jokes," says Pete.

Inspired by Mrs Holloway's tantrum in the Chemistry lab, he decides on Mental Elf instead.

"Isn't that a joke too though?" I point out.

"Yeah but serious as well," he sniffs, "ironic."

Nevertheless, fired by our shared sense of alienation, Mental Elf become quickly proficient. Our songs are promising, albeit a little one dimensional in tone. Foetus borrows a snare drum from a friend, and soon we can play our songs as well as key work by the Sex Pistols, The Jam and The Clash. We decide to make a demo tape – some of our own material and some cover versions – and make the most of the fact that some of the world's greatest rock stars live near us.

After trying to find McCartney's house in Rye, Pete takes us on a 30-mile detour east to Cotchford Farm in East Sussex. It's only twenty miles south of Croydon but a different world. We park outside a rambling house set near woodland. This is where Rolling Stones founder Brian Jones drowned in his swimming pool. Bannerman kills the engine, lights a cigarette and delivers another lecture on rock 'n' roll from the driving seat.

"You've got to admire the guy's guts," he says "Being a rock star's not like being a bloody plumber. It's all or nothing. Death or glory."

ON THE DRIVE home, Pete announces a new plan. "I'm organizing gigs for the summer," he says, "and then we'll all leave school."

Pretending to play rugby while I am actually banging a

tea tray in a band is one thing. Leaving school is something else altogether.

"Do you really think we're good enough to turn pro?" I ask.

"Pro? *Pro*?! Listen to yourself, you sad cunt."

"You know what I mean."

"You've got to want it more than anything," snarls Pete. "You've got to stop being such a lightweight."

Very soon there is something else in the way of playing our first gig. I get home from school one day. Charlotte leads me to our mum who is crying in the kitchen. An aunty has just called from America. My mum's mother has been taken ill.

"I want to see her," she sobs. "It might be the last time."

My mum's four sisters all left Bolivia when she did. They moved to North America with their husbands. My grandmother went to live with the youngest, my Aunt Charo, in New Mexico.

"You've never met the Bolivian side of the family, have you?" my dad says to me and Charlotte. "Perhaps it's time."

He can pull some strings and get some cheap air fares. We will fly to Albuquerque, New Mexico and meet the extended family.

"But what about the gigs?" demand Pete and Foetus when I tell them about the trip at our next rehearsal.

"We'll just have to get someone else to drum," says Pete viciously.

I have dreaded him saying this. I love being drummer and chief lyricist for Mental Elf. I don't want them to find a replacement. But neither do I want to seem needy. On the spur of the moment I hatch a counterintuitive plan, something which will turn the tables in my favour. I pretend that, actually, their tour ambitions are not big enough for me.

"Cancel the tour," I say boldly.

"Cancel it?! Why?" says Foetus.

"I'm going to America. I'll make some proper contacts there. We need to think bigger."

"What you mean think bigger?"

"My older cousin James is in the business. I'll go and speak to him and, then, when we've got something set up, we can all move out there."

It is a damned lie. I've never even met my cousin James, and I know for a fact he is not in the music business. He's still at school. But he's a senior, and he did pick the band for prom. Also, I have heard him down the phone saying to my mum, "Hope to meet y'all soon" and, for me, that is good enough. He *sounds* like an industry big-hitter. Compared to Croydon, everyone in America sounds like they work in the music biz.

"Are you serious?" demands Pete. "How come you never mentioned this before?"

"I didn't think we were ready," I say. "We'll only get one shot at this."

Peter Bannerman and Foetus cannot believe how big I am thinking. My kudos is massive. In fact, before I leave for America Pete rings me at home to make clear that he is ready for anything.

"Look, if they just want to sign me and you, I think Foetus will understand we are the talented ones," he confides. I laugh. He laughs. But then he adds: "Please make this happen. I really want to get out of here."

For the first time, I realise the power I hold. It's thrilling. But it's based on a lie and so there is also trepidation. I tell him I will do my best. I reassure him cousin James knows everyone in the record business.

But Foetus will not be outdone. He rings me at home too. "Pete is brilliant, obviously," he says, "but you've got to admit, he can be a stroppy git. If some manager just wants two solid and reliable musicians, then I'm sure Pete will understand."

"Pack nothing that isn't absolutely necessary," my dad says, sounding bullish and military.

We have stand-by tickets on British Caledonian to Houston in Texas and then onward to New Mexico on a local airline. We will have to hang around at Gatwick airport hoping for spare seats. We need to travel light.

I am only packing one necessary thing as far as I am concerned: a brick of cassette tapes wrapped in a t-shirt. These are the tapes which will be handed out to "the industry" that I am sure I will meet. On one side is Mental Elf covering songs by classic post-punk bands: The Police, The Skids, The Jam, XTC, the Pretenders – these will show the Americans the vibrant post-punk scene in England. On the other side are the Mental Elf demos, including "I Peaked as a Foetus".

In New Mexico, I meet my mum's family for the first time. My cousins are beautiful tawny skinned creatures with excellent dental work. They have a big house and a pool and, even at sixteen, drive fast cars and hang out at malls.

There is no nihilism in the air like there is in Croydon. There is no sense of potential riot or suburban torpor like in the UK. When I unzip my case and see a cassette tape marked "I Peaked as a Foetus", it looks like something from another world. During our very first evening meal, my Aunt Charo does not waste any time telling Charlotte and me she thinks we have made a huge mistake being born in England.

"I tried to tell your mother, don't marry an English, come to America!" she says, recalling the days of my parents' courtship in Cochabamba, Bolivia. "I have photos of your little house in Croydon! It's adorable, but it's the size of the hut where we keep the pool-cleaning gear! Ha! Come! It's not too late! Come to America!"

Uncle Jim even has the audacity to takes the piss out of how we speak. As he and Aunt Charo are preparing breakfast my dad shoves me in the back. "They may have a swimming pool, but what they don't have is manners," he tells me. "Show them how civilised people behave. Offer to lay the table."

"Shall I lay the table?" I ask my uncle. Jim chokes, his eyes fill with tears, and he leaves the room to call in the whole of family so they can hear me repeat this exotic offer.

"Ya hear that? Dude wants to LAY the table! Ha ha ha," he roars, slapping his thigh. "Now that's something I'd *pay* to see!"

I am depressed. I don't understand my American-Bolivian cousins. I am not sure I really understand America. For days and nights, I lie in the heat and ponder how I am going to make contact with the American music industry. Occasionally, I take the tape out of my suitcase, examine its scrawly handwritten song title card and then put it back again. *What if there just aren't any nihilists in America?*

While my mother is visiting her mother in the local

hospital, I sit in the car and check the radio. I swivel the dial for punk. I scan the airwaves for rage. Nothing. All I hear are vanilla drive-time rock bands: REO Speedwagon, Styx, the Little River Band and Toto. Mall music. Tunes to hum on the escalator. No one is angry in the heartland. Mental Elf won't make sense here.

But Charlotte has spotted my tapes in the suitcase. She thinks it is time to take a risk. "Don't be such a namby. Play the tape!" she says.

"Maybe I'll wait and see if grandma dies," I grumble. "They'll be more receptive to nihilism then."

But grandma doesn't die. She gets better. Soon I have been in America a whole week, and I am not proving a very committed nihilist. I have even begun to hang out with my cousins a bit. They have shown me their amazing video machine which means you can watch films at home. When the film *Grease* came out in 1978, I ignored it because it was emblematic of cheesy high school Americana and not very punk. Now I watch the video and, with creeping sense of dread, I realise I like it. I feel even less nihilistic after I've sat in a diner booth eating ice cream sundae with James and his friends. Additionally, I have a suntan and I have started saying, "Sure thing" and "dude".

Whenever Charlotte hears me do this, she rolls her eyes. "Play someone the tape!"

Then one afternoon, James offers to take me for a spin in his Camaro, a muscle car with a soft top and thick tyres. James is eighteen. He is a man of the world. In Croydon, a sophisticated eighteen year old drives a Yamaha FS1E moped if he is lucky.

James's car, I have already noted, boasts a state-of-the-art cassette deck with quad speakers. Before we head out, I grab my demo tape from the suitcase. I turn it over in my hand. I almost don't recognise it.

"What you got there, cuz?" James asks when he sees it in my clammy hand.

"Some English music, if you're interested."

"Awesome," he says, flicking on his Ray-Bans and gunning the engine. I have butterflies in my gut as the Camaro squeals away from the kerb. We cruise the wide, tree-lined streets and then pull over outside a big colonial style house. There is money here. And sun and youth and freedom.

"Go get a sundae at the mall?" James says to two beauties tanning themselves in a big garden.

"Sure," they trill and climb in.

Juliet is a golden-skinned New Mexican. Dana is her pale friend visiting from New York. Neither of these gum-clicking divas in cut-off shorts and hooped earrings resembles the undernourished, diamond-hard girls I have seen nicking clothes on George Street, Croydon. They do not have tribal cultural loyalties like British teenagers do. They are not mods, rockers, punks, skins or Goths. They sip Coke, hum idly to REO Speedwagon and gossip about boys on the football team, confidently or perhaps absent-mindedly blundering into the American Dream. They do not look like they will get Mental Elf.

"Is London in England or the other way round?" Juliet asks me.

I laugh, but it's not a joke. Then James cranks up the stereo, and they all sing along to Toto as the warm summer air blows through Juliet's Farrah Fawcett-Majors-style flick.

*There is no dark side here! Don't play them the tape!* As these thoughts form in my head, James slaps the dashboard with a huge paddle hand. "I nearly forgot! My cuz here is in a band. Let's hear the tape, dude."

My heart stops. I assess the scene: two hotties in boob tubes flicking their hair in the back of a muscle car. *This is not the ideal audience for a presentation on punk! Do not play the tape!*

"Maybe later," I suggest.

We turn into a mall and head to a parlour to get a sundae. We don't even have to get out of the car, like you do at the Wimpy on George Street in Croydon. A boy in a paper hat serves us through the car window.

"How big are the ice creams back in jolly ol' England?" asks Dana.

I visualise the local ice cream van turning into the estate. I hear its dismal jingle. I see the lab-coated nerd with a comb-over at the hatch.

"About the same size as here," I say.

"And does the music rock the same too?" enquires James, grabbing the tape out of my hand. "Come on cuz, let's hear it!"

The first thing we hear is the Sex Pistols' "God Save the Queen". It tears through the car speakers. Then it's over. No reaction.

"What *is* that dude bawling?" asks Juliet finally, working the last of a small tub of ice cream with a plastic spoon.

"We're angry with the Queen," I mutter, and then add half-heartedly, "the stupid lazy cow."

"We have the Pistols in New York," Dana says. "One of them is dead, right?"

"Yeah, Sid Vicious," I say. "He was crazy. Good thing too because your people couldn't have handled Sid Vicious."

"Oh yeah, a real badass, huh?" asks James. "What did he bench press?"

In America, you can only truly be a badass if you go to the gym, if you are a jock. Pale nihilists with bronchial coughs are not badasses. They are "bums". I can feel my whole punk thesis disintegrating when I enumerate the things that Sid Vicious did.

"He sneered and swore," I say. "He was totally mental."

"And who are *these* guys?" says James, suddenly wild-eyed with interest as Mental Elf hurtle through the first chorus of "I Peaked as a Foetus".

"I can't hear the words," complains Dana, frowning and holding her little ice cream spoon in the air daintily.

"Oh my God, he's saying he picked at a foetus?! That is dis*gus*ting!" says Juliet.

"Turn it off!" shouts Dana, "They make me want to hurl."

Dana and Juliet cannot hear my finely crafted lyrics. They do not "get" Mental Elf at all.

"You know, if you want to hear some decent British music, there is one guy that I like," Dana announces from the back seat. "Have you ever heard of Gary Numan?"

I feel sick. I have recently discovered Gary Numan and his work with Tubeway Army. Charlotte has played me his monolithic masterpiece *Are Friends Electric?* And she predicted that punk and even post-punk are on the way out. She has warned me that the music scene can undergo sudden yet seismic changes. When that happens, slow-movers get trampled in the crush.

"Listen, little brother, let me help you out here," she told me. "There's a new sound approaching. A new music played on new instruments and a new look to go with it."

I stole the Gary Numan record from her and played it to Pete and Foetus before my trip. Pete hated the new electronic sound. He wouldn't countenance any synthesiser experimentation at all.

"It's shit music for posers and girls," he sneered. "Gary Numan won't be around for long. Trust me."

Back in James's car that is not the impression I am getting at all.

"Gary Numan is awesome. He's so mysterious and handsome," continues Dana, nudging Juliet and licking her spoon. "He can get with me anytime."

I am shocked. Much as I like his music, Gary Numan strikes me as a pasty-faced snaggle-toothed dork. The idea that such a man could enjoy sex with a tawny skinned goddess in hooped earrings seems like a breach of the world's natural order. But in a good way. There is hope for us all.

## 15
# To Live and Die in Croydon

My family fly back to Croydon in early September. I am worried about going back to school and facing Pete and Foetus. I haven't made a splash in the American music industry. When I look in the bathroom mirror, I don't see a punk and I don't see a nihilist. I have eaten a lot of ice cream and have a suntan. This abdication of responsibility will require sensitive handling.

But when I get back to school, Pete isn't there. At first break, Foetus finds me by the pig bins where we habitually scuff the ground while talking about the future of the band.

"Pete's left," he says. "He couldn't handle it anymore."

"Seriously?"

"Yeah, even his mum and dad say he's wasting his time here. He's got a job at Argos."

"Argos, what's he doing at Argos?"

"It's good money. He's saving up to make a go of the band. We need to raise our game. He's totally serious."

On the following Saturday, I go and find Pete at Argos in Croydon's Whitgift Centre. I arrive at 1pm, reckoning on it being his lunch hour.

"I don't take a lunch hour," he says hefting boxes along the counter. "I need the extra money for my new guitar."

*Tell him to order a synthesiser! There's even one in the Argos catalogue!* I take a deep breath and then tell him about my abortive trip to New Mexico.

"The yanks just don't get punk," I say. "I didn't make the contacts I hoped I would."

Pete is not as angry and dismissive as I imagined he would be. "Not your fault," he says, stamping a docket and sliding a boxed teasmade to an old lady. "Americans are a bunch of spoilt cunts."

The old lady gives him a filthy look and grabs her box.

"We just need to keep going in the direction we're going and not listen to the doubters," he says, wheeling away a trolley to collect the next items.

I am surprised he is so understanding. But the new guitar worries me. I feel bold enough to try out a more daring idea. "One thing I did notice out there is that music is changing," I say. "I don't think people want punk anymore. Quite a few people I met like Gary Numan."

"Gary Numan? Are you *serious*?"

"Yeah, there's a new sound coming. Electronic. We're going to get left behind."

"But I've just put down a week's wages on a new guitar!"

"Punk's over," I protest.

"Is this what your cousin in the industry told you?"

"Yes," I say, "and a couple of girls he works with."

Pete slams a box down on the counter. I hear an ominous tinkle of something breaking inside. "Well, let me tell you something loud and clear," he spits, fixing me with a glare of unbridled fury. "This is my band! And Gary Numan is the Argos David Bowie; he's shit!"

⚡

MAYBE I WILL form my own band. Or maybe I will go it alone. But Charlotte tells me I should stick with Pete. I have noticed she goes a bit dreamy and pink in the cheeks whenever she talks about him.

"I think he's quite talented," she coos, "and when he sings in that angry voice he's quite sexy."

I tell her to shut up. I don't like my sister fancying the pig-headed lead singer in the band. Our band. *My* band.

At our next rehearsal, the Argos disagreement is not mentioned. Pete shows Foetus and me the fliers to our first ever gig:

*The White Lion*
*Saturday September 25th*
*Come and check your Mental Elf!*

They have been handwritten and then photocopied. In punk terms, they look perfect. He has taken care of all the other arrangements for our debut too. Transport. The instruments. And of course, the set list.

"I've spent all my wages on this," he says. "All you two have to do is not muck it up."

The gig will be at the White Lion pub in Bromley, not far from Croydon. It's only a support slot, but quite a coup for a band who have never played in public before and who do not even have a drum kit. Since leaving school, Bannerman has been hanging out at the local guitar shop, Rock Bottom on London Road, Croydon. One of the sales assistants is impressed by his playing. The assistant plays drums in a new wave band called Strange Fruit, and he offers Mental Elf the support slot for their regular gig plus the use of his drum kit.

On the drive to Bromley, Foetus and I joke around in the back of Pete's car. It's not a limo, there are no police outriders, and no floodlit stadium looms ahead but, nevertheless, we relish being driven to our first ever show. We wind the windows down and ask girls on the pavement if they want our autograph.

"Piss-takers or what?" they laugh. But at least we are getting a reaction, and one of them is smiling and bashfully twizzling her hair.

*This is great! This is what all those hours banging a tea tray have been all about!*

"Wind up the windows and concentrate," orders Pete. He chews a fat wad of gum like rock stars and people in the industry are supposed to do. But he is also rigid with fear. There's a desperation in his frantic chew-rate. Whenever Foetus and I turn up the stereo, he turns it down to make po-faced announcements.

"We stick to the core music – Who, Jam, Pistols – okay? Don't try and sneak any new crap in," he says loading more gum into his mouth.

"You've got twenty minutes. Less if you piss the punters off," says the singer from Strange Fruit when we arrive. He is not happy that his drummer has given a support slot to a bunch of untried teenage tosspots.

We amble up onto the low stage. There are probably twenty people present, but to us it's a stadium-full. I am in awe because I have never actually sat at a proper drum kit before. I smash at the biggest cymbal and giggle with delight. I stroke the drums reverentially.

"For fuck's sake, try not to act like a competition winner," Pete implores.

Then, visibly trembling and eyes floor-ward, he steps up to the mic. "Hello, we're Mental Elf," he informs the audience in a low mumble.

We start with Bowie's "The Jean Genie", hoping to suck up any goodwill towards the local boy done good. I hammer away at the drum kit. Immediately I am aware of a major problem. Honing my craft on a tea tray full of cutlery hasn't prepared me for the real thing. With a tea tray, there is no "bounce", and so you always hit harder. With actual drums, the skins have tautness and tension. I am quickly finding that when I whack a drum with the same force I do a tea tray, the sticks rebound and hit me in the face. I take several blows to the forehead. Hammering away through The Jam's "Eton Rifles", I look like I am self-harming. At the back of the pub the drummer from Strange Fruit frowns. Pete looks back at me furiously.

"What are you fucking doing?" he hisses at me.

When I have nominal control of the drums, we continue to set out our stall: the punk and new wave song book. Songs by Skids, The Ruts, Sex Pistols and the Pretenders. But we do not offer simple, faithful covers. Pete has reworked them slightly, adding lengthy "my time to shine" guitar solos.

We are hacking through our repertoire with a sullen, box-ticking diligence when I notice new arrivals at the bar. Young drinkers in exotic futuristic dress and eye shadow.

Some of them look like proto-New Romantic Steve Strange, the singer with Visage, or flint-faced Euro alien John Foxx from Ultravox. Others have gone for the robo-military chic of Gary Numan. These are next wave synth-pop fans, bored of punk worthiness. They watch, whisper and finally dismiss our performance with insolent skyward cigarette exhalations. My guess is, dropping into a pub for a drink before heading to one of central London's new clubs, they believe they have stumbled upon the actual death of guitar rock happening before their very eyes.

"We should do 'Cars' by Gary Numan," I suggest to Pete in a break between songs, "make 'em laugh."

"Except this isn't a fucking joke, though, is it? This is deadly serious," he says through gritted teeth.

"Lighten up," I say as the crowd gets restless.

"Fuck off," he replies.

"Stop trying to be a guitar hero," I sneer. "It's over."

I have never challenged Peter Bannerman before, but it occurs to me that, right here and right now, we are experiencing the notorious band break-up phenomenon, "musical differences".

"You're going to ruin this band, *my* band with your stupid ideas!" he says.

We don't do any Gary Numan songs. We finish with a doleful "This is The Modern World" by The Jam. Peter Bannerman is so pumped up, he keeps over-stressing the angst of the song's title. "This is the modern weld!" he shouts. It makes me cringe. He sounds like a teacher shouting instructions on a metallurgy course.

At the end, there is silence. It's too silent even for the crowd to bear and so, eventually, two people clap. One is the drummer from Strange Fruit who just seems relieved it's over and he can get his gear back. The other is a Numanoid at the back of the bar. Her applause is slow and ironic. Foetus and I swap sheepish glances. Then we start laughing. It's been a disaster, but the sort of disaster we can revel in. One day, when Mental Elf really make it big, we will tell a rock writer about it. *Do you remember that first gig when we got laughed off by a bunch of Gary Numan fans?*

We decide to try to get served at the bar and discuss just how awful we were. "Get Pete to order," says Foetus, "he looks the eldest." But, slamming his new black guitar into a flight case, Peter Bannerman shoulders through the thinning crowd of Numanoids and storms out of the pub into the night.

"Leave him," Foetus says. "He'll come round. He just wants it too much, that's all."

PETE IS MENTAL Elf's guitarist, its lead singer, and, by leaving school, he has proved himself its greatest risk-taker. It's his band. But at the same time, I have seen the future, and it doesn't involve guitars. I hope our first disastrous gig will be my chance to leverage influence for a new electronic direction.

On the quiet, I have written a couple of Numanesque songs. The first is called "The Beast Inside". It's a macabre dirge for keyboard inspired by Pete's annoying mood swings. But I won't tell him that. Not until it's in the charts and we are popping champagne corks. The second song is about Croydon and is called "Suburban Corrosion". This is intended for vocals, drums and keyboard.

I wait a week. I cannot bear it any longer. I call Foetus

and suggest a band meeting. "I've got some new songs," I say, "bit of a new direction."

"Pete doesn't want to see you."

"Why not? It's not my fault we made such a mess of it."

"He's in a bad way," he says. "First the gig, and then my mum found him in the van and kicked him out."

"I think we should confront him. I think we should tell him he needs to lighten up."

"Go easy," says Foetus.

"But he's taking us in the wrong direction," I complain. "I'm writing all this great new material."

"Personally, I think Gary Numan is okay," Foetus says. "I just think we need to explain it to Pete gently. He's given up a lot for the band."

"Shall I ring him?" I ask.

"Nah. He hates you. I better do it."

"Why does he hate me?"

"Just thinks you're pissing about. You don't mean it."

"I do mean it," I say, "but he just wants to control everything. And because you are his best mate, you let him."

Foetus says he will arrange a meeting. That's when I will make a case for our new direction. I am willing to shelve "The Beast Inside", but I'm not ditching "Suburban Corrosion". I think it's got potential. What's more I think I should sing it.

Half an hour later Foetus rings back. "Mick?" he says sounding agitated and trying to drag the phone from a noisy room, "are you sitting down?"

I smile. Something good has happened. But I feel a pang of jealousy too. It has happened to Pete and Foetus without me being there. Perhaps someone likes our demo tape, or a manager wants to take us on.

"Yes, I'm sitting down," I say.

I can hear a lot of people in the room. Grown-ups. Celebrating. *Jesus, he's gone and got a record deal!* Someone in the room tells Foetus to hurry up and get off the phone. "Shut up a minute. I'm trying to tell him!" Foetus says, his voice cracking with emotion.

I am excited but also despondent. It's always been about these two, with me trying to fit in. But then everything turns on a moment. I listen to the voices again. I realise I am not hearing celebration and laughter but agony. There are yodelling highs but also howling lows. A woman shrieks in a terrible guttural voice. "Oh my God, please, not my boy!"

"Look mate, I can't talk," says Foetus, "but Pete's dead."

⚡

IT TAKES QUITE a few therapy sessions to get it all out. Some of them are spent in almost complete silence. But when I finally get to the ecstasy of crisis, Mrs Henckel shakes her head in disbelief. Her little room has never seemed so dark.

"How did your friend die?" she asks quietly.

"Sleeping pills. Alcohol. Like a rock star."

"Where?"

"In a flat. He had got himself a tiny bedsit in Croydon. He was making a fresh start."

"But why did he do such a terrible thing?"

"He thought we wouldn't make it."

"But your band was just beginning?"

"I know, but he could tell it wasn't happening. Music changes. We were being left behind."

"And you feel responsible?"

"I didn't *mean* it like he did. I let him down."

"What a tragedy," she says, "to give up on life like that."

"Too fast to live, too young to die."

"Excuse me?"

"He wrote it on his book of lyrics," I say. "It's kind of the rock 'n' roll spirit."

"Well then, I wonder whether this so-called rock 'n' roll spirit really has any value."

# 16
# Dark Side of the Loon

A bed. South London.

"Stop shouting!"

"I'll bloody well shout if I want to!"

Nicola's face looms over me. She doesn't look like the pretty dark haired one from the Human League anymore. Her eyes are full of fury.

"Where have you *been*?!" she cries.

"Stop shouting! You'll wake Ronnie!" I plead in an anguished hiss.

"Ronnie's at school. It's nearly lunchtime, you moron," she replies.

"You're kidding," I say sitting upright.

Once more I have been away. This is my homecoming.

"No, I'm *not* kidding. Now, where the hell have you been?" she repeats, arms folded with matriarchal severity.

Confronting the reality of Pete Bannerman's death with Mrs Henckel was a big moment. I worked through half a box of her tissues. I howled so loudly, I actually got a "holler back" from her dog in the kitchen.

"I think this bereavement has had a significant influence on your life and decisions," Mrs H said.

I sniffled and nodded tentatively in agreement.

"And so, there is a lot of work to do," she added, "if we are to get you back on track."

I didn't want to hear that. I didn't like the idea of there being even more work to do. But I knew she was right. The death of Pete Bannerman was like a freak wave that sent all boats in the vicinity off course. If you don't re-set co-ordinates, you end up adrift.

After leaving Mrs Henckel's house, I found I couldn't get home.

"I walked back to the tube station and ... there was a problem," I explain to Nicola.

"A problem? A cancellation? Leaves on the line? What problem?"

"A busker."

"A busker on the line?"

"No. He was playing a guitar."

"That doesn't seem unreasonable to me."

Nicola's eyes are like flashing knives. Falteringly I plough on.

"He was playing 'Heroes' by David Bowie."

"And?"

"He sounded like Pete."

"Isn't it more likely he sounded like David Bowie? Not being funny, but Bowie wrote the song."

"He *reminded* me of Pete, and I couldn't bear it. So, I left the tube station."

"And what did you do then?"

"I walked to the next one."

"Kentish Town."

"Yes."

"And ..."

"There was a busker there too ..."

"Oh, for fuck's sake. Can we cut to the chase? Did you actually get a tube or not?"

"No. I went to the pub. And then later I walked to Victoria."

"From Kentish Town?!"

"Yes."

"That's bloody miles!"

"I know. And it's even longer if you have to navigate round all the street performers."

"What were you doing in Victoria for God's sake?"

"I got a train to Croydon."

"Why? Why would you go *there*?"

"I wanted to see the 130 bus stop where Mental Elf started."

Nicola narrows her eyes and examines me carefully. It's a hard, professional gaze, one which I imagine often culminates in the arrival of a trolley of powerful meds. "You went looking for a *bus stop*? I thought something had *happened* to you!"

Nicola is angry, and I can understand that. I went AWOL, and that was inconsiderate. However, this is not without precedent among committed rock 'n' rollers. The legacy affords me three immediate examples: Joe Strummer of The Clash once disappeared without trace just before a tour, later to be found wandering the streets of Paris. Liam Gallagher once ducked out of an American tour with Oasis so that he could go house-hunting in north London. And Noel once disappeared to San Francisco after Liam threw a tambourine at him during a gig in LA.

"I can just about get my head around you wandering off ..." Nicola says suddenly.

"Really? Okay. Well, that's a relief."

"But that's not all you did, is it?"

I don't like the look in Nicola's eyes. Her whole personality, the essence of Nicola, is reduced to two pinholes emanating malevolence.

I sit up and place a pillow on my lap as a buffer. "What do you mean?" I ask.

"Don't you remember? You *rang* me."

"Did I?"

"Yes, at 1am!"

"Really? About what?"

"To talk all kinds of your usual garbled crap and to tell me I've changed. *I* have changed!"

"Oh. Really? What else did I say?"

Nicola's eyes go misty with tears. She clears her throat for emphasis. "That I am a – what was it? – an enemy of rock 'n' roll."

I FIRST MET Nicola at a music festival in the late 80s. I watched her from a distance, and she stood out because she was setting up a trestle table in a tent. My first thought was: *How the mighty are fallen!* It seemed very menial work for the dark haired one out of the Human League. I was starting out as a rock writer and I thought I had a story: *Synth-pop backing singer now making ends meet as a festival roadie!*

But then I got closer, and it wasn't her. Her name badge said "Nicola", and when she'd finished putting up the table she opened up a box, took out some leaflets and fanned them out for public inspection. She had a kind, understanding face. You could tell the leaflets wouldn't be promoting veggie burgers or a dodgy rave. I went over and picked one up. It was for a mental health charity.

"If you meet anyone having a bad experience, then tell them they can come and talk to me," she said.

I sat in her chair. "Okay," I said. "Here I am."

"What seems to be the matter?"

"I want a girlfriend."

She blushed and told me this was not a mental health problem and to get out of her chair. When I refused, she said young rock fans experimenting with drugs were the people she was most urgently trying to reach.

"That's funny, me too," I said.

"What do you do?"

"I write about rock music."

"Perhaps we're competing for their souls," she joked.

"I like the fact that you pretend to be Mr Rock 'n' roll," she said on our first date. "But you're too nice. Even I can tell that you don't really mean it."

I was actually quite insulted. Once Ronnie was born, the tension over our respective jobs became more serious. We began to have regular arguments over whose work was more worthwhile. An afternoon I spent with Pete Townshend, my first Big Six assignment, proved a major flashpoint.

I had enjoyed lunch with him in his backstage Winnebago at Southampton County Cricket Ground the same day Nicola had been bitten on the arm by a young schizophrenic she had taken to the zoo.

"Does it not affect you that, basically, here I am helping these people who are forgotten by society, while you contribute, what exactly?" she said, dabbing her arm with TCP.

"You're upset," I countered. "Let's talk about this when the teeth marks have subsided."

"But doesn't it? You use your talents to amplify the thoughts and feelings of a bunch of egocentric arseholes."

I shouldn't have risen to it. I am mature enough to know one should ignore a populist screed delivered in the aftermath of a human mauling. But it is too obvious to assume that taking a group of schizophrenics to the zoo is innately more worthwhile than enjoying lunch with the man who wrote "Baba O'Reilly". And so, I laid forth my defence. I explained that while taking mentally ill people to the zoo is obviously admirable, my job is more useful in a wider, more incremental way.

"Evolution is advanced by unusual copies of the species. Rock stars are those unusual copies," I said. "They create the ambient cultural weather we live in. They have re-engineered modern attitudes towards love, money, sex and death far more than any other artists. We don't listen to painters or sculptors or film-makers or TV executives in the same way. Even politicians. Does anyone actually listen to what the government says about how we live? No, let those bean counters fiddle with the percentages spent on education, health and defence. But give them control of the cultural levers? No. Rock pulls on those."

There was a pause. Nicola looked up from her wound. "That's the biggest load of crap I've ever heard!" she exclaimed. "You get flown halfway round the world to lick their arses and swim in their pools, and they get to talk shit and sell their CDs!"

I had to admit that is sometimes true too. And yet, people still look up to rock stars. I had noticed it with our neighbours. When they would come around for a meal, they would quickly despatch their interest in Nicola's onerous work. "The work you do must be *so* rewarding," they would say, but, before she could elaborate on a recent punch-up or arson attack in the day centre, they'd quickly turn to me and ask in a louche, insinuating voice: "So, who have you been hanging out with this week, you glamorous bastard?"

Even when Nicola did get a word in, someone invariably would stagger back wild-eyed from the bathroom to exclaim: "Jesus Christ, is that really James Brown's half-eaten chicken sandwich you've got in there?!"

Whenever we have one of these fractious evenings the aftermath follows a distinct pattern.

"You use the bathroom to draw attention to yourself," Nicola will grumble loading the dishwasher.

"No, rock 'n' roll is using the bathroom to draw attention to itself!" I will say, my voice echoing in the marble as I check that no memorabilia has been stolen from the collection.

But if Nicola ever truly doubts that my job is more important than hers, I have the clinching evidence to prove it.

"I often see Ronnie playing air guitar on the sofa," I say, "but I've never seen him fantasise about being a mental health worker."

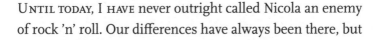

UNTIL TODAY, I HAVE never outright called Nicola an enemy of rock 'n' roll. Our differences have always been there, but

I had always believed they enhanced the relationship; they are disparate, perhaps even contradictory, elements which work in practice, like the duelling strings and guitar sections on ELO's "Mr Blue Sky" or the children's choir and deathly Mogadon vocals on Pink Floyd's "Another Brick in the Wall". But now I have launched the attack, and she wants an explanation.

"If you're going to be nasty, you need to back it up," she says. "If you're going through something major that's changing our relationship, then I need to know about it."

If men in their 40s are going to screw things up, it's more often with an affair or maybe an addiction to drugs, alcohol or gambling. They don't usually do it by fixating on something which happened when they were seventeen. But the story of Pete Bannerman feels live, and it is impinging on our relationship. I spend the afternoon telling Nicola the story of Pete and Mental Elf.

"You should have told me about him dying. This is awful!" she cries.

"I didn't think you'd get it."

"Oh thanks. Thanks a bunch. I only work in mental health, don't I? Arsehole."

"When I said you were an enemy of rock 'n' roll, what I really meant is ... you don't understand what an artist is," I say. "You want to make the whole world nice and normal."

"Don't kid yourself, Michael," says Nicola. "Peter dying had nothing to do with being an artist; it was a simple question of mental health."

"No, he was against the world," I affirm. "That's being an artist."

"That's what you tell yourself," she says, "and that's what has led to all this trouble."

"What do you mean, this 'trouble'?"

"You've kept Pete to yourself all this time. You never discussed him, and so now all of a sudden he's here, with us, this bloody *ghost* intruding on our relationship."

It's true. Sometimes I feel Pete's story is like a favourite morbid song I play over and over again on headphones. I won't share it. It's mine. And now it feels like Nicola is tapping me on the shoulder, warning me the house has caught fire. However, even though I might think this, I am not ready to admit it.

"I s'pose if you met him now you'd fix him up with some pills," I say.

"Is that what you think I do all day? Hand out pills? There is therapy. There is support."

"*Support*," I say acidly, contemptuously. "He was an artist. He wanted music to mean something. We need rock stars who are prepared to live out on the edge."

"Oh yes, and now that our son fantasises about being in a band, how is that going to work?"

"I hope he is true to himself," I sniff.

"And to hell with the consequences?"

"Not everyone is born to be an estate agent or a dentist," I sneer.

My eyes flash with anger. Nicola's widen in alarm. Ronnie has arrived home from school and is waiting just outside the bedroom door. He steps into the room gingerly, conscious that his arrival has brought a strained hush.

"For you," he says, with a soulful downward gaze and hands me a card.

I pull it out of the homemade envelope. On the cover is a picture of a grave. Above it flies a stick man rock star with wings. I read the words inside: "Sorry about the guitar. Sorry your friend is dead."

He watches me read. He is about to leave, but I stop him and give him a hug. "Don't worry about the guitar," I say. "It's fixed."

"Were you and Mummy arguing about me having the spare room?" he asks. "If you don't want to move all the stuff out yet, I can wait."

"That's very kind, little man," I say.

"And you mustn't worry about Daddy's friend," says Nicola crouching down to embrace him. "It was a long time ago."

Ronnie seems comforted. He turns to leave but then frowns as though bearing the weight of unanswered questions.

"Would he still be your friend if he was alive?" he asks.

"Yes, of course he would," I say. But my voice wobbles. It's a good question. A very good question. I just don't know the answer.

"Maybe it's good he's dead," shrugs Ronnie. "You like dead rock stars, don't you?"

"Oh, for God's sake, I can't listen to this," Nicola snaps and leads him towards the door.

After she has taken him downstairs, given him a pep talk and made him a hot chocolate to drink in front of his favourite TV programme, she runs back up the stairs and sticks her head round the bedroom door.

"You know what?" she says. "Maybe I *am* an enemy of rock 'n' roll."

That night I can't sleep. I go into Ronnie's room and watch him lying star-shaped on his bed, like one of the flailing airborne Beatles on the cover of *Twist and Shout*. I pull his AC/DC duvet back over him, take Pete's guitar downstairs and make an inspection of it in the dark.

*Would you be my friend now? Would I even like you?*

Nicola is right – the young ghost, for so long laid to rest, is now awoken. Thirty years after his death, through the painstaking emotional archaeology of Mrs Henckel, he is exhumed. I fall asleep with the guitar next to me on the sofa, but Pete Bannerman has heard my questions. He wants to provide answers and pose some questions of his own.

"I could see you didn't mean it," he says in new dreams.

"Come back!" I cry, as the spectre fades away.

"What do you want to talk to me for?" he sneers, looking around the place. "Aren't you happy with what you've got? A girlfriend. A kid, a house and a life. Plus, I see you meet all these big rock stars now."

The questions he asks are as challenging as ever. Pete knows how to get to me. He likes to press my buttons.

"I've got us another gig," he says slipping on his leather jacket, flicking cigarette ash onto the carpet. "Do you think you can be fucking ready this time?"

# 17
# The Teachings of Bowie

"Tell me," says Mrs Henckel during our next session, "exactly what happened following his death. How was it dealt with?"

It takes me a while to piece the aftermath together. I remember I dropped the phone like a hot pan. I must have shouted something because Charlotte ran downstairs and found me standing in the living room like a zombie and made me drink sweet tea.

"How could he do something like that to his family? He's a selfish *idiot*!" she said through her tears.

I sipped the drink and watched her cry.

"I fucking hate this place," she sobbed. "It's a dump. Nothing good ever happens here."

She was convulsed. But I just watched her. Grief wouldn't come to me then. Not properly. I didn't feel anything.

When my mum and dad got home from work, I told them that I had secretly been in a band and they listened, bemused.

"I know people play the comb and the spoons, but a *tea tray*?" exclaimed my dad. "Extraordinary."

Aged seventeen, he was in the navy fighting the

Germans, an experience which instilled a desire for an ordered, steady life. He simply could not understand a teenager sacrificing everything for music. Eventually, with a nudge from my sister, he was even able to concede that Peter Bannerman was a "very unfortunate young man".

My mother blamed England. "Is this the only chance they give the young ones in this country? To be a pop star or die?"

CHARLOTTE COACHED ME before I faced Pete's parents at the funeral. "Say 'Sorry for your loss,'" she said. "And it would probably be healthy if you try and let your feelings out a bit."

Foetus and I went to the funeral in school shirts and trousers with black ties. I didn't like the black tie. Even though Foetus said we looked like The Specials, it creeped me out. At the crematorium, I intended to utter my clumsy, rehearsed condolences, but when I saw Pete's family sitting in silence, looking through approaching mourners as though they were ghosts, I was too frightened.

I had only been to one other funeral. An aunty. She had an acceptable death: a well-lived life that had dwindled gracefully to nothing. At the funeral, they played Glenn Miller's "Chattanooga Choo Choo", a reminder of the night she met her husband at a dance during the Second World War. I wondered how their pop music could have been so light during a world war. Why weren't they angry? Why didn't they have punk? But the funeral was fond and tender. There was sadness but not grief.

Pete Bannerman's funeral was different. It was like an awards ceremony in negative. Everyone was nicely turned out in good suits. There was a trestled feast. People gave speeches. But the star of the show couldn't be with us. Instead of gracious thanks by video-link, he made his excuses with a short note. As we skulked around at the wake, Foetus told me one had been found at the bed-sit.

"What was the last thing you said to him?" he asked. "The note mentioned you said something important."

"It's over," I said. "There's a new sound coming. Something like that ..."

When I told him what I'd said, Foetus looked at me strangely. Part bafflement, part shock. Sometimes I recalled that look and interpreted it as: *Whatcha have to go and say a stupid thing like that for?* At other times over the years, its meaning has seemed darker: *Whatcha have to go and say a stupid thing like that for? You pushed him over the edge! You killed him!*

A WEEK AFTER Pete was cremated, I sat on my bed listening to an album called *Chelsea Girl* that Charlotte had leant me. She was listening to all kinds of miserable introspective stuff at the time. When the song "These Days" began and I heard the lyrics, I realised that Pete hadn't written them. It was written by, of all people, Jackson Browne.

While I listened, I heard the familiar rumble of a big petrol engine outside the house. I looked through the window. Peter's car. Stricken, I saw a familiar figure inside gathering cigarettes from the glove box. I swallowed hard. *Am I slipping into derangement?* No. An older greyer Peter got out.

His father was broken and slow moving, stooping to attend to freight in the car boot. His father found the body. His father had seen the note. *He must hate me! He must want to kill me!* But he wasn't angry. He was a ghost too.

"Sort it out between you," he said, laying a cache of Mental Elf memorabilia in the hallway. A box of records and tapes. Some books of lyrics. The new Stratocaster guitar, played at one show, that would stay zipped in its bag for the next 30 years.

Only as I watched him climb into the car did I notice another silhouette in the back seat. A body hunched in a great coat, staring aimlessly into space.

"Phil. Pete's brother," Foetus explained when we met to divide up Pete's stuff. "He's got learning difficulties."

"He never mentioned him. Ever," I said.

"He didn't like talking about him."

"Why?"

"He felt like Phil took up enough of the family's time. They struggle so much with Phil, he felt like they didn't care about him. That's why he never went home. That's why he was so obsessed with the band. It was his way out."

Charlotte tried to get me to talk about it, but I wouldn't. I just stayed in my room examining my collection of Mental Elf oddments and listening to music. In some ways, it was as though my sister felt the impact of the disaster more keenly than I was able to at the time. Within three months, she had packed up her life, abandoned a course she was doing at Croydon College, and left home for Brighton. She began various courses of therapy.

"You'll have to face it eventually," she promised me. "Maybe not now. But one day."

"Have you experienced tragedies of this nature in your work since?" asks Mrs Henckel.

"Yes," I say.

"Can you give me an example?"

I can. I can give her a lot.

In the early 90s, as they prepared to play in front of a crowd of approximately twenty people, I met Richey Edwards of the Manic Street Preachers at the University of London union. His PR introduced us. Edwards wasn't yet a star, but he was already carefully weighing every gesture. He understood that great rock stars are writing their legacy from day one.

"Hello," I said. "I'm Michael."

He nodded a wary acknowledgement but refused to shake my hand. I admired his truculence. I was scorched by his high-wattage charisma. It made me want to shake his hand. He *meant it*.

"Don't assume we are friends," he said.

When he disappeared in 1995, later presumed dead, I thought, *To those who fall! We salute you!*

And once, I shook hands with Kurt Cobain in a London record shop. He beamed earnest friendliness through piercing blue eyes.

"Thanks for stopping by, man," he said in his folksy down-home way. I hadn't stopped by; I had waited for hours. I was surprised at his easy charm. I couldn't connect it with the eerie dolorousness of his music. When he blew his brains out I thought: *Too pure for this ugly world!*

"And what about Nicola? Does she have a view about any of this?" asks Mrs Henckel.

The night Cobain died, Rex came round. We opened a few beers and turned on the news. Thousands of grieving rock fans spilled out onto the streets of Seattle.

"Imagine making music that has that much meaning

for people," I swooned, chugging a beer and watching the candles being lit at the massive public vigil.

"Too right," agreed Rex with boozy solemnity.

Nicola came and joined us, sipping an abstemious peppermint tea. "Someone could have saved him if they'd wanted to," she sighed.

"What do you mean?" I asked, eyes greedily consuming the TV footage as it cut to the flapping police tape outside the Cobain mansion.

"Someone could have stepped in," she continued, "but it's like the fulfilment of a mad collective wish. The fans are crying, but somehow they wanted it to happen."

It annoyed me, partly because she was right. Cobain's death felt almost like a relief. He had been a stumbling, disaster-prone junkie for too long. Finally, he had ascended to proper martyrdom and made Nirvana's music all the more powerful in the process. But I didn't like Nicola's dissenting voice pinning the blame on fans.

"Don't you get it? He died because he was an artist of unusual purity," I slurred beerily. "He died for rock 'n' roll!"

I tell Mrs Henckel that the only other dissenting voices I heard came from the rap community. I interviewed Ice-T shortly after Cobain's death. He was outraged that the most influential rock star of the time should take his own life.

"Aw man, that is some fucked up shit," Ice-T spat incredulously. "Reach the top and then kill yourself 'cos you can't handle it? No way! No black man would do that. We too busy tryin' stay alive to pull a stunt like that. In America, *other* people tryin' help put you inna ground. You don't off yo' *self*! That some self-pitying white boy shit right there."

Mrs Henckel isn't impressed with Ice-T's analysis. In

fact, she seems concerned that in the entire music community there don't seem to be many sensible voices who speak up for balanced mental health.

"You've never met a rock star who could talk *sensibly* about staying alive?"

"Actually, there was one," I say, "a local hero from near Croydon. He was quite passionate on the subject."

"Well, I hope you learned something from this person?"

"Sort of. After we'd had a bit of a row about it."

⚡

In May 2003, *Q* sent me to New York to interview David Bowie, the most elusive of the Big Six, the rarely seen white rhino of rock. It seems inconceivable now, but *Q* felt that Bowie wouldn't be able to sell the magazine on his own. The top brass felt the occasion needed to be lifted by the presence of another youth icon, and so they invited Kate Moss to sit in on our interview. Moss was a devoted Bowie aficionado, and thus they hoped she would help explore the nature of Bowie fandom as well as rock's crossover with fashion.

"You're all from Croydon, so you should get on," speculated Gareth Grundy.

"Sure," I said. Kate Moss had attended Riddlesdown High, the school from which the RLB stole footballs. I hoped this vague connection would help us bond.

But as the interview day grew nearer, I became concerned about what exactly this Croydon celebrity summit would be delivering to the 100,000. A one-on-one with either icon might be interesting. But together it might turn into cheesy love-in.

Also, I just didn't see the cultural equivalence between model and rock star. A cross-dressing alien junkie like Bowie opens up cultural possibilities, challenges the orthodoxy. Kate Moss has the face of a sexy working-class cat but uses it for what? To sell perfume, pants and eyeliner. *Get the London look!* It's really not the same thing at all. I looked forward to Bowie, rock's premier transgressive freak, making these differences clear and giving the world a proper lesson in deviance.

I FLEW TO New York and entered my high-rise hotel room. Before I'd even dropped my bags, a huge illuminated billboard on Broadway outside the window caught my eye: Kate Moss in a black see-through lace top lolling in the surf on a seashore. Her face was depicted the size of a house. Her mouth, about the size of my van, was composed in a defiant pout.

I felt sudden trepidation but also desire and awe. *You are going to meet this King Kong of Sex tomorrow!*

I resolved that if I was to approach Kate Moss with heightened critical acumen, I would first have to survive my own appetites. *A tactical hand-job would dissipate passing desire and put me in a better place from which to view her objectively.* But I was too jet-lagged to jerk off to a billboard. Besides, if I sat on the window sill, it was a seventeen-storey drop to the street. *Do you really want the NYPD to chalk the outline of a man giving himself a hand-job on the pavement below?!*

THE NEXT MORNING, I went to meet her at the Mercer Hotel as instructed by fax. The Mercer lobby gave onto a bar area throbbing with fashionistas, actors and assorted bastards holding cigarettes cocked at ear level. As I entered, they idly examined me with a quick up and down eye-frisk, then looked away again. *He is not famous!*

Outside door number 606, I gulped several litres of air-conditioned air. *Be cool. Her mouth is not really the size of your van! She is just a person from Croydon!*

I could hear Kate Moss inside speaking loudly in a gor-blimey accent. She was on the phone. I knocked but was immediately unhappy with my performance. A pathetic self-effacing knock. *Knock again! You are not delivering pizza, you are a gate-keeper of the culture!* The second time, I knocked with police-raid intensity. Moss's phone call ended abruptly.

"Bloody 'ell. Alright, no need to break it down!"

The door opened. "Hi, I'm Kate," she said, extending a hand. I looked at it and relaxed.

"It's not bigger than me. It's just a normal-sized hand," I said.

"You alright, mate?" asked Kate Moss with a perturbed look.

"Yeah fine," I said. But it *is* hard meeting a person whose body and face are the key assets in a multi-million-pound promotional industry. You can't help assessing whether they truly have the power to make you walk zombie-like into a store and buy expensive pants. She re-arranged the fit of a lovely, cherry red toga and slipped into some sandals, while I manfully resisted her branding power.

"God, my legs look so *bandy* in this," she sighed disconsolately into a mirror.

Her hotel room was full of disarrayed supermodel

paraphernalia: open trunks spilling fancy clothes; flowers from well-wishers; shoes which anticipated every possible social occasion, terrain and weather system.

"I have never been so excited to meet someone, *ever*!" she said.

"Thanks," I said.

"I mean *Bowie*, you moron."

Even her close friends Stella McCartney and Liv Tyler were envious and excited, she said.

"But their dads are legendary rock stars," I protested. "Aren't they used to all this?"

"But he is the best rock star ever," she exclaimed. "Come on, Bowie is the one."

Moss is a big rock fan. She cited her favourite bands of the time as Primal Scream, Queens of the Stone Age and The Libertines. On the bed there was a substantial trove of Bowie memorabilia, including a selection of photographs from photographer Mick Rock she wanted signed.

"These new bands are good and everything, but Bowie is the all-time best."

She gazed at one of the photos, taken in the 70s when Bowie lived in Berlin. He looked emaciated and bug-eyed. "He just looks amazing, don't you think?" said Moss, admiring the cadaver. "To me Bowie was ahead of his time."

WE WALKED TO a photo studio on Grand Street in Soho where the magazine cover shoot was taking place. The photographer, Ellen Von Unwerth, greeted us at the studio door, as excitable and kissy as a teenager.

"Mwah! Oh goodness, what an iconic day is in store for us today!" she trilled.

I kept my distance. I have always been sceptical of rock photographers. They are on the side of the icon, facilitating the mythology. They do not seek the truth. They do not serve the 100,000.

Von Unwerth and her crew went about their work, tweaking the set, preparing to lift their subjects out of the ordinary world and into the immortality of cover stars. Tailors and dressmakers, carpenters and make-up people fussed diligently over their specialities.

Then the room seemed to inhale collectively as a thin, middle-aged man in khaki jeans, brown hooded t-shirt, a fisherman's cap and glasses crossed the floor. All eyes flicked to the funky grandad. A classic case of celebrity inflation. *David Bowie has arrived and sucked all available star value from the air*!

An aide directed him towards me. The trick in such situations is to regulate breathing, set eyeball dilation somewhere below startled and get in a solid preliminary swallow.

"It's a long way to come," said Bowie. "So, thank you."

"Brilliant!" I said and immediately felt like a tosser.

But Bowie was used to civilians crumpling before him. He ambled about the studio, curious about the lights and camera, carefully avoiding full eye contact with the many people watching him. He wanted to be himself, even though for everyone else he was some Other.

Based on the way he strolled around, casually emanating charisma and engaging with the world only through furtive side glances, I held high hopes that Bowie was still a freak and weirdo. *I look forward to reporting to the slavering 100,000 that Bowie remains a nut job operating from the very outland of artistic possibility!*

Then, as the photo shoot got underway, he began chatting to Kate Moss, and my anxieties kicked in.

"You look absolutely delightful, darling, and, may I say, not at all anorexic, which people are very unkind to have said about you," he said to her. Moss looked confused and a little bit put out.

"No one has said I am anorexic, have they?"

"Well, that's *good*," said Bowie, recovering quickly, "and they are absolutely right not to have said it."

Bowie and Moss vamped for the camera. After a couple of shots, they paused. A technician touched Bowie's face with a make-up bud, and another fussed, pin between lips, with Moss's hem. All the while the pair chatted amiably. Moss told Bowie she had been out the night before and was still feeling a little tired.

"To be honest, I'm a bit fucked," she informed him.

"Oh, she's a little cracker, isn't she?!" Bowie frothed, delighted. "I think we've all felt that way from time to time. A bit fucked! Wonderful!"

I needed Bowie to be dark and dangerous, but he seemed less enigmatic to me now.

"I wasn't sure how we'd get on, but, may I say, you are an absolute delight!" he trilled.

Von Unwerth resumed, choreographing the compliant icons, her instructions making her sound like a dominatrix conducting noisy three-way sex – "Yes, David, just there!", "Good, Kate. Push it out baby!", "Do it again, brilliant!", "Fuck yes!", "Oh my God, fucking YES!"

The photos attempted to re-create 1960s glamour: short

skirts, sharp suits. In rock culture, everyone wishes it was the 60s – the beginning and, for some critics, also the end of the party.

In pauses between shots, Bowie and Moss chatted some more. Moss said she was going clubbing that night.

"Do you want to come too, motherfucker?" she said suddenly.

The atmosphere chilled. I have never heard an invitation offered with more brutality. I thought she revered Bowie. All eyes were on Moss. "What? Motherfucker is a *club*," she squealed defensively.

"Oh, you are a darling girl," Bowie exclaimed with renewed luvvie intensity when Moss had explained the faux pas. "Is your club really called Motherfucker? How wonderful! Wonderful! I fear, however, my dancing days are over."

Bowie and Moss twirled, battle-stanced, clenched their jaws, pouted and minxed, and the camera lens drank it all in with voracious clicks. The shoot drew to a close, and they changed clothes in preparation for the interview.

By now I was feeling desperate. The effusiveness of their interaction was going nuclear. I didn't know how I was going to control it enough to do an interview, and I couldn't face going back to the 100,000 with a stupendous serving of showbiz cheese. *You're going to need a hazmat suit to wade through this shit and find the rock star inside!*

We went to Looking Glass Studios nearby, where Bowie had recorded a new album called *Reality*. I felt this was a title which would help me press home my agenda. I have an enduring interest is the rock star persona, these exaggerated amplified versions of the self, dating from the time I discovered Sting was really called Gordon and Bono was really called Paul. It reached a crescendo when Duran Duran's pin-up bass player John Taylor admitted his real name was Nigel. *Who are these ordinary mortals really, and how do fake names help them ascend to status of priest-god?*

As we entered Looking Glass, the name of which itself is a hint that the recording studio is where the rock star transformative process is enacted, I made a decision. I would break up the quickly developing luvvie atmosphere with a hard-hitting grenade question based on the title of Bowie's new album: *How come David Jones from south London has recorded an album called Reality while operating under a pseudonym in Manhattan?*

But I was up against it. The atmosphere was dangerously light and fluffy. Bowie proved a gentle, affable and diligent host. He served tea and fussed over our chairs in a stark contrast to the usual markers of icon entitlement. He didn't take a caffeinated drink himself but instead appeared to be chewing a twig.

"It's a tea tree stick," his assistant Coco Schwab told me. "He's trying to give up smoking."

"I've kicked heroin, cocaine and alcohol, but cigarettes are the hardest," Bowie grumbled. "They put 50 chemicals in them to make it hard for you to stop."

"Oh yeah, fags are a bastard," chimed in Moss.

"Oh, that's adorable!" said Bowie. "'Fags are a bastard.' Oh, I absolutely love that!"

The congratulatory atmosphere was gaining further traction, and I sensed it would get harder and harder to gain a presence in the room. As they bantered, I thought of the gruesome Bowie photo Moss had shown me. I thought about Bowie's years with heroin and cocaine. I could feel my questions crystallising. I wanted to know what it's like to disappear so far up your own arse in destructive self-mythology that you almost kill yourself in the name of being a rock star. Why do it? And for whom? *I must wade through the celeb candyfloss and locate the inner alien!*

"I was looking at some photos of you earlier and—" I began.

"Shall we will listen to some tracks from the new album?" Bowie intervened suddenly. "Tony [Visconti] didn't want me to play them as they're not fully mixed, but ... as you've come all this way, I thought, we must give them *something*. I can't play the spoons for you. Ha ha ha."

My heart sank. This was not good. I was not in control, and an album playback with the artist present is always awful. But just the suggestion of hearing Bowie's new music sent Kate Moss into a spasm of record-breaking enthusiasm.

"Oh my God, fuck yeah!" she gushed.

*She can say "Oh my God, fuck yeah!" because she is a fan. But I am a rock writer! I need to listen to this music carefully, perhaps even a bit nerdily and with many repetitions. This isn't a dinner party where someone sticks an album on in the background while everyone chats over nibbles.*

"Nibbles?" offered Bowie, looming with nuts.

"Great!" I said and threw a fistful into my face in exasperation.

"And I'm rather hoping, Michael, that *you'd* like to hear the new music too?" he insisted. I caught Moss's eye, gleaming with anticipation.

"Fuck yeah!" I said "Let's fucking do this!"

Studio bods fiddled with equipment. Faders were raised

to maximum volume on the console. The music played. The first track was a flat-out rocker, and Moss gave herself over to it immediately and without hesitation. Sitting on a wheeled studio chair, she trundled round the room, long hair tossed over her face as she headbanged, narrowly missing the multi-million-dollar mixing desk. Then she stood and, like Rod Stewart in his heyday, began to thrust at a mic stand.

"This fucking ROCKS!" she exclaimed.

She was right. It did. But as a rock writer, the etiquette is different from that of a fan. It's unseemly to show signs of enthusiasm too early. At other album playbacks where the artist is present, I have found that amiably tapping a pen on a pad has usually proved a sufficient sign of endorsement because the danger is, when you come to play an album for the fifth or sixth time, it turns out to be a load of shit.

I felt trapped. As Moss continued dancing, I felt panic rising inside. Bowie looked at me with an inquisitive smile. I swallowed hard, put my arms above my head and flexed my fingers open and shut like a monkey grasping for hard-to-reach, treetop bananas. I gently swayed. I couldn't bear to see Bowie's reaction. *Dance, monkey, dance!*

"Wow. Just fucking *amazing*," announced Moss as the song ended.

Of course, I cannot simply call any new music "just fucking amazing" because there is a critical phenomenon called superlative inflation. If you use up "just fucking amazing" and then someone releases a new "Low" or "Diamond Dogs", where are you going to go?

"Yeah, very interesting," I said.

Bowie raised an eyebrow, the one above his blue eye.

245

He needed more. "Truthfully?" he asked, looking at me directly. "You can be frank."

"Oh my God," I finally capitulated, "you fucking KILLED it!"

We had been at Looking Glass for precisely fifteen minutes. I was already totally emotionally exhausted.

FINALLY, THE INTERVIEW began; it immediately lacked the rigour of a one-to-one encounter. I asked about *Reality*, but Bowie and Moss veered off into a chat about Croydon and modelling and mutual friends.

As I struggled to keep them off their social agenda, I became more and more exasperated. "Do you think the rock star or supermodel are comparable countercultural—" I began.

"We must see more of each other!" continued Bowie. "Come to dinner with Iman! Here in New York!"

"I love Iman!" Moss said, "and I love New York!"

"Oh lovely. When are you free?"

I had been grumpy for a while before this point, but I found my mood swung wildly on brazenly being left out of dinner reservations. *Why can't these bastards fix their social diaries when I'm gone? I am here to serve the 100,000!* I did not say it. But I felt it. They continued with their plans, reflecting how much easier it is to go out in public in New York than London.

"The fact is," continued Bowie, "New York is far more relaxed than London. I might get the occasional 'Yo! Bowie!' but that's it. In London the paparazzi simply won't leave one alone."

"Yeah London can be a hassle," Moss agreed.

I couldn't cope. In Mental Elf, we always promised we would be different. We would never become distanced from the fans. We'd always want them to touch us and talk to us. We'd always be true.

"Thing is, right," Pete used to say, "once you forget the fans, you become a different person, you become a tosser. We won't ever let that happen."

As Moss and Bowie commiserated over their invaded privacy, my mind wandered back to that Bowie party as a teenager. There we were, young kids partying in a house on the local hero's home turf. We were celebrating his greatest creation: Aladdin Sane, an alien, transgender junkie rock god killed by his own fans. I can picture Pete Bannerman in a huddle of young Bowies at the party. I can hear him whispering something outrageous and shocking about how the Aladdin Sane myth almost came true.

"So, Michael, shall we have a question then, sir?" asked Bowie, when he and Moss had finished bonding.

I picked up my grenade and lobbed it straight into the room. "Well, I was wondering: are New Yorkers really that relaxed around you?" I asked as he resumed chewing his tea tree stick. "'Cos my mate Pete once told me that, if he couldn't find John Lennon, Mark Chapman planned to shoot you instead. He had a list."

The question took a moment to register within icon synapses. "*What* did you say?" growled Bowie finally. I think it's fair to say he wasn't that into discussing it.

Even so, I heard my quavering voice relating to Bowie what Pete Bannerman had told me. In 1980, mentally deranged "fan" Mark Chapman was in the front row of the audience watching Bowie in a Broadway production of *The Elephant Man*. Afterwards, Chapman went looking for Lennon 30 blocks uptown at the Dakota Buildings. He wanted to kill a rock star. If he couldn't find the ex-Beatle, he planned to come back and shoot Bowie outside the theatre instead.

"How *dare* you!" Bowie barked, when I'd finished enumerating the details. "We don't talk about that, *do* we?! And I'd very much appreciate it if you didn't mention it in your article."

He wasn't the suave Thin White Duke anymore. His eyes, one blue, one green, looked like fires had been lit inside them. He became a scary monster.

"You have no idea what strange ideas people have about artists," he continued after a pause. "I don't discuss these things because it feeds the fantasy."

"Too right," said Moss daintily.

More tea was called for.

I excused myself to the toilet, where I composed an apology. "It's wrong to shoot rock stars, and I apologise for anything I have said which may have suggested otherwise," I mumbled on re-entering the interview room. "I just wanted to make the point that there are just as many unstable people on the streets in New York as London."

Bowie seemed to accept the apology with a low, patrician nod.

"But how did you get from David Jones, the south London schoolboy, to this?" I asked, gesturing to Moss's photos of the emaciated Christ-figure Bowie, waiting to be signed on the coffee table. *Show us what's out there on the edge of darkness!*

"These photos and others from the period are very

painful for me to look at," he said, carefully examining his old self. "I am so ill here. You can make all kinds of excuses for yourself as an artist. You think being extreme or living on the edge speaks of integrity. You claim it's for art. But then it's very possible you may die. That almost happened to me many times. Is art worth that?"

Bowie was calm, collected and sincere. In fact, he sounded like a different person; no longer the frothy, playful socialite but a survivor recounting extreme experience with sombre humility.

"See this?" he said and reached for a framed photo of extravagantly bouffanted 50s rocker Little Richard. It was a rather flea-bitten piece of memorabilia, much worse than some of my stuff. Bowie had sent off for it from the music magazine *Melody Maker* when he was a kid, when he was plain old David Jones and his fascination with rock stars was just beginning.

"I think it cost a shilling, and it has been with me everywhere since. At that age, I was looking for something to relate to, to bring me out of myself, and I just thought Little Richard was the best thing ever. I had a brother who was mentally very unwell. I came from a family where there wasn't a lot of love, and it was a lonely existence. I would lie in bed at night listening to American Forces Radio and imagining myself somewhere else, in this world of music. In an unhappy home, Little Richard was my guide. Mentally I used to try and climb inside that picture and get to a different place.

"And eventually I did get to the place. But I had to reinvent myself several times and take on new personas to do it. Now I can see there is a madness to what I do. The need to perform and be seen is a need, a compulsion. When I look back now, I feel faintly queasy at some of the things I've done. At one point around 1975, I weighed 90 pounds. I was surviving on a diet of green and red peppers and milk. I was so ill. When I look at the photos of me then, I am a walking skeleton. I am lucky to be here. And I am at a stage now where that is what I want more than anything – to be alive.

"Truly it's a world of primal fantasies and emotions, both on the side of fan and artist. The post-war generation really needed to invent rock 'n' roll. We needed to invent a new world to get away from the old one. It has been an amazing journey, but there has also been a huge cost."

MRS HENCKEL LISTENS to my account of the Bowie assignment.

"I am vaguely aware of this artist," she admits.

"Well, that's a bloody relief," I respond.

"And so it seems he managed to find his way out of self-destruction?"

"Yes."

"How do you feel about this?"

"Fine. I'm glad he's doing boxercise and chewing health twigs."

"But you took issue with the fact he now does not like to be bothered by fans?"

"It's just so disappointing when great artists, even when they have contributed something significant, just want to kick back and have dinner with other celebrities. In Mental Elf, we promised we'd never forget the people. And as a rock writer, it is my job to represent the claims of the fans."

"The fans or yourself?"

"I am a fan too. We are one."

"I suspect you simply felt left behind."

"Well, not *personally*, no. I was representing the *reader*."

Mrs H raises an eyebrow and shifts in her chair.

"Why are you looking at me like that?" I remonstrate.

She doesn't answer. And I ought to know she won't because I am very familiar with this use of eyebrow and adjustment of limbs. It means Mrs H has hit on something important. She never actually says this. She makes me draw my own conclusions.

I try to bore through the lull with laser-eyed indignation. She ignores me.

"Tell me about your friend Rex," she says suddenly.

"What about him?"

"You say he is committed to rock ideals but he will never succeed."

"His band is too hardcore," I say.

"If his band is called Cot Death, I sense they don't want to succeed. This in itself is self-destructive."

"Well, that's punk I'm afraid."

"I think you are repeating with him."

"Repeating what?"

"This Rex believes in rock 'n' roll like your friend Peter, and perhaps you admire his failure. But Bowie has succeeded, survived, and perhaps you resent this?"

"Oh, come on, that's crap!"

"I think you are deeply invested in the mavericks, the ones who stay on the sidelines."

"Bullshit!"

"I would suggest David Bowie has important lessons for

you," she says, "irrespective of whom he decides to eat his evening meal with."

"It was just plain bad manners to make dinner arrangements with a person from Croydon in front of another person from Croydon!"

"Bad manners?"

"Yes!"

"I didn't think you punk people observed such niceties," Mrs Henckel says, with a not very nice mocking tone, "but I do think you are anxious about being left behind."

"Oh, stop being so bloody annoying. "I say. "What is your point?"

"You must draw your own conclusions," she says finally.

# 18
# You're Fired!

It is 3am. I am sitting in my campervan outside the house to think things through. I decide I am going to sack Mrs Henckel. What the fuck is she *talking* about? Why does she think I am invested in Rex never having a hit single, and why does she try to convey everything with her eyebrows? I'm paying top-dollar, so why doesn't she just tell me the answers? With her oblique asides, she is like the pedantic bass player pointing out the problems in the tour schedule to the charismatic lead guitarist in an otherwise excellent band. Staring through the van's windscreen, I explore this image more closely. I realise that, in this scenario, *I* am the charismatic lead guitarist in the otherwise excellent band.

*If she was in Mental Elf Mrs Henckel would be pushing us to record a boring concept album called Magnolia Psyche. And as a rock writer, I would review it and give it 0/10!*

Staring out into the night I am angry that she has stirred up feelings about Bowie and Bannerman. I make coffee on my little stove. It supercharges brain function. I try to think more carefully about what Mrs H said. *Do I feel left behind?* The Bowie I met was an articulate rock 'n' roll survivor savouring the ordinary pleasures of post-lunacy. Family. Creativity. Dinner with new friends.

By stark contrast, I have to admit, I am hanging out in a van not savouring these pleasures because I haven't quite worked out what rock 'n' roll means to me. And now that he's been given a voice, Pete Bannerman is a part of that conversation. He is there when I shut my eyes. He is like my own unpredictable fan stalking me through the unregulated netherworld of the subconscious. "Did you get Bowie's autograph?" he sneers. "Did you tell him you impersonated him with felt tips on your face?"

I didn't tell him about the felt tips. But I did get an autograph. The signed album hangs in the bathroom. Bowie wrote: "To Micky: Questions, questions, bloody questions."

"JESUS, WHAT ARE you *doing* out here?" Nicola finds me in the van. She taps on the driver's side window, huddling against the cold in a dressing gown. "Michael, come on. This is *madness*."

I am in the driver's seat, staring though the windscreen. But the engine is off. I am not going anywhere, just sitting at the wheel with the stereo on.

"I can't sleep," I say through a gap in the window. "I need to listen to some music."

"Penny for your thoughts?"

I tell her about the session with Mrs H and how we revisited the Bowie episode. "I dropped a bomb into the interview that came from Pete Bannerman. I think she thinks it's because I was jealous."

"Jealous of what?"

"Of David Bowie. Because he courted self-destruction but is still alive."

"Blimey," says Nicola, "you're certainly getting your money's worth with her."

She opens the van door and climbs inside. I tell her I cannot sleep. I cannot face Pete Bannerman in any more bad dreams, so my plan is to stay awake tonight, tomorrow night, maybe for the rest of my life. Nicola does not think this is a viable plan.

"Why are you listening to Nico? She'll only make you feel miserable."

"Pete liked her. He could play this note-perfect."

"That's just wallowing. Turn it off. Come to bed."

"Wallowing? I'm not wallowing."

"I think you need to face up to the fact that Pete didn't make it but you ... you have a life and are actually okay."

"I want to feel music like he felt it. I want to understand what he went through."

"That's not really possible though, is it? You told me yourself," Nicola reminds me.

"Did I? When?"

"You said that music makes you *feel* like you are close to someone. But the reality is, there might be no real connection there at all."

It's true. You can never be sure that the meaning one person derives from a song will be the same as what someone else does; just as you can never be sure that when one person describes something as "yellow", they are seeing the same colour you see. The potential for misunderstanding is even greater when it comes to second-guessing an artist's intentions. With considerable mental excruciation, I recall telling Thom Yorke that I thought Radiohead's "I Will" was a cute paean to being a stay-at-home dad when, in fact, it was a song about the wholesale slaughter of children in the Iraq war.

As Nico drones on, I sip my coffee and watch a ragged fox zigzag down our street, propelled by frantic snout work. I am momentarily fascinated by this wild, untamed thing loping among the ordered bins. It probes for bones, scraps or perhaps a creamy lid poking through a burst bag. *Go for it, Mr Fox! How good to see a wild thing amid the municipal order!*

"Michael, I think we need to drop our differences and think about Ronnie," says Nicola, changing tack.

"Yes, of course. I know that."

"And if you truly believe that I am an enemy of rock 'n' roll, then ... perhaps we need to address that properly and in a grown-up way."

"How? How do we do that?"

"You're changing. At least, I am learning new things about you ... I guess what I am saying is I love you, but that doesn't mean we are always meant to be together."

My eyes leave the fox. I am jolted back to a place where I want certainty and order. "What are you trying to say?"

"I've tried to support you – the memorabilia, chasing the Big Six. I have tried to support you because I know it's important to you."

"Yes, you have. It's true."

"But if you think I'm not the right person for you any-more ... perhaps we should confront that."

"Don't say that," I mumble. "I just need to work out a few things."

Nicola takes my cup, sips my coffee and recoils. She doesn't like the jolt. She isn't trying to stay away from sleep forever. I watch her lick her lips with distaste, and I think how pretty she looks in the moonlight. Like Midge Ure in the video for "Vienna" by Ultravox, but with a more pleasing figure and without the moustache. It's a shame, this could be a romantic moment – if I were really here, that is. If I could be present.

"I don't want to sound like a baby," Nicola continues, turning the cup in her hands, "but you hear about people in relationships who suspect their partner is having an affair and ... I feel like that. I feel like Pete is taking you away from me."

"I am trying," I say. "I am trying to get back to who I was."

"Well then, let's both try harder. What's past is past. We can get over this."

"Yes," I say. "This is just a blip, something I should have dealt with ages ago."

Looking at Nicola's open, smiley face, I want to believe it. I want to move on. But at the same time, I feel so heavy, so leaden and despondent. I feel so lost.

"Come on, my little rock 'n' roller, it's bed time," she says and taking my hand yanks me up from my seat. I turn off the music and we stumble from the dark van into the moonlight. I am thinking we might kiss. It's definitely one of those moments where a kiss would be good.

"Jesus Christ, what was that?!" Nicola cries suddenly.

The startled fox ruins it. It's right by us now. With a glance of terrible accusation, it scrambles over our bins and slinks into the night.

➤

I AM NOT going to see Mrs Henckel anymore. She has served her purpose of helping me acknowledge Pete's death. I have blubbed in her chair, have used up her tissues and have sat willing the stumbler in her painting to get up and walk. I do not need a long aftermath of her poking about in my personal value system.

However, I do not want my relationship with Nicola to disintegrate, and I am going to fight for it. I reckon we are like Fleetwood Mac after their world-beating album *Rumours*. Some people might think we've delivered our best, that we are done, but we are not. We still have the slightly more experimental *Tusk* to come.

The next day, while we are both nurturing this more positive feeling, Nicola muses out loud that one day when we get the house sorted and our finances stabilised, we could even have another baby.

"Yeah, maybe a bass player," I say

"What a *weird* thing to say," she responds.

I still find it hard to conceive of my life outside of the rubric of rock 'n' roll. But I am going to try harder. I need to sleep again. I need to detach from the ghost of Pete Bannerman. In a sense, there is help all around me. Music is changing. Instead of synths replacing guitars, emotion succeeded hedonism. There is a new crop of sensitive, life-affirming rock stars I can talk to. They are the bands that Oasis hate. But they are the ones who talk the new language of mental health.

*Q* send me to interview Snow Patrol. They sing a lot of highly emotional, stadium-ready songs which hint strongly at male emotional fragility. Their singer Gary Lightbody is so self-flagellating and emotionally ravaged, I feel like sending him to have a couple of sessions with Mrs Henckel.

"I often reach a critical point in my relationships where I cannot bear the intimacy, the responsibility of that intimacy, and find the self-destructive urge to sabotage irresistible," he reveals. "That is, uh, also I suppose, where the songs come from. But eventually the goal is to be, you know, functional. And happy."

And then I meet the Killers. Their frontman Brandon Flowers, though emotionally angular on record, is determined to be regular, decent and normal in his everyday affairs.

"When I look at the love between my mother and father, I can get very emotional because that is such a deep and genuine bond. I want that," he says. "I love making music, but I have my own ideas about the lifestyle that goes with it. I won't let rock consume me. One day I'll just be a regular husband taking out the trash."

Rock's new intake seems to include a lot of sensible young men. Listening to them, I cock my head, crumple my brow and listen with empathy. *Careful, even though she's fired, you are turning into Mrs Henckel!*

One day I get a call from Rob Fearn and it seems my new empathic skills are in sudden demand. "I think we might put Keane on the cover," he says. "They seem to be having a few problems and they specifically asked for you to discuss them."

Since I first interviewed them over Dundee cake, Keane have become massive and sold 5 million albums. A band enjoying overnight success like that is always a contender for the front cover. A band that's having a few problems is utterly irresistible.

"Don't be an arse with them," advises Nicola when I get off the phone. "'Somewhere Only We Know' is a brilliant song. They are unpretentious. They're not trying to be anything other than who they are, and they still write really moving, personal stuff."

I know what Nicola means. I like their song "Bed-Shaped" and recently discovered it is about a childhood friend of theirs, Dominic Scott, who left the band before they achieved success. It's about childhood friendship, faded idealism and those who get left behind.

But Keane's success has become a cultural battleground. Other rock bands deride them. Rex becomes apoplectic at the mere mention of their name. "It's music for Waitrose shoppers," he snarls, "The middle classes have got the careers, big houses and cars. They've got the fancy toasters and fuck-off coffee makers. They can't have rock as well."

"Music is changing," I tell him. "Sensitive bands with pleasing melodies are the thing. Maybe that's the price of ... success."

"You're not getting to me, you know," he snaps, arms folded defensively. "I know you're just trying to wind me up, but you're not getting to me."

ACTUALLY, WITH KEANE things are not that simple. With the global success of their debut album *Hopes and Fears*, they have accrued fans like Scottish novelist Irvine Welsh and, even less likely, *American Psycho* author Bret Easton Ellis. As part of my interview preparation I contact Irvine Welsh, who is directing one of Keane's new videos.

"I think a lot of people who like the band are weirdos, twisted deviants, but very unhip," he offers, even though he concedes they are "quite posh cunts".

"I think it's pathetic that they even have to go through this frisking process to see if they are okay to like," says Nicola. "Why not just listen to the music?"

"We need to protect the legacy," I maintain tersely, packing my bags for the trip to New York.

"I thought the whole purpose of you seeing Mrs Henckel and talking about your friend Pete was to question this sodding legacy."

I don't respond. I have a pair of socks in one hand and a newspaper cutting in the other. I am reading in the *Guardian* that Keane have been seeing a brand consultant. I am shocked and appalled. Have they been instructed to hide their golf clubs and their Dundee cake and make friends with cult authors? There is a suspiciously loud fuzzy guitar on their new single "Is It Any Wonder?" and, thinking about it, this seems a very convenient time to be "having a few problems". I must be very wary. The klaxon at rock's border control is ringing loudly. I will be the first foot soldier on the scene.

"You've been much more relaxed these past few days," says Nicola as I run to the van. "Let's try and hold onto it."

I MEET KEANE in a bar in Manhattan. Tim, Tom and Richard are not the same people with whom I walked on a Sussex beach two years earlier. They look healthier, like they eat better food and go on better holidays. They have nicer wristwatches and have been on tour with U2. But in rock 'n' roll, the stats and trinkets don't add up to much. You have to mean something. You try to add something to the narrative. And because I am the rock writer carrying out this audit, Keane are warier than before.

I tell them that I have read that the band has seen a brand consultant.

"Oh well, whoever said that can fuck off," says Tom Chaplin. "We haven't. What a stupid rumour to spread around."

I believe them. In fact, their new album *Under the Iron Sea* actually makes them sound like they have been confronting some tough intra-band emotional conflicts. Many of the songs are about mending a troubled friendship, mostly concerning the creative angst between Tom Chaplin and songwriter Tim Rice-Oxley. It doesn't matter how big and successful a rock band is, there is often a key duo scrapping over control.

Over two days, I listen carefully to their story and frown empathically. I am sensible and mature in my approach. After the last interview, heading back to my hotel, I pass a big poster of Oasis in a record shop window near Broadway. A giant-sized Noel and Liam Gallagher, chins raised in belligerence, stare out at New York. I stop and address them above the city hubbub, "You too should confront your issues. *Do the work!* Keane have."

The morning I return home from New York I want to ring Mrs Henckel and tell her, even though I don't need her anymore, that I have learned to interact with rock stars in a mature and humane way all by myself. But I cannot bear the prospect of bleating all this into her answering machine, so I tell Nicola about it over breakfast instead.

"I think Tom, the younger one, has a complex relationship with Tim, and there's a sort of maverick/authority figure dynamic there."

"Go on," she says sipping her tea.

"Well, Tim is sort of quiet and serious, and he worries about artwork and tours and the business side of things, which can make him come across as an austere father figure."

"Hmmm."

"And Tom is younger, more bullish: the frontman who is suddenly hanging out with Bono and Springsteen and making the most of it."

"So, how did you deal with this ferment of emotions?"

"I didn't judge. I listened. Even when I thought about golf clubs, I found I could separate him from his father's nine iron. I had no agenda."

"It sounds like you reflected back completely congruently."

"What's that?" I ask.

"You reflected back a realistic, holistic view and actually addressed some of the emotional dynamics."

"Did I?"

"Yes, it's what I do at work. You don't judge, just listen." Nicola sinks the last of her tea as Ronnie shambles in for breakfast. "I'm actually quite proud of you."

"What's Daddy done that's good?" Ronnie asks.

"He just acted ... with good intentions."

I can tell Ronnie doesn't know what his mother is talking about, but he smiles anyway. It's a happy morning. Usually after an overnight flight, I crash into bed and stay there till the afternoon. But this time, I am not tired. We even have twenty minutes together before Ronnie has to leave the house for school and Nicola for work. After breakfast is cleared away Ronnie wants to play a game. He wants both of us to join his band and play air guitar together.

"What shall we play along to?" asks Nicola.

"How about The Libertines?" I say.

Nicola pulls a face. "Bryan Adams' 'Summer of '69', that's a good one?"

If Asda launched their own Bruce Springsteen, he would look and sound like Bryan Adams. "Summer of '69" is fun and fluffy but lacks depth, which makes it perfect for ironic air guitar. However, the song resonates with me more deeply than I care to admit. It tells the tale of a teenage rock band who didn't make it ("Jimmy quit, Jody got married!"), and the song's narrator grieves for the rock 'n' roll life he gave up on. In the video, Bryan Adams even consults a therapist to explore the issues arising from this.

We put the song on and rock out. Nicola and Ronnie are laughing together as they scream the chorus. "Those were the best days of our lives!"

But I don't sing those words because I know they are not true. Even so, there is a light and carefree atmosphere at home I don't recall experiencing for some time. Ronnie notices it too.

"Why are you so happy?" he asks his mother.

"Why am I happy?" she chirrups ruffling his hair. "Because ... that's what we're supposed to be aren't we? I don't need a reason. Everything is just ... okay."

"Stay like that, Mummy. It's cool."

"I'll be late tonight," Nicola says on her way out. "Can you take Ronnie to the dentist after school?"

"Sure," I say.

"Mummy said she's proud of you," says Ronnie with a smile when his mum has gone. "Has she ever been proud of you before?"

"Loads of times," I say, swigging coffee. But it's not true, at least I cannot remember the last time it happened.

I DROP RONNIE at school and then head home to my desk. I look at my laptop. It's a work tool but also a beautiful piece of rock memorabilia. I stroke the Oasis Access All Areas sticker on the lid. Then I reverentially touch the Radiohead and The White Stripes backstage laminates and the tiny, rock-hard nugget of gum once discarded by Robert Plant which is stuck on the lid. I open it and flex my fingers over the keys. When I sit down in front of my laptop to write an article, I feel like a rock star about to solo on his battered but beloved first guitar, the one on which he wrote his first hit. The "f" key has fallen off on account of writing up so many expletive-ridden rock interviews.

I open a new document. I begin writing up my Keane experiences. "I used to think there were rules about rock, but it's time to think more carefully," I write. And then I delete it. I try again.

"Noel Gallagher said that Keane looked like three estate agents, but that joke is not funny anymore," I write. And then I delete it.

I go and make more coffee and listen to The Libertines. Then I go back to my desk and have another go. "If we want our rock stars to live long and healthy lives, then we have to stop taking the piss out of them," I write. Then I delete that too and ring Rex because I feel really stuck. I don't know what to write. I don't know what to think. I tell Rex I am stuck writing bout Keane.

"I can't help you with that one mate," he snarls darkly. "You're on your own."

I get off the phone. I stare at the laptop screen. Nothing comes.

At 3.15pm I collect Ronnie from school and set off for the dentist. I insist on calling him "the dentist" even though Nicola and Ronnie prefer the overly familiar "Greg". It's a silent battleground in our relationship – for me, a justified retaliation for the fact that while I call Rex "Rex" Nicola calls him, with just a soupçon of disparagement, "your friend".

Also, I have always suspected Greg of fancying Nicola and her of mildly reciprocating. Evidence? First: the sheaves of extra stickers that Ronnie gets when he goes for a check-up. These stickers either depict smiling, dancing pieces of fruit or else the simple po-faced statement: "I Have Been Brave." Second: the armfuls of free toothpaste and mouth-wash samples Nicola comes home with. I never get them. (Having said that, I never go to the dentist.) In addition to all this, there is the lift home Greg once gave Nicola and Ronnie. It was raining, and he said it was no trouble because it was the last appointment of the day.

"He's a bit keen," I noted, as his tank-like German coupé sped away from the front door. "Don't dentists have to hang around and clean up the surgery?"

"Don't be silly. Greg is the big boss. His staff do that," Nicola demurred.

Most hurtfully, Ronnie once asked for a toy dentist's set

for Christmas and mentioned that he might like to work with Greg one day. It is a source of great concern. I don't know if I could cope if my son became a dentist.

Ronnie and I arrive at the surgery. I note the German coupé in the car port. I feel a pang knowing that Nicola's buttocks have revelled in the leather stitching of the front passenger seat.

We enter the consulting room. Greg is snapping on fresh gloves and consulting a computer screen. When he turns to say hello, I am sure the light in his eyes dims when he sees I am Ronnie's chaperone for this visit. "Hi guys. Come on in!" he says brightly.

*That Colgate smile isn't as wide as it could be!*

Ronnie clambers into the chair and proffers the pink cup of his mouth for inspection. I flick through Greg's car and fitness magazines and listen grumpily to the gunge emanating from his radio. He is a dentist. All dentist radios are tuned to drive-time rock radio. It's probably part of the training.

"Day off?" he asks jauntily.

"No, just finished early," I say without looking up. *Finished early? You haven't written a word!*

"Your wife was telling me last time that you have a damp problem in the bedroom. I gave her the number of my builder. Did he sort it for you?"

"Yeah, all done," I murmur. *Liar! That damp patch is now the size of the airborne pig on the cover of Pink Floyd's* Animals!

He begins prodding the back of Ronnie's mouth with chrome pincers. I hear Coldplay's "Fix You" begin. Greg hums along. *This song is the aural equivalent of sloshing with pink mouthwash!*

I look around his surgery: bright, antiseptic and ordered. There is no rubbish on the floor or blood on the walls. My mood starts to slide. *I'm not saying he needs to shoot up or start a fire in here but, Jesus wept, this is what the whole world would look like without rock stars!* I shut my eyes and see Slipknot running across the stage, boots sploshing in their own puke. *At least that was interesting!*

"It's getting rather crowded up top," says Greg, pointing at Ronnie's U-shaped jaw on an X-ray. He swings the screen around on its stem so I can see. I do not see a jaw. I see an auditorium where a rock band might play.

"You might need a brace, young man," Greg says. He looks up at me inquisitively, but I am suddenly lost in a reverie about rock bands and nice guys and the role teeth play in cultural resistance.

"Daddy, are you listening? Greg wants to give me a brace," Ronnie garbles through mouthwash.

"Not for a while, young man," adds Greg, "and only if your parents think it's a good idea."

I am thinking of all the bad teeth, the rebel teeth, I have encountered: Ozzy Osbourne, Ice-T and – *Jesus Christ!* – Shane MacGowan of the Pogues. I am especially thinking of Red Hot Chili Peppers guitarist John Frusciante. Once, Q sent me to his house in LA where he made me lunch, a huge juicy steak. As we ate, I assessed his teeth carefully because in photos I had seen his open mouth looking like a burnt-out garage, full of blackened stumps, the result of a terrible crack cocaine addiction. As we ate, I saw his mouth now looked like a newly renovated bathroom: shining white marble surfaces everywhere. I was glad for him, but my heart sank a little. It detracted from the story. I went into his garden and rang the Q photographer.

"Bad news. John's had his teeth done," I said.

"Oh, for fuck's sake," he grumbled. "That's the photos fucked! Doesn't anyone want to look like a proper fucking rock star anymore?"

"MR ODELL, WHAT DO you think?" asks Greg.

"No, I don't want him to have a brace," I hear myself say. "He'll end up looking like a robot."

Greg looks at me darkly. I can tell he has never faced this objection before. It's like a parent telling a doctor: I don't know if health is really what I want for my child. Or telling a teacher: I'm concerned at how knowledgeable she is becoming.

"So, you don't want young Ronnie having nice straight teeth?" asks Greg finally.

"Why should we make everyone have straight teeth?" I reason.

"People are far more judgemental about personal dentistry these days," Greg says. "I'm not saying that's right, it's just how it is. Kids especially."

"All the more reason to have rebel teeth," I say. "None of the people I work with have straight teeth."

Greg puts his implements down and rubs his chin thoughtfully. "What do you do anyway?" he asks suddenly.

"I am a rock writer."

"Really?" he says, eyes lighting up. "I used to be in a band! At university. Best years of my life."

We chat. Ronnie reads a car magazine and covers himself in stickers as Greg tells me the story of his band,

Sidewinder. They were a three-piece pop/rock outfit. Greg was the lead singer. They played three gigs but then disbanded because he had his exams.

"Dad, I think Mummy's going to get cross if I don't have a brace," says Ronnie suddenly, pulling at the corner of my jacket.

I don't respond. I am listening to Greg's rock 'n' roll war stories. The members of Sidewinder once slept rough when their van broke down near Hull. "I can still remember how brilliant it felt waking up under the stars!" enthuses Greg.

When he smiles, I notice he has great teeth. I reflect: the latent rocker is present under the surface of the most unlikely people – even Tony Blair was once in a band. But the thing is, people like Tony Blair and Greg the dentist know when the party is over. In a flash I realise this is why I resent Greg so deeply. *This guy took what he needed from rock 'n' roll, and now he's a dentist with a big car!* Greg moved on. I stayed because I didn't take what I needed from rock 'n' roll, it took things from me.

WHEN WE GET home, Nicola is already in the hallway. "So, Greg rang me," she says, arms folded, one eyebrow raised in war-like inference.

"Why?" I ask tentatively.

"Just to check I was okay with your radical new care plan for our son's teeth. That is, the *no care whatsoever* plan!" Nicola is talking so loudly even Ronnie cowers. She takes me aside to continue our tête-à-tête in whispered rage.

"I thought we were making headway here. How can you jeopardise your own son's *teeth*?"

"I just think there are more serious things to think about than good dentistry."

"That's the most bloody ridiculous crap I've ever heard!"

"Why don't you want me to have straight teeth?" asks Ronnie.

"You'll look like a soap star or ... an estate agent," I say, "or a dentist!"

"Oh," he says. "Do they earn a lot of money?"

"Yes," I sneer. "But they have no *soul*."

"You are talking absolute rubbish, Michael," says Nicola. "Greg is a really nice guy and he is very good at what he does."

"Greg?"

"Yes Greg. The dentist. *Greg*!"

"Why not just call him 'the dentist'? What's all this 'Greg' shit?"

"He's called Greg! He's lovely. What's the matter with you today? I thought we'd turned a corner."

"What corner? What's around this corner?"

"Sanity, Michael. Normality. Jesus Christ, what's got *into* you?"

"Sanity means I can't write my article. Normality means I don't know what to think anymore!"

Before she can respond Ronnie comes back into the room. "Why are you fighting?" he asks forlornly. "Why can't you agree about anything?"

# 19
# Magnolia Psyche

I take refuge in the campervan. I need space to think. I need space to write. But the van's little heater is broken and so it is very cold. I remember the story of Deep Purple trying to record the classic album *Machine Head* using the "Rolling Stones mobile", a legendary studio on wheels. In 1971 Deep Purple hired it and drove it to Montreux in Switzerland; while there looking for inspiration, they witnessed a huge fire at a casino across a lake which inspired the iconic rocker "Smoke on the Water".

I hum the famous chords. I imagine the fire to try to make myself feel warm, but it doesn't work because this isn't really the kind of cold that the imagining of a 40-year-old iconic rock fire can dissipate. It's an emotional chill. Nicola will not speak to me unless I apologise to Greg and also begin clearing my memorabilia out of the office. There is even a timescale.

"Today" her last text message said, followed by a link with directions and opening hours for the local dump.

This is a crisis. A real crisis. And I feel, reluctantly, it is time to consult Mrs Henckel once more. I think it's time to get the band back together. Sometimes a band can cope with one uncharismatic and pedantic member to keep everyone else's feet on the ground and the show on the road. I ring Mrs H and she manages to see me later the same day.

"So, since I last saw you I have tried, really tried, to view the world through a non-rock prism."

"Go on."

"But I had this revelation at the dentist's," I continue. "I just don't think I can accept a world which is so ... antiseptic."

"How did this opinion manifest itself?"

"The dentist said Ronnie might need a brace soon."

"Yes? And?"

"I said no. I just think having everything at right angles is so boring."

"And yet you say you are really trying?" says Mrs Henckel.

"I am trying! I thought you were supposed to be on *my* side?"

"Why will you not meet Nicola halfway?"

"She thinks it's so simple. She thinks this is just about memorabilia and Pete."

"What do you mean?"

"She thinks if I mope around a bit and feel sad, we can move on."

"And how do you see it?"

"It's not just about Pete Bannerman, is it? It's about the choices I've made since then; it's about *who I am*. Until a few weeks ago, I was a rock writer in pursuit of the Big Six. Now she's asking me, and *you* are asking me, to become a bill-paying, tooth-straightening, fucking ... *zombie*!"

"How are we asking you this?"

"I can't write anymore!"

"And why do you think this is so?"

"I used to have an interesting inner life, but you've turned my mind into ..." I look her around her plain consulting room and remember how worried I was by it when I first visited, "into a bland magnolia box with a pot plant."

Mrs Henckel doesn't say anything. She looks around her magnolia room. She glances at her pot plant. She looks a bit sad.

# 20
# Teacher's Lips

"Are these possessions very valuable?" asks the woman, glancing down at her clipboard. She looks like the blonde one from the Human League. Good hips. Big eyes. "Because if they are you might want to consider our premier insurance."

"They are priceless to me, but I don't think anyone else sees it that way," I say sombrely.

She peers inside the box I am holding.

"Jesus. Is that ... a *sandwich*?"

I have driven my memorabilia to a storage facility in nearby Rotherhithe. I am trying to meet Nicola halfway. However, I refuse to take my stuff to the dump. This is the compromise option. I have driven to the Elephant storage facility and I am investigating prices. It's called Elephant storage, I suppose, because an elephant is big and can carry a heavy load. But also, perhaps, because an elephant never forgets.

"Are you sure you don't want to filter some of this stuff out and save yourself some money?" the woman asks, sceptically examining my clump of Duran Duran hair.

"I *have* filtered it out," I say crossly and push it back down into the box.

She shows me one of the storage units. A small one will cost £150 a month and could accommodate my bathroom memorabilia and Pete's guitar, records and all my other Mental Elf mementoes. It would mean Ronnie could have a bedroom to himself. One day, when he has grown up, I could bring it all back home where it belongs.

"Are there security guards round the clock?" I ask.

"There is someone on site 24 hours a day," she replies. "They will also give you access."

I like that. I like the idea of 24-hour access to my personal Rock 'n' Roll Hall of Fame. We head to the office to do some paperwork. As we cross the forecourt my phone rings. It's Nicola. "Don't go home when you're done," she says. "Meet me at the school."

It's GONE 4PM when I arrive at Ronnie's primary school. I walk along the iron railings which have little lost gloves and hats dangling from their spikes. I pass through the gates and into the deserted building. I hate going into schools. They always smell of mashed potato, glue and conformity, and they make me think of the teacher who inspired Mental Elf.

However, I am pleasantly surprised that Ronnie's school is a vibrant place. Infant energy comes off the walls in waves: "Please help save our planet!", "Help those in war torn countries!" I tour the posters, paintings and papier mâché models in the main hall. I wander about looking for something with Ronnie's name on it. I see a poster showing a stick man holding a guitar. In vivid felt tip underneath is the legend: "Rock 'n' roll ain't noise pollution!" *That's my boy!*

I wander into the empty music room off the main hall. My nostrils twitch. I detect the sweaty fug of cooped little bodies recently dispersed. Inside the music room, guitar, drums and piano stand idle. The tools of a rock band. I stare at the mini drum kit. I can tell from the faint impact stains on the snare drum that it has never really been given a proper hammering. Just gentle tapping along to "Kumbaya", no doubt. My palms itch. I walk towards the little drum stool purposefully. *I must bang the drums!*

Before I can strike a single beat, Ronnie's teacher Miss Dunwoody enters with Nicola following.

"Ronnie is in the secretary's office drawing," Miss Dunwoody is saying to Nicola.

"Just in time for my solo," I say brightly, but I can tell from both their faces that this is not a moment for levity. I put the drumsticks down.

"Please, both of you, grab a seat," says Miss Dunwoody. We cram into tiny plastic chairs. Trapped by suction, I wonder if I will need surgical intervention to get out.

"Obviously, we take a situation like this very seriously," Miss Dunwoody begins. As she speaks, I notice her craning her neck slightly to get a view of the t-shirt under my jacket. It's an Anti-Nowhere League t-shirt bearing the legend "Let's Break the Law".

Nicola notices the t-shirt, shoots me a look of intense frustration and kicks me in the ankle under the table.

"As do we," she says, leaning in front of me to block the view. "Can you just tell us again exactly what happened."

"We were having music practice," Miss Dunwoody says, "and Ronnie refused to play the recorder."

"Why?" I ask.

"He said it wasn't a cool instrument."

"Oh my word, I am so sorry," apologises Nicola looking to me plaintively for support.

"Did he give a reason?" I ask.

"He said there were no famous dead recorder players," continues Dunwoody, looking straight at me. I am not sure what this look is meant to communicate. Perhaps that there were, in fact, a lot of famous, heroin-addicted recorder players loosely attached to the 1960s Bebop jazz scene and, as the son of a music journalist, Ronnie ought to know this? Or that our son is correct, there are not many noted dead recorder virtuosos, but this morbidity is worrying in a young child? I decide it is the former.

"Well, that is factually correct," I say. "*I* certainly can't think of any, and it's my job to know."

I hear Nicola's breathing change and she murmurs "shut up" very quietly under her breath.

"But more worrying is his general attitude," Miss Dunwoody continues. "When I told him he wasn't being very polite, he said no one can judge him or tell him what to do."

I examine her earnest, face. It's clean and milky, as suburban as a multi-directional lawn sprinkler. She is not from the city. *I bet she went to see Robbie Williams at Knebworth in 2003, bought a programme and a t-shirt and on the way home convinced herself she had supped from the jewelled goblet of rock!*

"I am sure you both agree that this attitude is unacceptable?" she continues.

"Yes, and we will work with you to get Ronnie back on track in any way you decide," Nicola says. But I am looking inside Miss Dunwoody's open bag on the floor next to her.

It's a large canvass shopping bag crammed with a plastic lunchbox, a mini umbrella, children's exercise books and right on the top, something which gives me hope: a pencil case with the famous Rolling Stones lips logo on it.

"What he said is a bit quirky, but he's not actually done anything *wrong*, has he?" I say firmly.

"No, that's true, he hasn't. And he's not actually in trouble. For me it's more a welfare issue. When I suggested he might later regret not learning an instrument he said, 'Who cares? I hope I die before I get old.' I think that needs flagging up, that's all."

"He said that? That's terrible," says Nicola.

"Well, it *is* from a song," I say. "*He's* not actually saying it, is he?"

"Yes," says the teacher, "but he told the class his dad thinks dead rock stars or ones with bad teeth are the best."

"Jesus Christ," says Nicola.

"Ronnie said rock stars who die for the cause are heroes."

"Did you tell him that?" says Nicola turning on me.

"Not in so many words, no," I say.

"Which words then? How *did* you say it?"

"We were discussing rock stars and life and, yes, teeth on the way home from the dentist, and I just said ... it's better to live fast than fade away."

"I think he's just a bit confused," Miss Dunwoody offers, "and perhaps those sort of comments are not really helping."

"What do you want me to do? Write out the lines to Motörhead's 'Ace of Spades' 200 times?"

"Michael!"

"Pardon me?" says Miss Dunwoody.

"I see you have a Rolling Stones pencil case," I continue.

"Yes," says Miss Dunwoody, glancing down at her bag. "So?"

"It's a piece of rock 'n' roll merchandise."

"I am not sure what point it is you are trying to make."

"Why that pencil case?"

"My boyfriend gave it to me, if you must know."

"People made sacrifices to make that pencil case cool. People *died*."

"It's been a long day, Mr Odell, and I don't really want to engage in a debate about the ethics of my pencil case."

"I'm just pointing out that you yourself have invested in rock 'n' roll culture while simultaneously displaying a very low outrage threshold."

"I work in an inner London primary school. I can assure you I do not have a low outrage threshold."

"Then why are you coming on like the fascist teacher in Pink Floyd's "Another Brick in the Wall"?"

"Michael, for *God's* sake, shut up!" says Nicola.

"I think we should leave it there," says Miss Dunwoody. "Let's just agree we need to keep an eye on things."

"Don't worry, Miss Dunwoody," Nicola says, rising from her chair. "I can assure you this will never ever happen again."

We leave the music room, and while Dunwoody goes to fetch Ronnie from the school office, Nicola and I stand in the empty school playground waiting for him.

"Well done," she smiles before darkening suddenly. "You've fucked it up!"

"I told the truth," I sigh.

"What kind of parent calls their child's teacher a *fascist*?"

"A concerned parent," I say, scuffing the floor with my toe.

"And what kind of parent visits a school in a 'Let's Break the Law' t-shirt?" she laughs incredulously.

"Well, I didn't know I was coming straight here, did I? I was loading my soul into a fucking *storage facility*, remember?"

"Go back and say sorry to her," orders Nicola.

"No."

"If you don't go back and apologise, I don't want you in the house."

"Fine," I say, "I don't want to be in a house where I'm being *conformed to death*!"

Ronnie arrives in the playground with a card he has made, but neither of us is in the mood to accept it. He puts it in his bag. He and Nicola walk off together. I can tell by the way he slips his little hand into hers and the way her shoulders are bunched as they head up the hill that she is sobbing.

# 21
# Man and Van

"When Sally's mummy and daddy split up, he went to live in a flat," says Ronnie. "Why are you going to live in a van?"

"I can't afford a flat. And Mummy and I are taking a break, not splitting up."

"Why are you taking a break?"

"Your mum and I need some time apart. It's like if you squabble when Jack comes for a sleepover and we put you in different rooms for a while."

"So why not just go in a different room then?"

"Because it's a slightly bigger argument than yours and Jack's."

I am going to live in the van. However, I am struggling to explain this to Ronnie. I want to tell him that moving into a vehicle is not entirely without precedent in rock. Once, I interviewed Mark Lanegan, guest singer with Queens of the Stone Age and now a solo artist. He was living in an ambulance at the time.

"Of course the social life suffers," he admitted, "but I got the essentials: a stereo and a cigarette lighter and a sleeping bag. An ambulance is just fine."

But Ronnie is too young to understand this. I will tell him this story when he is older. Also, the storage unit will have to wait. I will not be able to afford £150 a month while I am living in a van. All my memorabilia will have to come with me.

Once I have loaded all this stuff, I go into the kitchen and take all the tinned food from the cupboards. Again, rock provides me with some useful strategies. I interviewed Lemmy once, and he told me that in the early days, he survived on a tin of beans a day. Dewy-eyed, he recalled once eating a tin on the beach at Redcar in the north of England, scooping them into his mouth with a metal comb.

"I don't give a flying fuck what people think of me," he said. "I'm not trying to fit in."

When I have finished loading my provisions into the van, I go and find Nicola. She is in the living room slugging wine and listening to music. Not her own records. My records. Michael Bublé's work doesn't really accommodate visceral real-life situations, and so she is listening to Nick Cave. He articulates the dark side very well. As his doomy voice reaches the chorus of "People Ain't No Good" her eyes water and her nostrils flare.

"I actually think that this is what you have always wanted," Nicola says.

"What is?"

"Life on the road. No responsibility. No family."

"No, I like family life," I say tetchily, "but it depends how uptight that family is."

"I cannot believe you are choosing the ghost of your friend over us."

"I am not choosing him. I am being me."

IT'S DARK WHEN I leave the house. The van is parked about twenty yards down the street. As I pace towards it, I see our neighbour Lesley putting her bins out. When she comes over for a drink she is always very interested and respectful about my rock memorabilia. I do not want her to see me climb into the campervan loaded with these artefacts in case she thinks I am a loser. And so I wave, walk past the van purposefully, then, when she has finished doing the bins and has re-entered her home, I turn back and dart inside.

My heart pounds. I estimate that if Neighbourhood Watch really does work, the police will arrive in five minutes.

No one comes.

I put on a light and arrange my new home. To mark my leaving, Ronnie has made me another card. It shows an armoured Ronnie figure supported by helicopter gunships and a battalion of fighting cats twirling nunchucks. He and his furry friends are defending a castle. On closer inspection, the castle is our house and the cats are our cats. There is a grieving damsel surveying the scene from a turret who is wearing an Abba t-shirt. Nicola. I survey the scene more carefully: I am not in the picture.

THE NEXT MORNING I drive over to see Mrs H. I tell her that I face, *we* face, a stark choice: either I get a free session or I pay, in which case I won't be able to afford the petrol to get back to south London and I will have to live outside her house in my van.

Mrs H gives me a session on account.

"I suppose it hasn't escaped your notice that you are repeating the story of your friend," she notes, looking out of her window at my new home.

She is right. There is an uncomfortable symmetry with Pete in Foetus's dad's campervan.

"But this is my van and I can drive it, so I am in control," I counter. "Plus, it has a better stereo."

Mrs Henckel doesn't say anything.

I sit in the silence of her magnolia room. I study the uniformity of the paintwork. I glower at the pot plants. The interior of my van is definitely more bohemian and interesting, I conclude. I have memorabilia everywhere, while she has nothing but blandness and conformity. I am convinced that I have made the right decision, but I do not verbalise this. Today I think it's best to say as little as possible.

Instead I look at the painting. The cloaked figures have not made any progress stumbling away from the apocalypse. They are still exactly where they were when I first visited. I look at the frayed arm of the chair and the beady eyes of the dog. Nothing changes. Even the CDs are stacked in exactly the same—

Wait. I crane my neck. Something *has* changed. There is a new CD on the shelf next to Van Morrison. When I manage to read the spine, I can't believe it.

"Bloody hell, you've got a Slipknot album!" I exclaim.

Mrs Henckel glances up at it. "Oh, yes, I saw it in the supermarket," she says, a little bashfully.

"And you bought it?"

She nods. I am touched. Mrs Henckel, while loading her trolley with food and man-size tissues, has actually thought about rock 'n' roll.

"It was reduced," she shrugs, trying to lessen its significance. "My curiosity got the better of me. When you told me about your interview and said they were the most dangerous rock 'n' roll band in the world, I wanted to hear it for myself."

"And what did you think?"

"My dog was very frightened. It is quite something to embrace such darkness."

"You should try Anal Cunt!" I say. Then I apologise because Mrs Henckel looks stern and forbidding.

She frets the arm of her chair momentarily. "Michael, do you think you are making progress with me?"

"Sort of. Yes, I think so. Sometimes."

To be honest, I am not sure. I mean, I *am* making some bold decisions, but at the same time, I have just moved into a van filled with rock memorabilia.

"I took this opportunity to explore your music because I suppose I am not sure I fully understand you yet," she says, "which in turn made me wonder if I am the best therapist for you to see."

"What are you saying?"

"Simply that it is my professional duty to assess whether our work here together still has value."

"Is this because I insulted the décor of your room?"

"No. I have no problem at all with you expressing your anger."

"Well then, don't give up on me now," I plead. "You can't just bail out now because you feel like it. You have to do the work!"

"Of course I will do no such thing. If you are happy with your progress then we must continue."

"Yes, thank you. I'll try harder."

"But perhaps we must consider new strategies."

# 22
# Van The Man

Mrs Henckel's attitude worries me. *Maybe she thinks I'm crazy?* By the second night I am having doubts of my own about whether our sessions are working. At 11.30pm I get out of the van and walk past the house. There are lights on. And there are lights on in other houses along the street. Families preparing for bed. Adults preparing for sleep and, perhaps, a healthy dream-life that will burn off residual angst which, in turn, will help them awake afresh tomorrow morning. *I cannot burn off this residual angst in a night! I have been courting this darkness since I was seventeen!*

I get back in the van. Through a sliver in the ghastly oatmeal curtains, I watch the street's nocturnal life: people going into the late-night corner shop and emerging with fags, cheap vodka or perhaps a newspaper; single people from the flats; people who are not in families. I have been to that corner shop countless times as a family man. But now I must join the desperate after-dark clientele. I go into the shop. The shopkeeper Mr Roy has always been friendly and sometimes finds time while re-stocking the chocolate bars to discuss my latest work in *Q*, which he stocks in pride of place at the front of the magazine rack.

"You still livin' the dream?" he chuckles as I enter and opens a plastic tub on the counter to take out a lolly. "For your beautiful boy."

I feel a pang of guilt accepting it. *Thing is, Mr Roy, there have been some changes, and actually I am now living in a van.*

I take the lolly, say thanks and buy a bottle of wine. When I get back to the van I am overcome by sudden scruples: I cannot drink wine within sight of a lolly meant for my son. I put it in the glove compartment.

I further decide that I cannot drink in a van within sight of Ronnie's bedroom and so I move the van and park a mile away on Lordship Lane. The only parking space I can find is near Greg's dentist surgery. His car port is empty. I imagine him at home, teeth gleaming at the dinner table, Coldplay on the stereo and his son, covered in smiley face stickers, reporting excellent progress on the recorder.

I open the wine. I tilt and slug hard. I spill some down my front. *Tramp!*

This van is full of memories. I bought it second-hand because it reminded me of the one that Foetus's dad used to have. But it's full of family memories too. Like the time Nicola, Ronnie and I drove to the Sussex coast singing "Born to Be Wild" all the way, even on the grid-locked A27 when the sense of visceral wanderlust began to fade. The truth is, you cannot experience the widescreen, wind-swept glory of classic American rock in Britain. It's too rainy and poky. Just as you are surging towards an ecstatic chorus, you have to slow down for another roundabout. But we tried, and it's still a good memory.

In a cupboard, I find paper cups leftover from that holiday. Winnie the Pooh is pictured on each cup with a pot of honey upturned on his face. Basically, I am about to re-enact this scene except with a bottle of Merlot. Drinking Merlot from my son's Winnie the Pooh cup feels like a betrayal of childish innocence. Then I remember a macabre piece of rock 'n' roll trivia which makes it darker still:

*Winnie the Pooh was written by AA Milne, who bought a beautiful Sussex farm with the proceeds of his book. Later, Brian Jones of the Rolling Stones bought the farm and drowned in the swimming pool! Darkness will always trump innocence! Drink!*

Soon I have drunk enough to find this coincidence bleakly funny. I ring Rex to share the insight. He will get it. He too has devoted his life to rock 'n' roll.

"You stupid dickhead!" he says when I describe my current circumstances, but with a hint of kindness and affection, I like to think. "Did you know Bon Scott drank himself to death yards from where you are now?"

I had forgotten. In 1980 AC/DC singer Bon Scott died in a Renault 5 parked on Overhill Road in East Dulwich, less than half a mile from where I am now, after a late-night boozing session.

"Ring me if you need to. Don't do anything stupid," says Rex

I put down the phone. The doubts return. *Perhaps I have already done something stupid*, I reflect. I am drinking myself to sleep using a Winnie the Pooh cup while living in a van.

# 23
# Slash

I go and see Nicola and Ronnie each day. I do Ronnie's bath time, but he declines the air-guitar session afterwards. He is unusually pensive.

"Daddy, shall I make you the sandwich?" he offers earnestly and suddenly while towelling himself off.

"Excuse me?" I say. "Shall you make me the *what?*"

"The sandwich."

"I'm not hungry, sweetheart. And anyway, you say 'Shall I make you *a* sandwich.'"

"But I heard Mummy on the phone. She said to her friend you were one sandwich short of a picnic. That's the sandwich I can make for you."

I stare into my boy's eyes, clear pools of innocence.

"Oh, she did, did she?" I say thoughtfully, gulping back an exclamation of rage. "Well, I'm fine for sandwiches, thank you."

"Is that where you've been? On a picnic?"

"It's no picnic," I snap. "I am thinking about things."

"What things?"

*It's not just about Pete, it's about what rock 'n' roll has made me as a person!*

"Do your ears," I say ignoring the question, "and the back of your neck."

In the evening I go back to the van. I sit and listen to music, eat beans and watch the traffic. I like traffic. I like to see who is nodding or pounding the wheel to rock music as they negotiate the roundabout at Goose Green. Many people are, but the salarymen in classy German coupés are not. They are barking into hands-free sets, still working on their phones late into the evening. That's how they can afford classy coupés, I reason. But they have no soul.

I doze, but at night the rhythms of the South Circular keep me from deep sleep. Ergo they keep the ghost of Peter Bannerman away. That's where he resides, in the darkest trench of the unconscious.

Sometimes I sit up and watch my fox. She doesn't run now. She looks me up and down. *Ooh-aah-oo! You are one of us now!*

On the fourth day, Gareth Grundy rings.

"Sorry, Michael," he says, detecting the cramped acoustics of the van. "Have I caught you in a toilet?"

I step outside and say, "No, don't be daft. I was in a record shop. What can I do for you?"

I decide not to tell *Q* magazine I live in a van. I don't want them thinking I cannot adequately function as a rock writer, even though being a rock writer is one of the few jobs in the world that is not compromised by uncertain personal hygiene arrangements or flagging mental health indices.

Gareth wants me to do an interview. "It's Slash from Guns N' Roses," he says. "It's for a greatest rock 'n' roll stories ever issue. Up for it?"

One of the things the magazine finds is working are

lists. The readers are less interested in in-depth personality pieces than cooked-down lists of the most extreme madness.

I do not know what to say. Since becoming a bum I struggle to make the simplest decision. My brain is like an onerously slow bureaucratic institution: every question must be referred up to an array of understaffed, badly led departments.

Thus, "Should I interview Slash?" is laboriously examined by the Department of Fear and Paranoia – *What if I say no, and Q never ring me ever again?* It also gets a clammy probing from the Department of Nihilism – *What's the fucking point of interviewing another rock star, especially one who wears a top hat?*

"Michael, are you there?" asks Gareth.

"Sure. Why not?" I say finally.

"He's an interesting guy," says Gareth. "He's got loads of stories."

I stare at the rain-lashed, traffic clogged South Circular. "Don't worry, I'll make it crazy as hell," I say quietly.

That evening Slash calls. He is by a pool in LA. I am in my van. Due to the sizeable time difference and the fact that rock stars are always late, I am stooped over the campervan's two ring hob cooking beans when my mobile rings.

Slash is a nice man. Born in the Midlands, he is easy-going and likeable, even though he has absorbed certain LA traits like wearing a top hat and beads which might potentially make him a twat.

"Hey Michael, Slash. Sorry to call so late, man. Hope I didn't wake the house," he says.

"No, everyone's asleep," I lie. I chat to Slash while

cooking, a tea towel slung over my shoulder, mobile phone cradled under my ear. The interview, as with so many rock interviews, is about the "madness" of his rock star life. In Slash's case, this centres on his experiences with drink and drugs while also touching on the fate of bass player Duff McKagan, famous for having a pancreas which exploded due to his prodigious intake of vodka.

"So, tell me more about how you helped Duff through his, uh, issues," I prompt.

Slash begins to pronounce clearly and interestingly on the subject of rock stars and their appetites for excess, danger and stupidity. As he speaks, I marshal my ingredients (beans, cheese), nod and listen. I do not notice the dangling tea towel touch the hob flame.

"In a band, you are basically a brotherhood," says Slash. "You help each other 'cos rock 'n' roll is a dangerous game to play on your own."

I nod. Slash makes so much sense. You don't let a fellow band member's pancreas explode without at least stepping up and asking them if everything's okay. I feel a pang of guilt. *Duff's pancreas may have exploded, but at least the rest of him is still here!*

Memories flood back: in 2004, I joined Slash and Duff and their band Velvet Revolver on tour in Denmark. Slash was helping Duff who, in good shape, was, in turn, helping vocalist Scott Weiland through his issues with drugs and alcohol. I even watched Duff and Scott working out together in a forest clearing backstage.

"You're doing great and I'm right with you!" Duff encouraged Scott. Scott looked tired but smiled gamely. It was moving watching their brotherly love.

I recall this and gloomily think that all it takes is to spot someone in trouble and step in to help. *You missed the signs! You weren't paying attention!*

That's when I see fire licking around my elbow. I slap myself to put the tea towel fire out. I hope Slash doesn't hear because, despite everything, I want to remain professional. But Slash is not stupid. He has lived a rock 'n' roll life. He knows when the man he is talking to on the end of his phone is on fire.

"Everything okay your end, dude?"

"Yes. Everything is okay."

"I thought I heard a yelp."

"Actually, I'm on fire," I say breezily.

"Take a minute dude. Sort that shit out."

"Thanks, Slash," I say.

When the danger has been averted, we resume our chat. "Sounds kinda small where you are," notes Slash. "You're not doing this in the toilet, are you?"

"No. I'm in my kitchen," I say.

We finish the interview. Slash says he loves *Q* magazine, and he wants to have his publicist send me a CD of some new music. There is nothing unusual in this until he asks me my address. I am silent. I am not sure what to say.

"Actually, I live in a van," I confess down the line.

"Ha, funny dude. But really, where should I send this package?"

But it's not all bad. Slowly I am mastering the details of a subsistence existence. After a stand-off with the groundsman at Dulwich Picture Gallery who found me irrigating his rose garden, I have at last established a proper portable toilet: a catering-size olive oil container with a wide neck suitable for an adult penis head. I stole it from the back of an Italian restaurant in Dulwich Village and I am inordinately pleased with this scavenged item.

The same trip also yielded toilet paper, a catering box of little amaretto flavoured snacks and some dough balls I found abandoned on a child's plate.

*I am a town fox! I am a wild man living off-grid!*

"PERHAPS YOU FEEL you are yourself 'on tour'," Mrs Henckel remarks when I go and see her. "Perhaps you reject the norms of family life."

I do seem to have chosen an existence not unlike my rock 'n' roll heroes. I remember Pete Bannerman once telling us that members of Strange Fruit, the band who leant us their equipment, had collected and eaten road kill while on a tour of Northern France.

"You want it bad enough, you'll do anything," he informed me and Foetus grimly. "Death or glory."

However, I realise I am not in a band and I am not on tour. My bus never slides into the "Artists Only" bay at a venue, the air brakes wheezing as fans with camera phones materialise at the windows. On my tour, I get moved on by a parking warden or, if I am going to the toilet in the park bushes, get chased away by a groundsman in an electric buggy. Also, I never get offered an autograph book. I get offered a cut-price pizza leaflet under my windscreen. My suspension does not rock with the vigour of free love. It rocks to the sound of tantrums and jags of grief.

But sometimes I sit in the van and while away the evenings thinking of a name for my one-man non-tour.

I remember that I have a Sex Pistols' "Pretty Vacant" single with a picture of two buses on the sleeve. The destination board on one shows it is headed for "Boredom" and the other is going "Nowhere". I loved that artwork when I was a nihilistic teenager. I decide I am on The Tour to Nowhere.

## 24
# What's the Story?

On the seventh day in the van, because it feels like a significant milestone, I decide to conduct an inventory of my memorabilia. I am missing Ronnie and this will make me feel closer to him.

"One day son, all this will be yours," I used to say to him as we reviewed the collection together.

He liked to assess new items. He liked to discuss what kind of rock star he might one day be. But, most importantly, he liked to hear the stories about how I'd acquired each artefact. Like the time I had lunch with The Who's Pete Townshend in his backstage caravan. While Townshend offered a furrow-browed commentary on "the countercultural impact of Mod in the 60s", I slid the napkin with which he had been dabbing his mouth into my bag.

"Clever Daddy," Ronnie said, "but isn't that stealing?"

"No," I said. "It's recycling."

And he likes to hear about the James Brown sandwich. Brown and I had met in a London hotel. After many poignantly whispered reminiscences about his brutal childhood in a Louisiana brothel, he went to the toilet. While he was relieving himself, I put the remnants of a sandwich he'd been eating into my pocket.

"Dang! They cleared away lunch, and I wasn't finished yet," he said when he came back.

"Ain't nobody come in the room," his gigantic bodyguard demurred, looking down at me suspiciously.

"Anyway, it's been amazing meeting you," I announced quickly and left.

Great days. Ronnie loves that story.

But his all-time favourite anecdote isn't even about a rock star. It's about Nelson Mandela. He laughs wildly whenever I tell it, even though Nicola sighs heavily and wonders whether it sends "the right message".

"Oh, go on, please, Daddy, tell it again," Ronnie will say.

"Fine, *fine*," I say, palms raised in mock reluctance.

"Oh great," Nicola will hiss viciously. "Tell our son how you told Nelson Mandela, *Nelson Mandela*, for fuck's sake, that his release from prison was a great day for "our people" and then *robbed him!*"

My life as a rock writer has taken me on a wonderful but sometimes morally confusing journey. And, in terms of confusing moments, my brief and unexpected face-time with Nelson Mandela is right up there.

"Well, yes," I say, "but it was an *accident*."

IT WAS 1990, a heady time for black culture and politics. American rap group Public Enemy were raising the consciousness of black and white youth across the world, and gangster rap had emerged in LA. Nelson Mandela had just been released from prison in South Africa. In the UK, rock stars, as they so often are following major global events, were charged with organising the celebrations to mark his release.

A friend, Dotun Adebayo, music editor at *The Voice*, Britain's biggest black newspaper, asked me to cover the event for him. He had gone to LA to interview gangster rap group NWA. I was chuffed to be asked. Of course I said yes. It was only later that I fully registered the moral obstacle to accepting this historic assignment: *I am not a black man.*

I rang Dotun at his West Hollywood apartment. He had me on speakerphone with what sounded like a party in progress around him.

"Listen, Dotun. You sure you won't be back for the Mandela show?" I asked.

"No way. You do it."

"Fine. How is it going over there?"

"He's killing us with his James Bond accent, motherfucker!" came a snarling, girlish voice jammed up against the speakerphone. "Tell them UK gangsters we comin' over and smoke their sorry asses!"

"Give me the phone back, Eazy," said Dotun. Over a chorus of barracking from Eazy-E, Dr Dre, Ice Cube and the rest of NWA, he wished me good luck, and the phone went dead.

When I got home, I told Nicola about the assignment. She was inexplicably angry. "What type of message does it send out?" she demanded.

"That the music editor is busy with gangster rap?" I said weakly.

"You're a white guy!"

"I'm half-Bolivian."

"But this is Nelson Mandela, for fuck's sake."

I was taken aback by her vehemence. "What if I get you a plus one?" I said.

"No way. It's embarrassing."

And then, for some unaccountable reason, I began to feel angry that she was angry. "What right does a white girl from Leamington Spa have to tell a half-Bolivian that he cannot be a black man?" I raged. "I'm going. You're just jealous."

Nicola looked reflective, suddenly tired of the argument. "Fine, go and see Mandela," she said. "Just don't steal from him."

"Steal from him? Why would I *steal* from him?"

"I've noticed how you've started taking souvenirs from all these rock stars you meet and putting them in the bathroom."

"This is *Nelson Mandela*."

"Exactly. So, don't rob him. He's been through enough."

That hurt. I like souvenirs, sure. But I'm not a total arsehole. It had never even occurred to me that I might be able to pilfer a memento. Well, not until Nicola mentioned it.

AT THE WEMBLEY Stadium press accreditation Portakabin, I soon had more important things on my mind. I joined the line with journalists from other British papers. Papers read by white people. They got their press passes without a problem.

Then it was my turn. A potato-headed security operative in a fluorescent tabard thumbed through a box of envelopes. There was no pass for me. A simple mistake easily rectified, I reasoned.

"I am representing *The Voice*, Britain's biggest black newspaper," I grumbled as he riffled again.

"Sorry, mate, nothing for you here," he shrugged.

"But I am from *The Voice*, Britain's biggest black newspaper," I shrieked. "This cannot be so!"

"No pass I'm afraid."

"You've got to be bloody kidding me!" I honked in righteous fury.

Mr Potato Head radioed his superior. He then handed me the walkie talkie, and I made my case for a media pass, getting spittle all over the little perforations of the handset. "How can this be? This is plain RACISM!" I shouted at the little voice at the end of the line.

Then Mr Potato Head intervened. "Mate, try pressing the Speak button on the side," he advised. I had been shouting "This is plain RACISM!" at the perforations on a piece of Taiwanese plastic. If you don't press Speak, the person with the other handset cannot hear you.

"Fine," I spat.

"Actually, it would help if you said 'This is plain RACISM. *Over*,'" counselled Mr Potato Head.

I eventually screamed into the walkie talkie and watched Mr Potato Head wince at the language I used. And I could tell he was thinking: "Easy, mate, you're not even black."

THE HARD-PRESSED SUPERVISOR came to the Portakabin, apologised and issued me with a laminate. I was waved into the stadium by security guards with a noticeable extra flourish of deference. Then I looked down at my pass. The supervisor had given me the wrong one. It was not a press pass but an Access All Areas one. I could go anywhere.

Suddenly I was in an enclosure jostling for lunch with familiar faces: Terence Trent D'Arby, Youssou N'Dour, Neil Young. And there, sipping a drink, was another: Lou Reed. Lou Reed is an important rock star. He influenced punk. He influenced glam. He collaborated with Bowie.

*Black readers won't give a shit about Lou Reed, especially after he called black girls "coloured girls" in "Walk on the Wild Side", but allow yourself this one indulgence. Harvest a quote!*

I approached Lou Reed with my tape recorder offered at arm's length, like a gift.

"Lou. Michael Odell. Acting Music Editor from *The Voice*, Britain's biggest black newspaper. A great day, no?"

It took Lou Reed less than a tenth of a second to process me as a hostile. "*Please*. Fuck off and leave me alone," he said.

I couldn't believe it. *So* rude. I do not believe he would have said this to a black person. "Just checking that's your only comment to Britain's biggest black newspaper on this historic day?" I said jauntily.

He turned to me wide-eyed and exhaled heavily. "Look, buddy, I just want to watch the—"

He stopped talking and looked at me. Looked past me, actually. There was a rising hubbub behind my back. In Lou Reed's mirrored sunglasses I saw something amazing, terrifying and awe-inspiring all at the same time: Nelson Mandela and his entourage. The South African President-in-Waiting had been led backstage to say thank you to the rock stars taking part in the concert. A gaggle of security guards and advisers led him through to the corral.

I knew my presence was unwarranted. I knew this was not my moment. But, by some reverse alchemy, all the rock stars were suddenly mere fans. They rushed towards Mandela, and I didn't want to miss out. *Look! Lou Reed is breaking into a run! Push him out the way and get to Mandela!*

It was clear Mandela hadn't really been keeping up with rock music during his 27 years in solitary confinement on Robben Island. To all intents and purposes, I might have been a rock star. I put my elbow into Lou Reed's chest and got there first.

"Michael Odell, Acting Music Editor of Britain's biggest black newspaper," I said breathlessly.

Mandela poured his beatific gaze on me. It was a gaze of patience and wisdom, truly something to behold. But at its very core I thought I could detect a dawning scepticism. A look of deep query in the freckled old man's eyes seemed to say: "The Acting Music Editor for Britain's biggest black newspaper? Aren't you a *white* guy?"

"It's a great day," I said, the tape recorder quivering in my hand, "a great day for our people?"

I felt Lou Reed's elbow in my spine.

Benignly, with beautiful rolling South African r's, Mandela said "very good, very good," and then I reached for his hand, grabbed it and shook it. Mandela was then led away by his aides to speak to some proper rock stars. When I began breathing properly again, I looked down and saw that I had taken a napkin which had been balled up in his hand. Inside was the remnant of a snack. I couldn't believe it. I had robbed Mandela of a half-eaten sausage roll.

IN THE VAN I tell the anecdote to myself over a beer, looking into my rear-view mirror. It's a good one. It's a really good one. I picture Ronnie cackling happily and slapping his little thigh whenever I tell him this story. But he is not here. He can't hear me. I have sometimes comforted myself that, although I sometimes struggle to pay the electricity bill, I am a wealthy man, paid richly in anecdotes. But alone I suddenly feel the worthlessness of this currency. I have no one to tell stories to in the van.

## 25
# An Enemy of Rock 'n' Roll

I have been in the van for nine days. I have grown a beard.
A reduced variation in diet is now reflected in the yellowing whites of my eyes. I am shocked by what I see in the
rear-view mirror. *You look like one of those Vietnam veterans
who didn't hear the war is over and is still living off coconuts in
the jungle!*

I am almost relieved when Nicola calls and asks me to
"babysit". There'll be food in the fridge. And I can't wait to
use a proper bathroom. But I am annoyed that she calls it
"babysitting".

"You don't need to call it babysitting. I am Ronnie's
father," I say tersely.

"But you left us to live in a van," she says. "So, it *is*
babysitting."

She saves the killer blow for last. She wants me to
babysit while she goes to a concert.

"Who are you going to see?" I ask.

"Michael Bublé," she announces grandly. No two ways
about it, this is a definite kick in the nuts. She could have
tried some mild antagonism, like selling Ronnie into child
slavery. But no, she has gone nuclear.

When I get to the house I see the Michael Bublé tickets lying on the kitchen table.

"What a waste of money, I could have got you those for free," I say.

"The way you behaved to him? I doubt that very much," she counters with a sneer. "But also, you wouldn't, would you? He's an enemy of rock 'n' roll." Nicola makes ultra-sarcastic air quotes when she says "enemy of rock 'n' roll". I have rarely seen her so belligerent.

When she and her friend Vicky have set off, I sneak into the bathroom for a shower. It looks different without my rock 'n' roll memorabilia. It's just a bathroom. There is a new Ikea print of a yacht bobbing in azure water, a piece of bland water-themed art whose function is to re-establish the bathroom as a place of aquatic interests. However, the more I stare at it, the more it reminds me of the yacht Shakira flounced by in her press photos. The one she totally upstaged with her groin.

I run the shower. My range of international bathing unguents has also been cleared away, and so I have to improvise with Ronnie's Bob the Builder shower gel. Afterwards I smell like a bag of sweets.

When I meet Ronnie on the stairs he sniffs the air suspiciously. "Have you used my Bob the Builder soap?" he asks me crossly.

"Yes," I say, with a coaxing ruffle of his hair. "Can he fix Daddy's smell? Yes he can!"

"Well, don't use it again," he grumbles. "You don't live here anymore."

I go downstairs shaken by this animosity. *You are trapped*

*in the burning building of your youth! Get out before you lose everything!*

I eat everything I can find in the fridge. Then I fall asleep on the sofa.

I AWAKE TO the purr of a cab engine outside. Nicola and Vicky stumble into the house.

"How was the show?" I ask unfurling myself.

"Oh my God, he was so great," Nicola says, in a voice intended to convey a sense of total satisfaction bordering on the erotic.

"He was *quite* good," moderates Vicky with a significant eye-roll. She is trying to quell the excesses of Nicola's enthusiasm. "But we were sat quite far away and—"

"No, he was great. Fantastic," says Nicola sharply.

I am not sure whether to enter this vexed debate. But when Nicola takes off her coat and I see she has bought a tour t-shirt I am riled beyond endurance.

"Bublé is a throwback to the pre-rock 'n' roll era," I pronounce. "He's trying to evoke the 50s, an age of supposed innocence and romance – Eisenhower-era bullshit. It's basically hiding from modernity and reality, the dark side."

"Blimey, I'd never really thought about it like that," Vicky says.

"Well, I'm not in the mood for a rock critic lecture," yawns Nicola. "I'm going up."

Vicky solemnly begins taking out the folding bed and I head for the front door. I find a card waiting for me out in the hall. I open it. Ronnie, Bob the Builder and I are all holding hands. "Sorry I was cross, Daddy," it reads. "You smell nice."

## 26
# O, Daddy of Rock!

I am in a meeting room at a South London sixth form college. There's an oval table with some ergonomic chairs, plus a jug of water and glasses. I am nervous and tetchy because there is more personal space than I am used to. I live in a van. Also, I have a history of under-performing in conference-style settings. Put me in a room with an ergonomic chair and an oval table, and vital mental functions begin to shut down. *Only Satan could feel at home in such an antiseptic corporate environment!*

But I am here because Rex asked me to be. We had a heartfelt talk, and I told him I don't think Cot Death are ever going to make it and maybe he should think of the band as more of a hobby.

"It's not *me* that's saying it. As such. It's a friend. She knows a bit about music and that was her opinion. She said you should maybe try something else."

Rex said my friend was an arrogant, negative bastard.

"Couldn't agree more," I nodded firmly. "She's German. They can be very negative sometimes. As a people. But still, it's something you might want to think about."

Within a week, Rex had accepted that I may have a point.

He has now picked up some extra work running a part-time music and media course at a local college. He has boasted of his industry "connections" and asked me to come in and address a group of young students thinking about being rock writers.

"Will you help me, bro'?" he said. "My mouth is writing cheques here that my arse can't cash."

"Sure, no problem," I said, though I did feel a bit sad about Rex selling out.

"They'll cover travel expenses and provide sandwiches," he said brightly, but covertly, as though a stern Punk Judge was listening in.

"I'm in," I said.

Actually, I jumped at the chance to help Rex. I felt that, having colluded with him remaining in a nihilistic rut all these years, I owed him support in a new and positive venture. Also, sitting alone thinking about Nicola and Michael Bublé, I felt a sudden urge to man the barricades on behalf of rock. For a man living in a van it is also not insignificant that there'll be travel expenses and sandwiches.

When the day comes, I blow the expenses on a couple of drinks in a pub around the corner to steel me for entry into the college's music and media department, which involves a five-storey journey in a lift.

I enter the conference room. I see keen young faces, lots of leather, hair sculpted with gel and numerous piercings. I take a sip of water, fix my gaze on the most nervous looking student, a young man with hair tousled multi-directionally like a mauled hamster and address him.

"One day the Big Six will all be dead, and young writers will have to spot and nurture new icons," I say. "*You.*"

When I point my finger at Hamster and say "*You*", I notice it quivers a little. But for a vagrant entering the world of public speaking I think I am doing okay.

"What do you think offers the best long-term media career prospects, magazine work or TV training?" a young man asks me intently.

He is a good-looking blond young buck in a leather jacket. This presents a problem. As a teen punk I remember being schooled to mistrust both Billy Idol of Generation X and Paul Simonon of The Clash, high-cheek-boned blond rockers with pin-up good looks. Nihilism mistrusts narcissism. Narcissism can go and fuck itself. *Sorry, bruv, the last thing we need is a square-jawed Adonis taking a free ride to fame on the legacy of rock 'n' roll!* I give him a long look which I hope conveys all this, plus my belief that he deserves a firm, back-handed blow to the head.

"What I mean is, I've dabbled with writing, but magazines seem to be a dying industry," he continues.

I arch an eyebrow. I hope this communicates my fantasy of dragging Career Boy from his chair, frog-marching him to the lift and then throwing him out of the building into the traffic.

"Bollocks," I say and take a sip of water, then continue. "Who said this? 'Don't ask me why I obsessively look to rock 'n' roll bands for some kind of model for a better society. I guess it's just that I glimpsed something beautiful in a flashbulb moment once and perhaps, mistaking it for prophecy, have been seeking its fulfilment ever since.'"

"Lester Bangs," says a keen young woman with a broad smile and attractively domed forehead, which makes her look a bit like a dolphin bobbing playfully in the water wait-ing to be thrown a fish.

"Excellent. *Good*," I say and then direct all my conversa-tion towards her.

"Rock writing is not a job. It's a *calling*. Lester Bangs felt the legacy of rock more keenly than any other writer. If he were here now what would you ask him?"

I can see Career Boy conferring with a young man dressed in combat fatigues sitting next to him. He looks up with an impish smile. "Er, why were you found prematurely dead in your apartment in 1984?"

Career Boy is beaming at me. I want to punch his beau-tiful face.

"Do you *want* to be here?" I ask him sternly. "Or is some-one *paying* you to annoy me?"

"Actually, no. It's just I have this hunch that it's over for rock journalism. Also, the tutor said there'd be lunch."

I feel so angry I imagine biting Career Boy really hard on the arm. My fantasy is interrupted by Rex bringing in a platter of sandwiches. I pull it over to me and eat them all, tearing off hanks like a wild animal so Career Boy can savour the injustice.

"Real rock stars are rare and exotic beasts who live on the edge. To tell their stories you must get inside their minds, using ruses and wiles," I say, like some backwoods hunter, wiping remnants from the meal off my face with the cuff of my shirt.

Dolphin asks me if I have ever interviewed Pete Doherty.

"Not yet," I say, nonchalant as hell, with a piece of crust hanging from the corner of my mouth.

"I just think he is a really interesting rock star. I think there's a lineage there with the Romantic poets."

"*Good*," I say. "Pete Doherty is one of a rare breed with any *substance*."

"Unfortunately, a lot of that goes up his nose," says Career Prick, looking around the room hoping to receive waves of kudos. I ignore him and focus on Dolphin.

I wish I had a Pete Doherty anecdote for her. He is the great rock 'n' roll hope for this generation, but I have never actually met him. However, I have interviewed a ton of other junkies, and I am willing her with every fibre of my being to ask me about one of them.

"What about Nick Cave?" she says brightly. "Have you done him?"

I want to cry I am so grateful. I was just thinking of Nick Cave!

"So, yes, in 2004 I was on tour with Nick Cave and the Bad Seeds," I begin. The air in the conference room electrifies. Nick Cave is solid rock currency.

"I had just arrived at Athens airport to join their European tour. Now, joining a band mid-tour can be tense because rock bands cultivate a gang mentality. The writer has to break into that."

"Oh, come on, most bands are desperate for the PR, otherwise they wouldn't let you on tour in the first place," ventures Career Shitbag.

"The. Work. I. Do," I enunciate in a slow snarl, "cannot be described as *PR*!"

"So, anyway," Dolphin intervenes helpfully, "what happened next?"

"At the baggage carousel Nick wondered out loud what

was behind the rubber flaps where the luggage emerges,"
I say. "Nobody knew so ... I climbed on and rode it out of
the terminal building and back inside again with all the
suitcases just so I could tell him."

There is an awe-struck silence.

"And what was out there beyond the flaps?" asks the
young man in combat fatigues. He is the friend of my
enemy. He will not get a proper answer.

"*Aeroplanes*," I say with acid hatred. "And *luggage*. What
the fuck do you *think* is out there?"

I look at the boy's crestfallen face. I feel a pang of shame.
Why did I come here? What am I trying to achieve?

Suddenly I don't want to give a talk. I want to get back to
my memorabilia. I want to get back to the heavily plasticised
interior of my van.

I gabble through some basic rock writer principles. Why
rock writing was needed to liberate the minds of post-war
youth. When to drop a grenade question into the interview
situation. Why Pete Doherty might become the Big Seventh
if he pulls his finger out.

Then, sweating like a stressed pig, I take questions.

"Who from the Big Six have you yet to interview?" asks
Dolphin.

"McCartney," I say immediately.

"And if you got the chance, what would you ask him
above all else?"

I feel hot and tense. I feel like running for the door. "I
don't fucking know," I say.

"Oh, come on," says Career Boy. "Your grenade question."

"What do you really think of Linda's vegetarian saus-
ages?" I say weakly.

"Oh, come on," he pushes gleefully. "What is the one thing you really want to know?"

"Okay," I say, feeling both faint and belligerent at the same time. "Forget Beatlemania and mop tops, why don't you just tell me who you really are, you fucking arsehole?!"

The conference room falls silent. I can hear ice cracking in the water jug on the table, and one or two of my audience wipe spittle flecks from their faces. Through the plate glass I see a hunched Rex turn around and remove his shiny new tie from a plate of sandwiches. I realise I have been shouting.

# 27
# LOW

I am two weeks into my Tour to Nowhere. I now look like Australopithecus, an early evolutionary protohuman with bent spine and gaunt visage, on constant lookout for fruit, vegetables and small lizards. However, it's my regular tea time visit to the house, and I am determined to see it through.

Ronnie answers the front door but his gaze avoids mine. I am looking hard for the welcoming light in my boy's eyes. It's not there. And then I see a large pair of shoes in the hallway. Smart brogues indicative of an elevated professional standing. The footwear of someone with a proper job. *Greg! That fucking dentist has been here putting smiley face stickers on my boy!*

"Why are you looking at me in that weird way, Daddy?" asks Ronnie. I grab him and spin him round by his shoulders.

"What are you *doing*?!" he cries.

"Looking for stickers!" I growl.

"Stickers?! Why?!"

"Is he here?" I snarl. "The dentist?"

"No, Daddy! There's no dentists here!"

"Then whose are these shoes?!"

"They're your dad's," says Nicola, arriving from the kitchen at the end of the hallway. "You wore them with his suit to the awards, remember? I was going to chuck them out, unless you still want them?"

Nicola has a sensible new haircut. She doesn't look like either of the girls in the Human League anymore. She looks like Enya. She checks her new haircut in the hallway mirror. It's a new mirror without Elvis etched onto the surface. It's the kind of mirror where you don't look like you are standing next to a rock star when you look in it. You are just an ordinary civilian. You are on your own.

"No, I don't need the shoes," I say. "Chuck them."

"Good. Now we have some news, don't we?" Nicola says to Ronnie.

"Yes," he agrees a little sombrely.

"What is it?" I say, smiling because I am satisfied it has nothing to do with handsome dentists.

"It's my name," says Ronnie, "I want to change it."

"Your name?!" I yelp. "What's wrong with it?"

"Nothing. It's just ..."

"What do you want to be called now?" I say joshingly. "Ronnie Spector? Da Doo Ron Ron?"

"I don't want to be named after a rock star. I want to use my first name. I want to be Tom."

It's like a hammer blow. I quickly do the rock arithmetic. There are very few good rock stars called Tom. Tom Petty. Tom Verlaine. I don't rate Tom Jones or Tom Tom Club.

He sets out his reasons. He and Nicola have been having deep and meaningful conversations about rock stars and their value in society. "I'm not being horrible, Daddy, but

I've grown out of it," he says, while Nicola looks on proudly behind him.

"Grown out of it? What do you mean you've grown out of it?"

"I don't want to be a rock star anymore. They're silly. They're not real."

"Don't take it personally," Nicola says. "I'm just trying to show him that your world is not the be all and end all."

I don't know what to say. Rock was our thing that we did together. But now even Ronnie has taken what he needs from it and moved on. I feel lost, left behind.

"Fine," I say bitterly. "Let me know of any other changes you decide to make."

I turn for the door but in a slow, faltering *Why doesn't somebody stop me?!* way.

"Before you go, I found another bag of stuff that belongs to you," Nicola says behind me.

I turn and pick up the bag. It rattles. I look inside. The bag is full of interview tapes – hundreds and hundreds of hours of rock star testimony. Every interview I have ever done.

"Do you want them?" she asks.

I feel the sudden morbidity of the collector. Old tapes of people talking in hotel rooms. *What am I shoring myself up against with all this crap?*

The only reason I can think for keeping them is that Rex covets them. That gives them a value. It's always nice to have something which someone else wants.

"Go on, play me that tape of Bowie shouting at you!" he will giggle sometimes during a boozy evening. "Play me the bit in Milan where Liam Gallagher is licking your face."

The tapes have served as dependable little party pieces. But now the party is over.

"I'll bin them," I tell Nicola and then walk over to the green box and drop the bag inside.

"Not in there; they don't recycle hard plastic," Nicola says from the front door. "You'll have to take them to the dump."

When I began therapy, Mrs H told me it would be helpful to make a mental note of both the events and surroundings when I felt particularly depressed, especially if I hit a new low. I make a mental note now. Nicola telling me that even the bin men will not accept the legacy of my life in rock is definitely the shittiest I have ever felt.

# 28
# Reasons to Be Fearful

"My son has changed his name," I sob in Mrs Henckel's little chair, plundering the box of tissues beside me. "Everything I ever believed in, it's fucking *over*."

"This changing of names seems to be a family theme," Mrs Henckel sighs a little testily. "Perhaps you feel left behind because others have given up something in which you are still heavily invested."

Sometimes I find Mrs Henckel really fucking annoying. Especially when she is not on my side. Especially when she is right. I am finding it hard to cope with her insights today, so I totally ignore what she is saying. I study her shelves instead.

"Bought any good albums lately?" I ask wiping away the last of my sniffles.

"What?" says Mrs Henckel.

"After Slipknot? Bought any good albums?"

"I think this is a little tease you make," she says with a half-smile. Then she reaches across to her desk, grabs a file, opens it and leafs through some notes inside. "But perhaps in some ways my understanding of rock 'n' roll is only just beginning," she says suddenly. "I have consulted with a younger colleague who is interested in popular culture. She tells me there is an interesting therapeutic subtext to your music."

"Oh yeah, tell me about it," I say sarcastically. I'm not really in the mood to hear a Freudian interpretation of rock 'n' roll by some intern.

Mrs Henckel leafs through her pages once more and pulls a sheet out. "Are you aware of the famous rock 'n' rollers named Bono, Bob Geldof and Sinead O'Connor?" she asks.

"Of course," I say, "I've got one of Bono's biros in my van."

"Each of these artists suffered the trauma of a prematurely deceased parent," she says.

"Oh," I say.

"And this troubled man, Pete Doherty," she continues, "grew up in a peripatetic military family, another common theme among these artists."

I want to speak, but she holds up a flattened palm of commandment.

"And this man Gary Numan, who you compared with a robot?"

"What about him?"

"He suffers from Asperger's Syndrome."

"Fuck me! You're joking! He never told me that!"

"And these people – Foo Fighters, Oasis, Amy Winehouse, Mick Hucknall – all experienced early family break-up or abandonment."

I sit in silence. I do the maths. My dad was ex-military. We certainly moved around a lot.

"And so you see," continues Mrs Henckel, "the music is

not self-destructive in itself, it just seems to draw a certain profile of person to it."

"What are you saying?"

"Do you not see how prevalent negative mental health experiences seem to be in your field?" she demands finally.

"Oh, come on, this is just you trying to suggest my whole world is dysfunctional," I snap angrily. "There's a lot of desperate people in rock 'n' roll. Big deal. There's also a lot of anorexics in ballet! What are you gonna do? Ban Swan Lake?!"

"You misrepresent me," says Mrs Henckel.

"You are just down on rock 'n' roll because you don't like it."

"This untrue. I am merely speculating. Perhaps Peter Bannerman did not die for the rock 'n' roll dream. Perhaps he was already badly wounded emotionally and merely chose this music as his resting place."

⚡

I sit in the van. I open the bag of tapes Nicola gave me. I scrabble through the interview cassettes. Oasis in Italy. Blur in LA. Killers in Paris. I am particularly fond of my Chemical Brothers interview in Tokyo because in the middle of our conversation there was an earthquake. Crockery smashed as our hotel moved on its rollers. You can hear a man in our hotel restaurant yell in terror, but the Chemical Brothers simply continue talking about the transformative power of dance music.

I have done a lot of interviews.

I need something to distract me, so I put them on the van stereo one by one. At the start of each interview I hear the convivial clink of glass and the manic click of gum as I become the other person. The rock writer. I imagine Mrs Henckel's disdain and ready my defence.

*At least I have done my bit to keep 21st-century Britain edgier and more interesting than ... than ... Germany! The Germans didn't even bother to have a proper post-war pop culture, and that's how they ended up with Nena's "99 Luftballons" and the music equivalent of the mechanically reclaimed meat that goes into frankfurters: the Michael Schenker Group!*

When I have had this spasm, I have a terrible realisation: I am turning into my father. Despite trying to assert a difference between our respective generations with rock 'n' roll, I am aping his mistrust of Germans.

Then I begin listening to the tapes and hearing other things I don't like. I have soon taxonomised four types of rock star. The first are the businessmen. They rock, but then they leave the stage and lock themselves in the dressing room with their accountant. They have detached themselves from the dark side. They don't die.

"We had a good time sticking it to the establishment of post-war Britain," says Mick Jagger in Toronto, "but if we had actually done half the things people said we did, we'd be six foot under."

In Amsterdam, just after I have taken Sting's chips off his plate and challenged him about "meaning it", he says: "There was a time when I was very young and I thought a rock star sacrificing himself was cool. But making yourself a martyr is stupid and boring. I'm not harming myself for the fans. Or for you."

A few tapes further on, I identify a new group: the maniacs. They do not have dinner with their accountant. They have an appointment with the coroner. These are rockers completely seduced by rock's legacy of madness and feel the need to emulate it.

"We wanted to out-rock 'n' roll all contenders!" Nikki Sixx from Mötley Crüe says in an interview I did when the band re-grouped in 2004. "You come after The Who, the Stones, the New York Dolls and Iggy – and there's a sense that 'We're going to go places no one has before.'"

Mötley Crüe certainly achieved that. Their combined life experience includes overdose, manslaughter, rehab, jail, divorce, devil worship, child death, rape and degenerative illness. In 1987 Nikki Sixx had been pronounced dead in an LA hospital following a drug overdose at a party. However, he later "came back to life", walked out of the hospital and asked two stunned Mötley Crüe fans who had been keeping a tearful candle-lit vigil outside for a lift home.

Inevitably there is a downside. Further along on the tape I hear the voice of Mötley Crüe singer Vince Neil recalling the night he drunk-drove his sports car into an oncoming vehicle, killing his friend Razzle from the band Hanoi Rocks and causing brain injuries to the occupants of the other vehicle. Neil sounds hollowed out, ravaged, when recalling these events. But it is not the accident and his survival which he recalls with guilty amazement so much as his treatment while serving 30 days in jail in Torrance, California. He was allowed beer, and visiting groupies could have sex with him.

"I wrote a $2.5 million cheque for vehicular manslaughter when Razzle died. I should have gone to prison. I definitely deserved to go to prison. But I did 30 days in jail and got laid and drank beer because that's the power of cash. That's fucked up. But you're twenty years old and you've got a million dollars in your pocket and drugs and drink and women and fame, and there are lawyers to protect you. Even if they cannot get it for themselves, there are people who believe totally in the rock 'n' roll lifestyle and they want you to have it, even if they can't."

Vince Neil sounded chastened and regretful. But not as chastened and regretful as John Taylor, the bass player from Duran Duran. In their pomp, they were the biggest band on the planet and Taylor their most eligible bachelor.

In 2003 I interviewed him and he described the chaos at his apartment on New York's Central Park West in the mid-80s. Boy George was his neighbour. Motorbike despatch riders delivered drugs and, although supermodels came and went, his most constant companion was a rare designer parrot, allowed to roam free around his apartment, which kept squawking "Delivery at the door!" During this madness, Taylor developed an artistic rationale which I feel sure has motivated more than one rock star:

"You convince yourself that madness and appetite are creative. Look, 'Exile on Main Street' wouldn't have happened without Keith Richards's heroin addiction. 'Young Americans' wouldn't have happened without David Bowie's cocaine addiction. Alcohol played a big part with Vincent van Gogh. You need that edge. The trick is to find that edge without killing yourself."

When we finished talking, Taylor gave me a most earnest, post-interview salutation.

"You got kids Michael?" he said. "You got your health? Then you don't know how lucky and how free you are. Cherish it. Hold it. People in this game are always looking for something. If they're dumb they start gambling with their most valuable gifts when the fact is they had already won."

I never imagined I would be sitting in a van taking lessons from Duran Duran. But Taylor's voice hits home hard. And then I have to admit that Mrs Henckel has a point, for here, a few tapes further on, are the third group: the rock 'n' roll desperadoes.

I pull Pete Townshend out of my Big Six interview collection – stored in a separate, ribbon-tied box – and listen to him talking about Keith Moon.

"He was a brilliantly talented guy, but rock 'n' roll disguises so much unhealthy behaviour, it passes as normal. People think music promises some sort of eternal youth, and sooner or later they get frightened to grow up. I think Keith was one of those guys."

Afterwards, I rediscover a 2002 interview I did with John Lydon. He is in tears over the death of Sid Vicious. "Really Sid was just a kid," he sniffles in the bathroom of The Hyde Park Hotel. "He had a shitty start in life [his mother was a drug addict who supplied her own son] and he tried to make something of it. He shouldn't have died. No artistic statement is worth a life. Somebody should have helped him."

And I also listen to James Dean Bradfield of the Manic Street Preachers talking about the aftermath of bandmate Richey Edwards's disappearance in 1995. "People were angry with us, and when you are grieving that's a heavy extra burden to bear. I remember this one guy came up to me in the street in Cardiff and said, 'He had more talent in his little finger than the rest of you put together'. But the fact is he was ill. And none of us knew how seriously until it was too late."

And finally, I listen to New Order's Bernard Sumner talking about the death of Ian Curtis when they were both in Joy Division. Curtis's mental health problems are the most mythologised in rock. His suicide has sometimes been portrayed as an extension of Joy Division's artistic mission.

I joined New Order's tour in Vancouver in 2002, the assignment which ended with the stolen underpants. Sumner met me for lunch by the harbourside and we watched the seaplanes come in. He was in a good mood and seemed to be enjoying himself. *How am I going to shoehorn a question about Ian Curtis into a chat over a convivial seafood salad?* I asked myself. While we were eating, a massive seagull swooped down over us and tried to grab a chip from Bernard Sumner's plate.

"Hello, Ian," Sumner said to the seagull, "I was just thinking about you."

I laughed out loud even though I wasn't sure if this was appropriate. Sumner took it in his stride.

"People are fascinated, aren't they?" he said. "By the dead ones, I mean. They get very serious and reverential about the guys who die in bands. It was a horrific thing to happen to us and to him, especially as we were just starting to find proper success. But you can't let it dominate your outlook. I think about Ian a lot, especially getting older, but I don't want to feel weighed down by his tragedy forever."

New Order bass player Peter Hook is, perhaps unintentionally, the most moving when he recounts the moment he heard about the death of his friend: "I was eating my tea. We were supposed to be going to America the next day. A big deal for us. I mean we didn't start the band with great expectations, and there we were ... going to fucking

America! But the phone goes and someone tells me Ian's hung himself. He's dead. I just said 'Okay then', put the phone down and went back to the table. Shock. It was pure shock. I didn't know what I was doing to be honest."

When I have spent the night listening to all these tapes, I realise I am in a last, fourth group: the left behind, the survivors who must spend their lives bearing witness for those who perished. Except I don't have any gold discs or a yacht to show for rock 'n' roll. I only have a van full of memorabilia from a band no one has ever heard of.

The sun comes up. Over morning coffee at my tiny hob, I decide perhaps I will at least consider what Mrs Henckel said. Did Keith Moon, Richey Edwards, Sid Vicious and Ian Curtis all bring their problems to the party with them? Is that the role that rock 'n' roll serves in our culture, warehousing the damaged and mentally ill? I see Brian Jones floating in the swimming pool at Cotchford Farm. *Did rock 'n' roll really make him an "arsehole"? Or was he a gifted but damaged guy who limped into the party?*

# 29
# Foetus on My Breath

I am in the local library. I am among pensioners, the homeless, and stressed mothers barnacled with children. These are the people who use local libraries. On a weekday it is especially full of homeless men making use of free heat and light and newspapers. Before he started school, I used to bring Ronnie here for story time, and he was always scared of them. We'd sit on little mushroom-shaped stools, and he'd grip my hand tightly when he heard their terrible pterodactyl cackles. Now I feel I am close to joining them. When your mental health falters, it is so easy to slip between the cracks.

But I am not quite there yet. Today I am on a mission. I have not been in contact with Foetus since just after Pete Bannerman's funeral. We divided Pete's stuff between us. There was an argument over who should have Pete's guitar. I got it, he left and we soon drifted apart.

Now I am going to find him.

"Foetus, Foetus, where are you?" I mumble to myself scrolling through Facebook pages.

It doesn't take long. In fact, it takes less than fifteen minutes to get a decent lead. But the profile picture is baffling: a cloaked figure in woodland, not unlike one of the pair in Mrs Henckel's apocalypse painting or a questing character from *The Hobbit*. For me, Foetus will forever conjure up the urban dystopia of 80s Croydon, yet Facebook says he now lives in the Cumbrian mountains where he carves wooden walking sticks, bowls and occasionally owls for a living.

"Hi Foetus," I write, "long time. What's up?"

I wait for an answer. The screen gives me nothing.

"Come on, you stupid bastard, answer me!" I say to the computer. I am tired and hungry. I am a man who has forgotten that other people have lives, jobs and commitments.

"Keep the noise down *please*!" hisses Carol the librarian.

I fall silent. This is her library. Her word is law.

Eventually the blackened nails and the yellowed fingertips of a nicotined hand appear on my shoulder. I whiff the tang of tobacco and the sweetness of lager at my back. One of the homeless lads says they're going off to find lunch in the dumpster round the back of Subway and do I want to come?

➤

I DO NOT hear from Foetus. I am estranged from Nicola. My son is no longer Ronnie but Tom, a boy who shows scant interest in rock 'n' roll. I need to unload on someone. I call Charlotte.

"Wye aye, lad," Bob answers the phone.

"What's that screaming I can hear in the background?" I enquire.

"It's ya sis," he says. "She's in the new therapy suite. Sounds like she's working through the last bit of Croydon."

Charlotte comes to the phone. I hear panting through overworked lungs.

"Talk," she gasps. "I'm knackered."

"I did the work and now I live in a fucking van," I say in as non-accusatory a way as possible.

"What? What are you *talking* about?"

"I did the work," I say. "I faced it." I tell her that I've woken the ghost of Pete Bannerman.

Where *are* you?"

"I left home too, like you did. What do I do now?"

"I think about Peter too you know," says Charlotte. "And it's long overdue you dealing with it. But go home! You've got responsibilities, for fuck's sake."

"He would be 42 now. He might've have been something really special."

"Yeah, and he might have ended up Area Manager for Argos. You just don't know. Go home!"

"And do what?"

"Write a book! I keep telling you, it would be good for you."

PERHAPS I WILL *write a book*, I think. *A compendium of rock, classifying each artist, not by their usefulness to the nihilistic revolution, but by indices of mental health.* I leave the van and go to my local pub. I find a corner seat and order a half of bitter which I nurse carefully. I try to pitch my appearance somewhere between struggling writer and all-out desperado. Occasionally I catch sight of myself in the pub's large Victorian mirror. I do not look like what I think a man writing a book should look like. I look like a maniac trying to look like a man who is writing a book.

The pub doors crash open. Three young men and a woman enter, hauling drum-shaped tubs and black flight cases.

"Okay if we set up now?" one of them asks the barman. Here is a hopeful band at the very beginning of their rock 'n' roll journey, just like Mental Elf.

I have an urge to talk to them. I want to enquire about their mental health. *I am the ghost of rock 'n' roll past! Do not make the mistakes I have! Perhaps there is a problem you would like to discuss with me?*

They begin to sound-check. They are much better than Mental Elf were in Bromley. The drummer does not hit himself in the face with his sticks for a start.

But they are too accomplished for my taste. The way the singer holds her mic with one hand and raises the other in a traffic stopping gesture, all the while singing with her eyes shut, suggests she has done a performing arts degree or has been watching too much *X Factor*.

"Okay, let's do 'Delete All'," she commands the band. The song's subject matter – a scorned woman emptying a mobile phone SIM card of all her lover's contact details and then overdosing on pills – does not sound personal but imagined, like she heard about it from a more mental friend.

And the guitarist looks like the sort of person who has an ISA and a dental plan. While I am thinking this, I hear an internal voice. A critical voice. *Stop judging rock stars by how insane they are! Just accept that extreme rock 'n' roll is finished. It's over!*

The band takes a break. The barman gives them complimentary beer and they sit in a corner opposite. I watch them watch me with my full beard, half-pint and an abandoned pie crust I have taken off a plate from a nearby table. I know what they are thinking: *Our audience tonight consists of one tramp. We'll remember this and tell it to a rock writer one day when we are successful.*

I AM BACK in the library. One of my tramp pals is in trouble with Carol for drying his washing on a radiator. While they argue, I slip onto a computer to check my Facebook account. There is a message waiting.

"Foetus!!!!"

My cry shatters the scholarly silence. Even the other bums cough and splutter. But I can't help it.

"I didn't answer straight away because I was so pissed off you called me Foetus," he writes. "But I s'pose you weren't to know. I am not called Foetus anymore. I am back to Darren Stitch."

I message him back immediately and show an interest in his woodwork. A response pops up. He says he can carve me a four-foot wooden owl for £200. I tell him I'm going through a bit of a lean patch right now but maybe later. He asks what I do. I tell him I am a rock writer.

"You're having a laugh!" he says, and wants to know if I've met anyone really famous.

But I am not in the mood for pleasantries. By the fifth or sixth message I have asked for his number and then I am on the phone asking him about Pete.

"It has taken me years to get round to dealing with it," I say. "What about you?"

"I haven't really thought about Pete for ages," he says.

"But maybe it affected me less. I was definitely less surprised at what happened than you."

I want to know why.

"I could see how fucked up their situation was. His brother Phil was so needy, and his dad was struggling for work and always so angry with the mum for having a disabled son. Pete was caught in the middle. He was always so angry, and they couldn't contain him. The more I think about it, there's no way you can expect music to fix all the damage done by a screw-up family."

"Were Mental Elf really as crap as I remember?"

"No, actually we were alright."

"Oh, come off it. Really?"

"Apart from those cardboard boxes and the tea tray you used to bang, yes."

"Sorry, mate," I say.

"You really should've got some drums, you know," says Foetus. "Who knows? We might have actually got somewhere."

It's really good to talk to him again. I just don't believe Mental Elf were ever any good.

⚡

"WHEN PEOPLE SEND you records and CDs can you at least tell them to put on the right stamps?" moans Nicola. "Making me pay is taking the piss."

I am at the house. She hands me a pile of post. The underpaid parcel catches my eye. It's not from a record company because the address label is handwritten. The return address is in Cumbria. I can feel a cassette tape inside.

Back in the van I scrabble through the wrapping. There's a short note: "I'm still making music by the way. See what you think. And there's a little bonus on the other side."

I put on side one of the tape. There are three synth-heavy demos. Not bad. In fact, Darren's music is a bit like the early work of Gary Numan.

On the other side there is nothing at first. The tape squeals. And then there is the vague sound of an old fashioned nee-na police siren, the one the British police used to have before introducing the American woo-woo-woo one. A police car passing Foetus's house in 1980. Then through the aural murk I hear chords, voices. Pete Bannerman's voice. My voice. Laughter.

I stop the tape and stare at the machine. I know what it is, but I don't believe it. Darren has sent me a tape of a Mental Elf jam session.

To me, this is like finding a lost Beatles tape, a priceless artefact from music history. Tears fill my eyes. It doesn't matter this is a band that no one has ever heard of.

I press Play again. The mood is euphoric. It's the afternoon I convinced the band that my trip to America to meet my Bolivian in-laws would launch us into the big time.

"So, you reckon this could be the start of something really big?" asks Pete, full of hope.

My heart gives a jolt.

"Yeah, it could get pretty crazy from here," I say.

I hear him counting us in to The Clash's version of "I Fought the Law (and the Law Won)". As the percussive rumble of my tea-tray intro reaches a climax, I can hear Foetus's mum stick her head round the door and ask if we can keep the noise down.

"How are we supposed to rehearse with you butting in all the time?" demands Foetus.

We resume and play very fast, almost manically, through our set list. Songs by the Skids, The Who, AC/DC, Thin Lizzy, The Ruts, Sex Pistols, the Pretenders.

The tape makes the "drums" sound tinny, and the bass is all over the place. But even with this quality you can hear that Pete Bannerman knows what he is doing. You can tell he has talent.

Nevertheless, I stop the tape. Something bugs me. And then it hits home. The bands we have chosen, and the young men playing in them – Stuart Adamson from the Skids (later of Big Country), Keith Moon (The Who), Bon Scott, (AC/DC), Phil Lynott (Thin Lizzy), Malcolm Owen (The Ruts), Sid Vicious (Sex Pistols), James Honeyman-Scott and Pete Farndon (two members of the Pretenders) – these people are all dead now. They all checked out early. That's a lot of dead personnel, and no other line of work would put up with health and safety odds like that. What also strikes me is that we chose them. We looked for bands to emulate and chose such an ill-fated bunch. We are laughing teenagers in 8os Croydon mastering the songs of the doomed.

The rehearsal ends. Foetus says he thinks Mental Elf sounds great.

"This is the start of something big," he predicts.

"Good, cos I'm not hanging around in this dump forever," Pete says.

Silence.

I rewind the tape a little. I listen intently again. I don't say anything. I want to hear my teenage voice chime in with enthusiasm. Or else I want to hear my teenage voice ask Pete Bannerman why he is so desperate, and if there is anything I can do to help. But I don't. Why don't I say anything? Perhaps it is because I don't believe we are ever going to make it. Perhaps I already know we are not rock stars but anonymous dreamers in the suburbs.

# 30
# Paul McCartney

"I keep wondering if I should go home," I tell Mrs H, "but I cannot make decisions. I am at a total loss."

"Yes, that's exactly where you are," she says, low and meaningful.

When you are at a loss, you just trudge through it, like the figures in her painting. And so, I sit in my van debating whether my life constitutes a valid act of cultural resistance or whether I am actually just a tramp.

One rainy afternoon my phone bleeps and offers me a single line text: *Can you do Paul McCartney?*

I put down the phone and punch the air with excitement. But I forget I am in a van with a steel roof. My triumphant fist clangs on metal. It hurts and feels symbolic. Meeting McCartney will complete my Big Six rock writer quest.

But it doesn't feel as good as I thought it would. I once imagined it would validate my life and that there would perhaps be some sort of civic reception, even an open-top bus tour of Croydon town centre. It doesn't feel like that now. Interviewing McCartney will mean I can afford a new tax disc and a rear off-side tyre, which the police have warned me needs replacing. The magic of my quest has gone. I sit nursing my right hand and crying.

However, I still say I will go. I just want to cross the line and say that I have met Paul McCartney. My e-mailed brief for the interview is simple:

"He's done an experimental album. He wants to stake his claim as a maverick, a rebel – I think he's sick of everyone thinking John was the interesting one. Find out if he is."

It is beginning to feel like every rock star big or small can be located somewhere on a spectrum of cultural one-upmanship. They want to be considered subversive, dark and dangerous, and if there's two of them, there is invariably a ruckus over who is the ultimate badass.

Paul McCartney has done more than enough with The Beatles and, yes, Wings to assure himself legendary status. But he has recorded a new album under his pseudonym, The Fireman. There's a bit of screaming on it, and the cover artwork is cryptic and a bit DIY, which I suppose makes it nominally experimental and edgy.

I listen to the album. *I suppose this atones for "Ebony and Ivory", but really, what is he trying to achieve here?*

Then I go to McCartney's office in London's Soho Square. Once I was walking past it with Ronnie on our way Christmas shopping, and I fancied I could see his silhouette at the large desk on the third floor.

"One of the world's greatest songwriters is up there in that room," I told him gravely.

"I can't hear any music," he replied, with the irrefutable logic of the child.

I am thinking about this as I approach McCartney's HQ.

He has been world famous for 40 years now, but I wonder, what he is actually doing today? Practising his jaunty thumbs-up salute in a giant mirror? Counting his money? I don't hear any music either.

INSIDE THE BUILDING, I am told to wait in an anteroom. The walls are upholstered with memorabilia. Not fag butts, clumps of hair or a pair of trousers, real memorabilia: framed photos of The Beatles as the Fab Four, as kaftaned hippies. There are commemorative books and an array of guitars.

"Come and sit in Paul's office. He'll be with you in a moment," an assistant says. I am shown into his room overlooking Soho Square and offered a seat in a nook next to a jukebox and an easel. McCartney is interested in art – a huge Willem de Kooning hangs above his desk, and Linda McCartney once gifted him a pair of spectacles which belonged to the surrealist painter René Magritte. The spectacles are on McCartney's desk. It strikes me that, for McCartney, always considered the "straight" Beatle to Lennon's maverick, the spectacles represent a portal into creative weirdness, alternate thinking, even madness. It further strikes me that these spectacles should not simply languish on a desk, a collector's item. They should continue their surreal odyssey. They *want* me to take them home and give them a new life. As I prepare to pick them up and put them in my pocket, I imagine the impact they would have at home.

"Magritte wore them, then Paul McCartney owned them," I would tell amazed dinner guests as Nicola stabbed herself in the forehead with a fork. "Now you are looking through lenses which have helped shape the edgy culture of the modern world."

"Hi, I'm Paul."

Paul McCartney has slipped into the room unnoticed. I stand up, dropping my pad and recorder onto the floor. Bending down to retrieve them, I hit my head on his jukebox.

"Hello, Paul," I say. However much you prepare yourself, it's still disconcerting to be spoken to by the actual vocal chords that sang "Yesterday", "Eleanor Rigby" and "Blackbird".

I have a mad urge to say: "Those are the actual vocals chords which, audible from a transistor radio in Bolivia, lured my mother to Croydon in the 60s!" But I don't. I swallow hard and remain calm. *Even though the gushing fan believes the rock star somehow knows them, there is no real contract between them!*

I comfort myself with the fact that the situation could be a lot worse. At least I have not been caught stuffing Magritte's spectacles into my coat.

"Sorry I'm a bit late," he says. "Bit of hassle on the road up from Sussex. Someone spotted me in the car and sometimes it's hard to get away."

"Who needs that?" I offer empathically. Then I squirm internally because I remember Pete Bannerman driving Mental Elf down to Rye, thinking we could ambush McCartney in his local Chinese takeaway.

"No one hassles me down in Rye," McCartney continues. "That's why I like it down there. For the most part people are pretty cool."

I switch on my tape. McCartney's publicist warned me

that he wanted to focus specifically on his new experimental record and that any mention of The Beatles would be unwelcome. But that is not my experience. We discuss the new album, but McCartney soon introduces the subject of John Lennon. As predicted, the tweaking of the McCartney legacy soon begins.

"John is always seen as the maverick, the agitator who sent his MBE back, merited a 400-page FBI file and a deportment order from President Nixon," I say. "Has your image suffered as a result?"

"Sometimes I am Sir Paul McCartney who got the Mega Lifetime Icon Award from Bono at the MTV Awards and was knighted by Her Maj," he says. "But I am also James Paul McCartney, a school kid from Liverpool who got sort of ... *elevated*. Sometimes I have to let go of Sir Paul just to achieve creative freedom. That's when I become The Fireman. And this is not something new. John was always very far-out in his creative instincts, but I was on the same page. I was always trying to shrug off the stifling weight of The Beatles' reputation."

*He really wants to be remembered as a badass!*

McCartney chats on amiably about his radical past, hanging out with Allen Ginsberg, Andy Warhol and William Burroughs. I feel another strong subconscious tug. Lennon is the ghost at the feast, but there are others close by too. I see Pete Bannerman and Foetus kicking me off the Mental Elf tour bus of my dreams. Sometimes they said I was a lightweight and that I didn't want it enough. Sometimes they said I didn't rock.

I wave the vision away and ask McCartney if he feels he and Lennon had unfinished business together.

"We did some very good work, I think. But who knows what more we might have done?" he says mournfully. "A friend like John doesn't come knocking on your door every day."

⚡

LENNON'S LIFE WAS claimed by the murderous fantasies of a nutcase. For McCartney, it must have been a devastating loss. The loss of a childhood friend as well as one of the greatest songwriting partnerships ever. McCartney is one of the left behind. He has had to survive while the life and work of his friend are mythologised. Is there a sort of rivalry with Lennon's ghost?

When I am back in the van transcribing McCartney's words I think about this. *Even when they are gone, do the dead ones still enforce their legacy, find a way to have their say?*

I call Foetus to say thanks for the tape. There is something I really want to know from him.

"After Pete died and you came over to look through his things, you gave me a look. I've never forgotten that look. I thought you blamed me."

"Blamed you? Why? It wasn't your fault."

"The band was his life. I always felt guilty that I didn't mean it like Pete did. I always felt I let him down."

"Oh, Pete always knew your heart wasn't in it," says Foetus. "He used to say to me: 'That cunt wants to be a writer. We'll make it big and then get a proper drummer.'"

I put down the phone and stare into space. *This is worse than believing a Bolivian rebel was actually a fascist cop!* We were not a great lost partnership. Pete was going to kick me out of the band anyway. I wasn't dark and dangerous enough.

*He always knew you didn't mean it!*

This calls for a binge. I crash through the door of Mr Roy's shop. He sees my raised arm and raises a hand to complete a high-five.

"Wassup, Mr Rock 'n' roll?" he says.

"No. Wine," I say, leaving the high five hanging and pointing past him. "Top shelf. The good shit. Two bottles."

Back in the van I open a bottle and tip the contents of Pete's box of mementoes onto the floor. I swig then pick up a brick of paper, yellowing at the edges, held together with a rubber band. I pull out a single sheet and immediately recognise Pete's handwriting. A homemade flyer for Mental Elf's gig in Bromley. After all these years, I still have a bundle of them, handwritten in marker pen and photocopied.

I stare at the flyer. I drink more. Why am I holding onto this stuff? He's gone. It means nothing.

I open the second bottle. It's late now. The streets are empty. I stagger outside into the night and stick one onto a lamp post using parcel tape. (Parcel tape is an essential for all manner of van emergencies.)

*The White Lion. Saturday September 25th. Come and check your Mental Elf!*

And then I get into the van, drink the rest of the wine and put on the Mental Elf rehearsal tape again.

THE NEXT MORNING I wake up early. The tape is squealing at the end of its spool once again. The van's speakers buzz faintly. There are tapes and memorabilia and two empty wine bottles on the floor of the van. As soon as I sit up I know two things.

First, I should probably give Mrs Henckel a call and ask her to re-join the band. I mean, re-join me as my personal mental health roadie.

Second, I must get to a toilet within 30 seconds or explode. My toilet bottle is full.

Once, Ronnie was caught short in the van as we bombed up the M6 motorway to the Lakes. There was no developing gradient of need. He simply raised the alarm when he was already at panic.

"I am desperate for the toilet right now and it's already coming out!" he cried.

We had successfully improvised with an empty squash bottle.

I do the same with one of the empty wine bottles, but in the midst of triumph comes disaster. I hear voices outside the van. Ragged, honking semi-broken teenage voices. One of them has spotted my Mental Elf poster on the lamp post.

"Mental Elf. That's a stupid name," one says.

"This advert is for a gig from before I was even born!" says the other.

I am shallow-breathing and gritting my teeth to maintain bladder control, but there is a thump against the van chassis. My piss-jet goes everywhere: the walls, the seats. I am spraying the van. I want to scream. I emit a tiny mouse squeak of agony.

"There's someone in there," a voice whispers outside.

I try to exert pelvic floor muscles, but they are out of shape.

The whispering continues right up against the van's sliding door.

"Is that someone having it off?" one giggles.

"I think it might be an old man dying," says the other.

It is 7am, way before the school run. Why are they on the pavement now? God knows. All I know is: only the thickness of a door panel separates me, a grown, naked man squatting with his penis in the neck of a wine bottle, and the curious gaze of young teenagers.

And then I remember Breakfast Club at Ronnie's school: providing breakfast for hungry kids from overworked single parent families. When I dropped Ronnie off in the mornings I always felt bad for them.

*It could be boys from his school!* It is too awful a prospect. Ronnie has suffered enough. Still gurning in agony I peer through a sliver in the van's oatmeal brown curtains. One of them sees me.

"I just saw a naked old man looking at us!" he shouts.

"Paedo!" says the other.

They start to rock the van. I squat in terror while gripping the oven hob.

"Paedo! Paedo!" they cry.

Eventually the rocking stops, the voices retreat, and I am left alone in a van doused in my own piss.

*This is the nadir of nihilism motherfucker! If you are lucky enough to survive this moment, you must renounce rock 'n' roll and rebuild your life!*

# 31
# The A-Rockalypse

"Can I get another one on the tab?" I beg Mrs Henckel.

"Can you get another what on the what?"

"Sorry, I mean can I extend my credit?" I say. "It's just that I am broke, but I think I am having a real breakthrough."

I want to see Mrs Henckel again. I feel like I am on a badly financed tour drawing to an end. She frowns but agrees that I can have a couple more sessions on account.

"So, I think I can answer your basic question," I begin.

"Go on."

"I remember you asking me when we first met, 'What is ze nexus of interest in zees rock stars?'"

Judging from her face, Mrs Henckel thinks it's a bit rich giving a freebie session to a client who then proceeds to mimic her accent. I start over: "Sorry, you asked why I so strongly identified with rock stars?"

"Yes, in many ways this has been the underpinning to our work together."

"Particularly the angry and nihilistic rockers," I add.

"And you have an answer to this now?"

"Yes. I see now it has been grimly fascinating, perhaps even a relief, to see madness and self-destructive urges in others. I used rock stars to cover up my own madness."

"Yes, I think perhaps you have hidden in music to keep your own issues at bay."

"Perhaps that's what rock stars do for society," I say. "Perhaps that's what rock magazines do for the readership – give them a vicarious glimpse of the dark side."

"It's true, one does not get this thrill reading *Good Housekeeping*," she says.

"I think my agenda was even more specific."

"How so?"

"I think subconsciously I was telling rock stars: 'Go on, you pussy, die like Pete did!'"

Mrs Henckel seems to exhale and relax. I feel good. I feel like I have solved something big.

"I'm giving up," I say. "I'm not going to be a rock writer anymore."

"Really?"

"Fuck the Big Six! They're only the Big Six because they still happen to be alive!"

"Perhaps there is a new generation of icons you can explore," suggests Mrs Henckel. "My colleague tells me about the promising young singer James Blunt."

"For fuck's sake," I mutter under my breath.

"Pardon?"

"Nothing. I just need to move on that's all."

"Let's work this through sensibly," says Mrs Henckel.

"No. There's nothing to work through. Rock stardom is an expression of ultimate Western decadence. Live fast, die young! Rock stars can fuck off!"

Mrs Henckel advises me against making any grand gesture. But I will not be persuaded. Fuck rock. Screw nihilism.

"I am an all-or-nothing type of guy. I have given my all to nothing, now I couldn't care less," I conclude.

"How will you live?" Mrs Henckel asks.

I pause. I have done some deep in-van thinking on this subject. Having listened to hundreds of hours of rock star interviews, I believe I have identified a suitable role for me in society.

"I thought maybe I could become a therapist," I say. "My speciality could be talking to wannabe rock stars about the dangers of the rock 'n' roll dream. I could be like the cloaked figure in your painting leading them away from the A-Rockalypse. As it were."

Mrs Henckel spends the rest of my pro bono hour telling me why I should consider my plans more carefully.

"Let's not have running before there is walking," she advises.

⚡

IT'S A MOST satisfying sound. The clank and the crash of memorabilia hitting the bottom of a black bin liner. Inside the bag I catch sight of the jar of peanuts I stole from the Bee Gees. I see Roger Daltrey's sock. These things now disgust me. Especially the sock.

Mrs Henckel thinks I am being rash, but I realise now I have been looking at rock 'n' roll through a false prism. I decide to throw away all my memorabilia and all of my Mental Elf keepsakes except the tape and the guitar. I am not ready to ditch those yet.

While I am purging my van, I call home. "It's me, Michael," I say. "I've had a breakthrough."

"Oh, really? Well, that's nice," Nicola says. She doesn't sound sincere. She sounds like she is humouring someone with mental health problems.

"Pete Bannerman was unwell before I even met him," I say. "Rock was a diversion. He needed proper help."

"I think I said that, didn't I?"

"Did you?"

"Yes."

"Well, thank you," I say. "Now I have finally felt it."

"Good. I am happy for you. What is that awful racket?"

"It's me chucking crap into a bag."

"What crap?"

"Rock 'n' roll. Can I come over?"

The phone goes quiet. I hear Nicola and Tom discussing something in a fevered whisper. Then Tom takes the handset.

"Daddy, happy birthday," he says. "I made you a card."

⚡

"Do you want to see my stickers?" asks Tom when I reach home.

"Stickers?! What stickers?" I retort sharply.

"Football. I'm into football."

"Hmm, that's another sublimated male desire," I mumble. "A load of men channelling their dreams of transcendence into the up-field movement of an inflated leather bladder."

"Well, we all need something," says Nicola sounding tired. In fact, on closer inspection, it looks like *she* has been sleeping rough.

"Someone threw a bowl of rice pudding in my face today so I'm going to get the last bits out of my hair and then have a big fat glass of wine."

I chat with Tom. He says Miss Dunwoody has given him three house points this week because he has been making excellent progress on the recorder at school.

"Good boy," I say. "What else has been going on?"

"We had a talk from a policeman," he says. "There's a paedophile on the loose."

Nicola soon emerges freshly showered and pink. We eat dinner and drink wine. We agree we should not make any rash decisions about a proper homecoming. I know I need to tread carefully. Coming off the road represents a dangerous time, even when there have been no fans or gigs and the tour has effectively been to "nowhere". I have spoken to many rock stars who have gone mad after a stint away from home. It's only been a month, but even so, I feel as ravaged as the members of Guns N' Roses after their legendary *Use Your Illusion* world tour in the early 90s which ran for 192 shows.

"People think you must be a pretty cosmopolitan dude after travels like that," Slash once told me. "But you're just a wreck. You're a zombie."

"I find those first few days after a tour hell," Ron Wood once told me when discussing the end of a Rolling Stones world tour. "There's no structure. There's no timetable. There's no show in the evening and no applause. That's when the bad thoughts can kick in."

I feel a bit like this. The Tour to Nowhere is drawing to a close. I must prepare carefully for family life.

"I think you need a complete break. A fresh start," suggests Nicola.

"Yes, exactly," I say, and I tell her about training to be a therapist. There is a flurry of involuntary blinking and I notice her temples begin pulsing.

"That could be a possibility, I suppose," she says unconvincingly.

"I know I can't expect to just walk into your world. It would take time."

"Sure," she says. "I wholeheartedly support any attempts to move on in a positive direction."

I feel good. I imagine my fresh start. Some books and lectures and then my own consulting room painted as near magnolia as I can bear.

I am sipping my wine in this reverie when my phone rings. I see the caller ID "Q mag" flash on my screen. *You are no longer a rock writer. Beginning right now!* I don't answer.

"Maybe you could come and volunteer at the day centre, get a feel for the work," offers Nicola.

My phone bleeps. Q have left a message.

"Do you want to get that?" Nicola says.

"No," I say. "It's Q, but I haven't got round to telling them yet."

"The thing is about the younger clients I work with," she continues, "they would absolutely love to hear some of your music stories. Especially if you laid bare the truth that lots of these artists are such troubled people or chasing a false dream. I think it would be very powerful if you warned youngsters not to hide their problems within the hedonism of rock 'n' roll."

The phone screen lights up again. Nicola's eyes meet mine. I cannot resist. I grab the phone and stand up.

"Look, the magazine deserves to know that I have decided to retire," I say. "This won't take a minute."

Nicola tips back a huge gulp of wine, wipes her mouth and clasps the balloon of glass so tightly it looks like she might shatter it.

"Hi," I answer as brightly as I am able.

"Michael. Can you interview Pete Doherty?"

# 32
# Pete, Come Back!

Each generation creates its own heroes. The noughties want Pete Doherty to be one of theirs. His name comes up again and again, among both readers and other artists as their last great hope.

And he is one of the few rock stars with a cogent explanation, an artistic justification for rock 'n' roll. His music invokes a lost, mythic England he calls Albion. It's a place peopled by cheeky urchins, lags and troubadours.

"I see myself like one of those Romantic poets," he once said. "The Romantics put people back in touch with their inner feelings during a time of social conformity. And people today also get so stuck in their lives. They are so stifled, so trapped. I want to give them a state of what's beyond that. Sensuality, beauty and pleasure. A world without scope, a world without laws."

Since that first meeting, Doherty has definitely shown us a world without laws. He has been arrested fifteen times: for drink-driving, drug and flick-knife possession, even for breaking into his bandmate Carl Barat's flat and stealing his TV. There is YouTube footage purporting to show him feeding his pet cat crack cocaine.

I am not sure how I feel about Pete Doherty. But I have an urge to meet him and share my recent findings about the extremities of rock 'n' roll.

"I think I'm going to do it," I say to Nicola when I have thought about it.

"But you've just retired!"

"I'm struggling with retirement," I say. "Too much sitting around. Besides, I think I have some important things to say to him."

"But Michael, he fed crack to his cat!" Nicola exclaims, with an unmistakeable final straw yelp to her voice.

I can tell Nicola is inviting me to endorse or condemn this degradation. We have a cat which I sometimes shoo off the kitchen work surfaces with an oven glove or tell to shut up its pathetic, greedy mewling. Nicola wants me to confirm it's wrong to feed a cat Class A drugs.

"The guy needs help," she says, "and you're going to ... Jesus, after all we've talked about."

"I'm serious. I want a chance to say my piece."

"Oh yeah, sure."

"So, you're angry?"

"I give up," she sighs.

"Why don't you trust me? This would be my final goodbye."

"Don't ask me," sighs Nicola. "Maybe you should ask your therapist."

"Now *that* is a genius suggestion," I say and dial the number.

"I AM NOT against this development," Mrs Henckel says, "but what is it you want to say to him?"

"I dunno. It's just a feeling at the moment. He is supposed to be the last of the great rock tribe but he's ..."

"What?"

"He's going to die before he achieves anything great."

"You feel this?"

"Yes."

"Then go. Ask him. Why not?"

"Really? You think it's okay?"

She offers a hesitant throat clearing. "Well, yes and also it is work and ..."

"What is it, Mrs Henckel?"

"You do owe me quite a bit in fees," she says finally.

I HAVE A few days to prepare, but a major problem presents itself. I am trying to bond with my son who is now called Tom. That means getting into football. But I have been subsisting on bad food in a small van and so I'm out of shape. While we are in the park having a kickabout, I make a run and fall to the ground in excruciating pain. I have snapped the Achilles tendon in my right foot.

I get a cab to the hospital. I sort of expect the blazered reception oldster to palm a klaxon and announce a hospital-wide Code Red as I hobble in, but the old bastard just shrugs obligingly and nod me towards A&E. There, the young medic attending me is surly and seemingly unimpressed with the mundanity of the injury I am presenting. I have never met a doctor whose bedside manner more clearly indicates she would rather be doing CPR on a vulnerable infant or transplanting a brain.

"Does this hurt?" she asks, manipulating my foot.

"Sister, morphine!" I yodel to a passing nurse, writhing and squirming on a chair while the doc tests my foot's mobility.

"You'll live," she states coldly, and says the foot must be plastered, placed in a heavy orthopaedic boot and rested for eight weeks.

"No, that's impossible," I plead with her. "I am a rock writer and I am going to interview Pete Doherty tomorrow."

At the mention of Pete Doherty, she ignores the urgent bleeping of her pager and becomes instantly more animated. It's amazing. I have found her, the latent rocker located deep within everyone, even the most dedicated professional stiff.

"I think he's great, really original and passionate and *free*," she enthuses.

"Yes, I think he gives people permission to experience their inner outlaw," I say.

"I'd give anything to dissect him," she adds. "He'd make a fascinating toxicological study after all the crap he's put in his body. How is he even still alive?!"

She tells me I must still have the plaster cast and boot, but I will probably get away with travelling to the interview on crutches.

"How will you get to his house?" Nicola asks, looking at the directions to Doherty's abode when I get home. "There isn't a train station for miles. It's in the middle of nowhere."

She is right. The address provided sits in rolling Wiltshire countryside, miles from anything. What's more, Doherty has asked that I get there for 9am in time for breakfast. I will have to drive. With one foot in plaster it will be a dangerous, not to mention illegal, undertaking.

"Isn't it against the law to drive with one foot in a plaster cast?" Nicola asks as I clamber into the campervan early the next morning.

"Probably," I say but think, *Damn the law. This is rock 'n' roll. I must go!*

"I thought you were going to try and be a bit more mature about this job?" she adds as I start the engine.

"I am trying my best," I say, lifting up my leg by the plaster cast that covers everything from my foot up to my right knee joint. "Trust me!"

Then, letting go of the leg with both hands, I drop my plastered foot onto the accelerator and, harnessing the explosive power of the engine with frantic clutch work, I set off. In my rear-view mirror I see Nicola standing outside our house gradually swallowed by diesel fumes. Pale and severe, she looks a bit like Gary Numan swathed in dry ice at the end of his Replicas tour.

I manage to get out of London by virtue of high-speed cornering and liberal fist slams on the horn. As I hurtle along the M4, the van's handling characteristics are, I reflect, a little like the spirit of rock 'n' roll itself: I can go forwards very fast, attracting awestruck looks from bystanders. However, stopping is almost impossible.

Pete Doherty has asked me to be at his mansion by 9am. I am surprised. This is early for any rock star. To be honest, I am sceptical that Pete Doherty even knows what 9am is. Perhaps he has lately heard of this mythical time of day when people get things done. He said he would leave a front door key for me in the glove compartment of a Morris Minor on the driveway.

Deep in the Wiltshire countryside, the van's deafening

progress scatters flocks of sheep to the hills. I easily identify Doherty's house. From a distance, it's a substantial country pile, a typical rock star abode. But as I get closer it looks more like a National Trust property after the zombie apocalypse. There is a Union Jack flag hung at a jaunty angle in a smashed upper window. There is a broken-down Morris Minor on the drive, which itself is strewn with hundreds of promotional badges for the comedy cockney duo Chas 'n' Dave. In a large ornamental pond by the front door I can see a tray of cat litter, a blanket and a baby's feeding bottle. There have been several inconclusive bonfires on the lawn, with charred remains still smouldering.

Having slid the wildly revving van across the gravel at the front of the house, I come to a halt. I exhale. I lift my plaster cast foot off the accelerator. The world is silent. I am excited to have got here alive but also a little disappointed Pete Doherty has not emerged from the house to remark on my incredible driving skills.

I go to the Morris Minor. There are no keys in the glove compartment. I stumble on crutches to the front door and ring the bell, but there is no answer. I circle the house, tap on windows with a raised crutch and rattle at bolts. Nothing. *I nearly killed myself getting here and that fucking junkie has forgotten me!*

Peg-legged fury and a deep sense of cripple injustice drive me on. Lurching about on crutches I search the garages and stables. Exhausted, I stand watching the progress of a man on a distant sit-on lawnmower moving across a field. *Those lines are mown perfectly straight. No way is that Pete Doherty!*

I go back to the front door and knock again. There is no

answer. In exasperation, I kick it. The door squeals on its ancient hinges. It's been open the whole time.

I go inside and begin calling "Pete!"

There is a distant patter of tiny feet. First a few and then many. Someone, something, is coming. I am frightened. *Get the fuck out of here, peg-leg! This is starting to feel like a Scooby-Doo mystery!*

But I cannot hop away fast enough. Cats, a dozen or more, mewling with hunger, race down the vast wooden staircase towards me, eager paws drumming on the wood.

"Pete!" I cry again. I spin round and stumble. I put a crutch down in the sea of writhing cats. I feel a bony tail.

*Riaaooow!*

"Jesus Christ! Get away from me!"

It's easier to go forwards than backwards, and so with an extended crutch I push through the first door I see. In here I am confident I will find Pete Doherty busy on the phone or perhaps with headphones on.

I stumble into a large room. It's a mess. Not just untidy, but eviscerated, as though abandoned in a hurry to avoid approaching invaders. There is graffiti on the walls. Indistinct words in a troubling dark red script. *Fucking hell, it's written in blood!*

Someone has been burning stuff on the floor: the carpet is scorched. There are clothes and rubbish strewn everywhere. But there is also evidence of a recent human presence – in one corner an electric heater whirrs and a laptop screen glows. The place stinks. *He must be upstairs. With any luck taking a shower!*

I turn to leave. But then I notice in the corner of the room under a cracked window, eyes closed, naked and motionless on a dirty mattress, a sleeping man. Pete Doherty. Horror and fear crowd in. I hobble over and look down at him for a long time, urgently drinking in details. His body is grey. His eyelids are pink. His mouth is open. His hair is pasted to his forehead with sweat, and his fingernails are blackened. There is blood on his right hand, the fingers of which are closed around a disposable lighter. I look for rising movement in his chest cavity. Nothing.

"Pete!" I cry. My voice is cracked, brimming with near hysteria. I hear hungry cats entering the room behind me. I hear the heater whirr. I hear the wild rhythm in my own chest.

*Yes, this is really happening right now in real time and you have to deal with it!* Several thoughts occur at once:

*Jesus Christ he's dead – you'd better call the cops!*
*Jesus Christ he's dead – you'd better get a selfie!*
*Jesus Christ he's dead – you're going to jail!*

I hobble closer and stoop over him. He is dead. I am sure of it. *Fuck!*

I exit the mansion and scroll through my phone for the *Q* office number. I rehearse the words I must say: "Gareth, Pete's dead and we need cops, coroners, photographers, documentary makers, historians and maybe also some lawyers down here *right now*!"

But as I am about to thumb the Call button I am overcome with guilt. I hear Nicola's voice in my head: *I thought you were taking a more mature attitude!*

And then I recall grave thoughts. Mrs Henckel has been encouraging me to think about where I had been and what

I had been doing the night Pete Bannerman died. I was at the cinema in Croydon. I was barely half a mile away from his bedsit. I even walked home along the adjoining street about the time he took his fatal dose of booze and pills. And I had thought: *I'm not calling for that loser! He's messing up my band! He'll soon come crawling back!*

And here I am twenty years later with another Pete. But I am not walking past his house at the critical moment. I am here, on crutches, surrounded by cats. I scroll past Q and call Nicola instead.

"Nicola, listen to me, I'm at Pete Doherty's," I cry, voice shaking.

"Glad you got there safely. Now, be responsible and don't ask him a load of stupid laddish questions," she says.

"I can't. He's dead."

"What do you mean he's dead?"

"I mean he's dead! As in, RIP! Not alive!"

"What are you *talking* about?"

"I got to the house and let myself in, and his cats attacked me, and there's blood on the walls and ... He's fucking *dead*!"

"Holy shit!"

"What do you think I should do?"

"Are you sure he's dead?"

"I'm not a doctor but ... yes!"

"Calm down! What are the symptoms?"

"He's not breathing! Death! Death is the main symptom here!"

"Don't shout at me! Check, for fuck's sake! You might be able to resuscitate him."

I re-enter the house. I scare away the cats and stand over

the body. Immediately I am consumed by doubts. Hasn't his head moved slightly to the left since I went outside to make the phone call? Wasn't the disposable lighter in his other hand before?

No. He still looks dead. And in the absence of formal know-how, the cheesy protocols of Hollywood now suggest themselves. I decide I will do what they do in films: solemnly push his jaw up to close his mouth and then draw a sheet respectfully over him. Then I hear Nicola's stark words: "You might be able to resuscitate him!"

I must check beyond all doubt. There is only one thing for it. A poke in the face with the crutch. That's the only definitive way to know!

I hold my right crutch over Pete Doherty's grey doughy face. I take a breath. I grit my teeth. I jab the end firmly into his right nostril.

*You see, he's definitely dea—*

The room explodes.

"What the FUCK?!"

Pete Doherty is not dead. In fact, his vital signs are suddenly quite good. He springs out of bed cupping his genitals with one hand and gathering a blood-stained sheet around him with the other.

"Who the fuck are *you*? What are you *doing* here?"

I am stunned. I am terrified. But it seems appropriate to attempt some sort of defensive belligerence.

"Michael! From *Q*! You *told* me to come here!"

"You could've knocked!"

"I *did*," I plead. "I knocked several times."

"What are you doing, poking me in the face with that fucking walking stick?"

"It's a crutch actually."

"You hurt me, man!"

"Sorry. I thought you were dead."

There are cats everywhere now, writhing around our legs, uneasy with the commotion. Still meowing and still hungry. One of them in particular sounds broken, desperate.

"What's up with that cat?" asks Pete Doherty.

"I accidentally put a crutch through it," I say. "Sorry."

"If I said to come for breakfast, I said it," he concedes eventually. "But I need to sort myself out first, man."

He grizzles in an indistinct mumble while climbing into some trousers and lighting his first cigarette of the day.

"Don't s'pose you could go into the village and find me some breakfast? And some cat food?" he asks needily, sounding pained and vacant.

I exit the house and crunch through the sea of Chas 'n' Dave badges to the van. After a short burst of hysterical accelerator work, I reach the village shop a couple of miles away. There's no one around. The Lotto sign outside the shop squeaks on its hinges and the awning flutters in the breeze. I enter to an ominous bell ring.

It's a general store, the only one for miles. I load up on cat food and milk and cigarettes. Turning the aisle, I notice two teenagers hunched over at a magazine rack. They are looking at a copy of Q.

I have sat in meetings and discussed readership graphs and market research reports, and heard grave discussions about how we can better serve the 100,000, the true believers in rock 'n' roll. But I have never actually met a reader, much less witnessed them flick through the pages of the magazine drinking in its vicarious thrills. But here are two of the 100,000, living among the deadening baa of sheep and the grind of agricultural machinery, seeking the dark side.

Clutching my shopping, I edge closer and stand at their shoulders, fascinated to witness actual memes of rock 'n' roll culture enter their eyes and soak into their young brains. They finish reading it and toss the magazine back onto the rack.

"Total legend," says the elder.

"Nutter," says the younger.

They are reading about Oasis. I cough theatrically behind them. They look at each other.

"There's a price to be paid for that," I announce, stepping forward.

The older, taller one turns round to face me. I see zits, misaligned teeth and food trapped in a dental brace such that it looks like someone has thrown a takeaway at a chain link fence. I see fear giving way to belligerence.

"You don't even work here," says the younger one.

"No, I don't mean the magazine. I mean the *lifestyle*. There's a price to be paid to bring it to you, so that you can enjoy it."

I am smiling. I offer them imploring, upturned palms to show my intent is peaceful. They have no idea what I am talking about.

"You on summink?"

"I *am* that price that had to be paid!" I say.

They look at each other perplexed.

"Dad," says the younger one.

"What son?" says a burly man further along the display.

A farm worker in dungarees. His shaved, pock-marked head is stooped into *Ultimate Cage Fighter* magazine.

"Okay, just forget it," I say crossly and leave with Pete Doherty's shopping. When I am halfway through the door I turn back and wave a crutch at them.

"Don't you see, I am just trying to *help* you people? It's OVER!"

I STAGGER BACK to the van. My phone rings. It's Nicola. "Jesus Christ, Michael, why didn't you ring me back?!"

"Sorry, I'm at the shops."

"Why are you at the bloody shops?!"

"We need milk and fags. And cat food."

"But what happened at the *house*?!"

"Oh yeah, turns out he wasn't dead. He's alive. And he's hungry."

"You might have rung and told me! I was petrified."

"Sorry."

"What are you going to do with him now?"

"I am going to make him some breakfast, and then I'm going to interview him."

"Is that wise?"

"It's my job, Nicola. It's what I *do!*"

"Okay," she says, "but don't indulge him."

"Don't *indulge* him? I've just done his bloody shopping."

"Michael, he's not well," urges Nicola. "This is your chance to make a difference. This is your chance to do something good."

"So, LET'S TALK about the new record," Doherty says, accepting the groceries with pained, wraith-like movements. He clears a space in what could nominally be described as a living room. That is, if the carpet didn't bear witness to a major fire, if there weren't food containers, empty bottles and hundreds of disposable lighters strewn about the place, and the crunch of broken glass underfoot and blood on the walls.

"So, with this album I am putting forward my idea – my vision, if you like – of a modern troubadour lifestyle," he begins, settling back into an armchair whose seams have burst. "A lifestyle of pleasure and beauty and no rules." The new album is full of songs about drugs.

The armchair reminds me of the one I sit in at Mrs Henckel's. But while hers has been unstuffed by clients fretting and picking at the seams in the search of enlightenment, Doherty's has been burnt by wanton nihilism.

Doherty sees himself as a Romantic conjuring the spirit of an old, lost England. The Romantics didn't have guitars or amps but, like him, they asserted human passion and individual experience over the homogeny of the industrial age. His band is called The Libertines, and libertines laugh at the squares and do what they want. At least that's what I *think* Doherty is trying to communicate. But I am finding it hard to engage with the details of his personal philosophy because the place smells so bad. I am soon having my own artistic vision: carpet-cleaning operatives lining up outside the door, cat rescue agents abseiling down the side of the building.

I look around the sad, broken room. I look at his wan, tired face. *This is your chance to do something good!*

"I'm sorry, but I'm not seeing much of a lifestyle," I say, putting down my pad, tape recorder and pen.

"What's that, mate?" says Doherty exhaling smoke richly.

"Why don't you get this place cleaned up?"

"Sorry?" he says, setting his mug down with the jitters of an old man.

"You're living like an animal. Why don't you sort yourself out?"

"I didn't invite you down to give me a lecture about my lifestyle," he says.

"I know. But I didn't come to babysit you either. I've never seen such a shithole."

I can hear the words coming out of my mouth, but they don't feel like mine.

"You don't know what you're talking about," he says. "This is daft. You can write what you like, but this is my home and how I live, and I am being true to myself as an artist."

"An *artist*?" I laugh horribly. "Is this what you think artists do?"

"What do you know?"

"I've seen how this bullshit ends. It just leaves a lot of crap for other people to clear up."

I think of Charlotte crying as she looked into my stark, tearless eyes after the phone call about Pete Bannerman. I think of his parents at the funeral. I think of his dad delivering the box of personal effects and the guitar, and about the depression and nightmares, and an emotional blast wave rolling out and engulfing all those standing close by, like the Civil Defence video they once showed us at school of a nuclear bomb going off and leaving nothing but an arid wasteland.

Pete Doherty doesn't like my critique. I can tell because

he has some colour in his cheeks at last. He is angry. In his own way, he is a conservative, a firm believer in rules, and I have breached what he sees as accepted interview etiquette.

"You've got a bad attitude, man," he says, shaking his head. "I don't need to listen to this. If this interview isn't about my work then you can leave."

"Don't you want me to run a Hoover over the place first?" I sneer packing up my things.

"Get out of my house!"

He escorts me up the rubbish-strewn hallway. A guard of cats falls into step next to us. He still hasn't fed them.

"Get some help," I say out on the drive, gesturing with an indignantly raised crutch to the many Chas 'n' Dave badges on the gravel, as though they symbolise the true depth of his fall. "And feed the cats!"

I climb into the van and start the engine. Then with two hands I drop my plaster cast onto the accelerator once more.

"You've got a bad attitude!" he repeats as the engine roars. "You're not my fucking *dad*!"

"Your funeral!" I shout and lift the clutch. But I'm angry and flustered, and so the van lurches forwards and delivers a firm blow to the stone pillar at the end of the drive.

"What the *fuck*!" cries Doherty, showing a sudden and belated concern for the preservation of historic country buildings.

With him remonstrating in my rear-view mirror, I reverse out of the pillar and then slip away. I have to pull over at a service station on the M4 to calm myself down and assess recent events.

*You just stuck a crutch into the nostril of Pete Doherty, a rock 'n' roll star! Then you performed a one-man intervention and got thrown out of his house! Not a typical day's work, but you did the right thing!*

When I get home, I place the smashed wing mirror on the kitchen table.

"What's that?" Nicola asks.

"It's a memento of me doing something good."

# Postscript

In 2009, shortly after I began thinking about writing this book, Oasis split up. It was such a shame. Being part of a combustible creative partnership is hard work and fraught with dangers. I thought about writing to them and offering counselling. But then again, I thought, counselling might solve their problems which, in turn, would negatively impact on their music.

At least the Gallaghers are still alive. Many others have succumbed completely to rock 'n' roll's dark voodoo. Once I'd started writing, Paul Gray (aka "the Pig") from Slipknot died, and so did Anal Cunt's Seth Putnam, Amy Winehouse, Robert "Throb" Young from Primal Scream, Lemmy from Motörhead and Scott Weiland from Velvet Revolver and the Stone Temple Pilots. They all died earlier than they should have. They died from complications arising from rock 'n' roll.

The statement issued by Robert Gillespie from Primal Scream after his bandmate's death caught my eye. Part of it read:

*He was a true rock 'n' roller. He walked the walk. He had Heart & Soul tattooed on his arm and I'm sure on his*

*heart too. He once said to me "When we go on stage it's a*
*war between us and the audience." He never let go of that*
*attitude.*

The tone was not entirely of loss. It was a eulogy to a compatriot fallen in conflict. Is that healthy?

It contrasted starkly with a statement made by Mary Forsberg, the ex-wife of Scott Weiland, after he was found dead on his tour bus in 2015.

*I won't say he can rest now or that he's in a better place.*
*He belongs with his children barbecuing in the back yard*
*and waiting for a Notre Dame game to come on. We are*
*angry and sad about this loss, but we are most devastated*
*that he chose to give up. Let's choose to make this the first*
*time we don't glorify this tragedy with talk of rock 'n' roll*
*and the demons that, by the way, don't have to come with it.*

When I met Weiland in 2004 I thought he was just another rock 'n' roller who'd taken too heartily to the lifestyle. It wasn't until after his death I discovered he'd brought something pretty major to the party with him: he had bipolar disorder.

When David Bowie died at the start of 2016, a newspaper asked me to write about my interview with him, one of the last he ever did. They wanted me to focus on his experimentation with drugs and sex, not to mention his fear of rock fan mental ill-health in the form of Mark Chapman.

I sat down with my laptop but then suffered one of those moments of creative paralysis. I knew what they wanted: tales of daring, extremity and madness. But really, he was one of the Big Six who'd come to understand the insane risks of rock 'n' roll and to value his mental health. I didn't write the piece.

When I consider rock's death toll, I think about Pete Bannerman and the fact he never got a chance to live the life of his alter-ego Pete Virgo. In fact, he never got to live his life. I agree with Foetus: he did want it too much. No one wants to be an "entertainer", a stage-school or *X Factor* muppet, someone who doesn't "mean it", but you can invest too much in rock 'n' roll. More dangerously, you can bring stuff to the party which doesn't belong there and which people like Mrs H ought to sort out.

I didn't stop interviewing rock stars altogether after being thrown out of Pete Doherty's country pile, but increasingly I came to view my subjects through Henckelvision. That is to say, I was less likely to collude in their tales of rock 'n' roll mayhem and ask more probing questions. For example, "How would you assess your mental health at the time you shot your brother aged twelve?"

That's what I asked Jay Z in 2010. He was very nice about it and highly articulate on the huge changes he'd made in his life since being a drug dealer in Brooklyn, New York. He had since evolved into a global star and exuded a smiley, Zen-like calm. He told me his new positivity had in part been nurtured by a close friendship with Chris Martin, a man often derided among rock writers as insufficiently Satanic to protect the legacy.

Was Jay Z in any way undermining the legacy when he described his ideal evening as "good wine and laughter with friends"? I'll be honest. There was a tiny, residual part of me that thought *Stop. The thought of you sipping Chardonnay at a barbecue offends me*, but I have to accept that Jay Z cannot be dysfunctional on my behalf.

I have made a lot of progress creating a healthy boundary between myself and what I expect from rock stars. For one, I sold the van. It's not healthy to create a private world of rock on headphones or in a vehicle. A guy called Jeff gave me £800 for it. As I walked away, he was poking about in the glove compartment of his new purchase.

"Hey," he called out to me, "there's a jar of peanuts in here."

"Keep them," I said. "I'm allergic."

# Acknowledgements

My sister Charlotte died in 2010 and Bob the year after. I will always remember them for their love and kindness in dark times.

Thank you to Anna Power at Johnson & Alcock for picking this out of the slush pile, and a big devil horns salute to Kiera Jamison at Icon Books. Editing is a bit like being a music producer. I was the wannabe howling and yodelling in the booth. Kiera tirelessly worked the knobs and faders (occasionally suggesting "more cowbell") until a tune emerged. I was aiming for "Bohemian Rhapsody", if it ended up more like Clive Dunn's "Grandad we love you" the fault is mine alone.

I had some very astute early readers. Mark Swallow gave the first draft a sceptical eyeballing, and Guy Pearson also came in and solo'd with virtuosity while I shook my head in awe, a bit like Eddie Van Halen dropping his gilded fretwork on Michael Jackson's "Beat It".

I would like to thank my wife Susanna, who read this account of a previous life and did not flinch. Well, not in front of me anyway. Finally, a shout-out to Tash and Freya.

Boop, Biscuit and Bean: I love you very much.